UNBREAKABLE(ISH)

Ali Ingersoll

WRITEWAY
PUBLISHING

Raleigh, North Carolina
www.writewaypublishing.com

ISBN 978-1-956543-70-4
Printed in the United States of America

Book layout by CSinclaire Write-Design LLC
Front cover by Dave Bryand
Back cover by CSinclaire Write-Design LLC

WRITEWAY
PUBLISHING
Raleigh, North Carolina
www.writewaypublishing.com

FOREWORD

ALI HAS OFTEN BEEN described as a Force of Nature, though she acknowledges only that her insatiable curiosity has been her saving grace as well as the foundation of her superpower resilience. She has long lived by the mantra: "What's Possible?"

Obviously, I've known Ali since childhood, and observed on her 3rd birthday that there seemed to be something preternatural about this child, youngest of our four children.

For the next 20 years she ricocheted around the world from one daunting adventure to another, exhibiting an extraordinary appetite for both risk and pain.

Rather than start college in California at 16, Ali chose to depart on her own to China where she learned to speak Chinese in a Beijing kick boxing gym and had almost too many travel adventures to recount. She even ended up spending an arctic winter week in an unheated Chinese jail up near the Mongolian border due to having forgotten to travel with her passport.

The next year found Ali on a solo survival hike deep

in the Australian outback where she was compelled to eat live mussels after losing all her food.

Nor has breaking her neck seemed to quell Ali's appetite for hazardous adventures. As a quadriplegic without even the use of her fingers, Ali has been scuba diving with sharks off the coast of Florida, zip-lining high in the Costa Rican rain forest, and recently skydiving with the All Veteran Group elite parachute team in North Carolina.

Meanwhile, though severely injured 15 years ago in a shallow water dive on a remote island in The Bahamas, Ali has overcome seemingly insurmountable setbacks to evolve as an exceptionally articulate and forceful public advocate for the disabled.

So here is Ali's own account of what's possible, illuminating how she came to be who she is today and what drives her to thrive beyond paralysis and the incessant neuropathic pain with which she daily contends. Undaunted, her curiosity about What's Possible remains well intact. And here's to hoping as many readers as possible get to meet Ali in person.

R. M. Ingersoll
July 2025

CONTENTS

PROLOGUE

OH MY GOD! *I can't move my body! I can't feel my body. I can't lift my head. I think I'm in water. Yes, yes, I'm in water. Why can't I move? Why does no one see that I can't move? I must look like a drowning mermaid right now. I'm running out of breath. I'm not Aquaman. I can't breathe underwater. Is this it?*

Did I tell everybody in my life I love them? If I die in the next few minutes am I happy with my life? I don't want to die. Wait, there's more, come on, Ali, FIGHT! Keep holding your breath. You can do it!

Will people remember how I lived my life? I survived jail in China at 17, I frolicked with monkeys on trampolines at the Playboy mansion, and I survived exploring hundreds of kilometers in the Australian Outback on my own. It can't end like this. Dammit, it's not going to end like this.

Wait a minute. I know what's happening. I'm trained in medic first aid. Just think, Ali. Stop struggling. Oh, right. I broke my neck. I know it. Okay, now if someone else would just figure it out and come flip me over.

I don't think they know I'm not joking. Please. Please. Please. Someone help me, I'm drowning.

Such was my inner monologue with moments to live. I was fully conscious, holding my breath, and waiting to be saved after taking a shallow water dive off a small tiki bar in The Bahamas, where I lived. I hit pure white sand headfirst. This was my first, but by no means, as it turned out, my last, brush with death.

My mother, who witnessed my ill-fated dive, jumped in and flipped me over, saving me from drowning.

I frequently hear stories about those who took a shallow water dive, woke up in the hospital, and did not remember what happened to them. Nope, that's not me. I'm one of those "lucky" ones who remembers every moment of breaking my neck and the seemingly forever twenty-two-hour journey involving multiple ambulance jets dodging huge lines of August thunderstorms to fly me back to a trauma center in Miami.

I also had to direct much of my own medical care on the island before an emergency jet came to fetch me. I think Darwin might be proud as it was undoubtedly a survival-of-the-fittest scene. Without knowing it, I'd been preparing my whole life for a life I didn't see coming.

How should I tell the story of my hard-to-imagine life? Perhaps I'll be a bit too transparent for some. What I will relate here comes from my experiences, my memories, and my perspective, which is not to say that there may not be other recollections and perspectives different than mine.

Nonetheless, in many ways my life is about the story! Our stories matter. Humans were telling stories long before we had written language. Stories connect. They teach.

They are how I have turned pain into progress and my ideas into action.

And so, dear readers, I am sharing my authentically transparent story with you. I have shared selected stories throughout my life with legions of my blog readers and message listeners, but perhaps never as I am sharing in this book. My family undoubtedly will think my story is way too much sharing, as they generally prefer discretion and anonymity.

I am sharing so many aspects of my life. The good. The bad. The ugly. The ridiculous. Some X-rated (but not detailed!). The borderline unbelievable. All that and more, no kidding, with a dose of dark humor that helps me through life.

I am who I am, and it's okay with me for you to learn who that is. We can get all that out of the way so, later, when I'm speaking from the stage or sharing (hopefully resonating) thoughts in books or consulting, we'll be past all the crazy stories, wondering, and questions, and we can get to work. But, first, I recommend a cup of tea or maybe an adult beverage, perhaps a bowl of popcorn, a sense of humor, and an open mind! If you want a little more medical information, see Ali's Medical Notes at the end of the book that correspond to the end note superscripts in the book.

If you would like to "see" a bit of my life from fun to adventure to medical and advocacy in photographs, there is a digital album you can access here:

https://aliingersoll.com/photo-album

PART 1

CHAPTER 1

My First Lesson in Preparation for Life

FEW EXPERIENCES IN EARLY life compare to being strapped to the stern seat of a 30-foot Grady White powerboat with twin outboard 250 horsepower engines at eight years old while my brothers motor headfirst into 25 foot waves in Exuma Sound in The Bahamas. My older brother cinched up the bungee cords as he strapped me to the back of the boat with a devilish smirk and sang the theme song from the TV show "Gilligan's Island." You know, the *Minnow* and crew and the three-hour tour at sea in a violent summer storm.

I looked left, I looked right, and I looked up. All I could see was the ocean on each side of me as the six members in my family weathered the storm of my early lifetime. With each wave, Dad and my two brothers braced for impact, knowing full well we might not be getting out of this one. I, on the other hand, was only thinking about how hungry I was. I reached for a little tangerine that I watched rolling back and forth on the boat as my mother was trying to hold onto my sister and me for dear life while our little vessel was being pounded.

I had no idea what the grown-ups were so anxious about. To be fair, I had enough cushioning as an overweight child to bear the brunt of the impact as the boat crashed downward, crest to trough, in the waves, only to be lifted again. I distinctly remember catching the tangerine mid-slide as our boat almost capsized.

Nearly eight hours later my body was worn out from the waves pounding on the boat. We were too far out to sea for the Coast Guard to reach us. I remember watching my dad and brothers stand against the storm. Their knees nearly buckled every time we crashed down one side of the wave. Our boat groaned like it was going to crack in half at any moment.

Somehow, we made it to a safe Bahamas Out Island harbor, bruised and battered. But our spirits were flying high to find a port quite literally in the middle of a storm. Back in the 1980s, we didn't have fancy GPS navigation or weather technology like we do today. When we started out on that trip, we didn't know what weather we were in for until we were in the middle of it, but we found safety at a port in the storm. Gotta love that.

The Ingersoll Clan

I HAVE TO ACKNOWLEDGE from the start that I had a rather unusual upbringing, including travelling frequently overseas, but it all began for me on a remote island in The Bahamas. Cat Island is fifty miles long. It has a population of around sixteen hundred, which has remained constant for many decades. Cat Island has a two-lane, pothole-ridden road, Queens Highway, running north-to-south.

These days there are a few local food and general store shops but no malls or movie theaters, and it is a magical place where being able to adapt to the unknown with imagination and some creative MacGyver skills is a must on a daily basis.

In the early 1970s, my father was flying himself around The Bahamas, exploring for a holiday destination for Mom and my two then-very-young brothers. From the air, Cat Island looked interesting, and he spotted an unmanned mid-island airport. The so-called Bahamian Family Islands (aka "Out Islands") were in those days rather like the old Wild West. With no Customs or Immigration services, they were an ideal shelter for drug runners from South America.

Sighting a house and car adjacent to the nearby Fernandez Bay beach, my father dropped down to fly tree tops at 50 feet to see if he could catch the interest of whoever lived in the house he'd spotted. That's how aviation worked in those days with no airport radio contact. The tree-buzz signal worked, and the homeowner drove out to the airport to pick up, she believed, her son, but she instead met my father and invited him over for tea. Thus did our now more than 50 years on Cat Island begin as a case of mistaken identity. Talk about karma!

My family fell in love with the remoteness of Cat Island and even more so with the lovely Cat Islanders, and long before I was born my parents purchased some land on Cat Island from the family of the lady who met Dad at the New Bight Airport. And further karma had it that this lady's son knew how to build local houses with native limestone. Over time, we ended up with several small houses situated just above the high tide line on 600 feet of pristine beach and crystal-clear water, the limestone sand as white as table sugar.

I never could have predicted that my favorite place on Earth and my sanctuary for inner well-being would also turn out to be the place where I'd break my neck a few decades later. Cat Island and my clan-like family shaped the character I am today.

My German mother and American father afforded our entire family the most incredible opportunities, from traveling to attending excellent schools, learning first hand to appreciate so many different cultures.

Our parents were in their early twenties when my two brothers were born. Then they waited nearly thirteen and sixteen years to have a set of girls—my sister and me.

Whenever I ask Dad why he decided to have a second round of children later in life, he always jokes that he needed to restock Mom's balance sheet with more to do because my brothers were old enough to take care of themselves!

I am blessed with the most incredible parents. Mom is one of the most loving and committed human beings I have ever known. She is a five-foot-one ball of high energy. I tease her about being a monkey because she's incapable of not climbing on something that is dangerous, even in her late seventies. She's the kind of mom all my friends wanted to hang out with. She's very beautiful, has the most loving heart, will have a rock out 1950s dance party any day of the week, is always the life of the party, and oftentimes forgets that she is not thirty anymore.

In contrast, Dad is six foot two, a slender gentleman with the keenest intellect of anyone I've ever met in my life, and I'm not just saying that because he's my dad. He's one of those people who knows a lot about a lot, not just a little bit about a lot. Frankly, his photographic memory was sometimes rather annoying when I was growing up. He is gentle, kind, pensive, thoughtful in every word he speaks, and he's a mentor most folks would kill for.

No matter where I was in life or how much trouble I was getting into—and I got into a lot—my parents were always there for me. Sometimes they had to let me figure things out for myself the hard way, and I have been known to be quite stubborn. But they knew exactly how and when to pick me up when I fell.

Island Lifestyle

CAT ISLAND WOULD NOT be everyone's cup of tea. If you want entertainment or shopping, go to Miami. However, being bored was not an option growing up in our household and on a remote island. As a child, I would follow my brothers and sister around like a little puppy while they would teach me useful things, like how to fix water pumps or even how septic systems work when we were knee-deep in having to fix ours.

When you live on an out island, you must learn how to fix things yourself. There is no one to help you. Self-sufficiency is a key to success if you choose to live a life more or less off the grid. We even generated our own electricity for the first 20 years before the European Union gifted Cat Island its own large generator. That meant no hair driers or toasters or air conditioning in those early years!

When I was nine years old, my brothers taught me how to use a Hawaiian sling for spearfishing so that we could bring home dinner each night. Think of this like a slingshot where instead of a stone you have a long, sharp steel spear that you pull back, aim, and shoot. I spent countless hours trying to hold my breath, using my flippers to swim down to 25 feet, which, I might add, is really hard to do when you have excess weight on you as a chubby child. When I could get down to a reef, I needed to identify the fish I wanted to eat, pull the sling back, aim, and shoot. Admittedly, I was an utter failure at this for quite some time, but, eventually, I got the hang of it. When I speared my first grouper, it was as if I had been initiated into the top level of the hunter-gatherer Ingersoll clan!

My mother waited on the beach during these expeditions and would fillet the catch right there on the spot. She taught me how to scale fish properly and get all the bones out. At night we would gather around a small tiki bar we built, grill the fish, light a bonfire, bring out the joke books, and enjoy such pleasures life had to offer.

An important tradition in our family was sandcastle building day. Oh no, this was not a competition for dilettantes. My brothers would be in fierce competition with each other, while my sister and I would be their helpers. When I say helpers, I mean we were told to go fetch a nice cold Bahamian beer called Kalik, collect little sticks to make fires on top of these massive sandcastles, fetch buckets of sand, and sabotage the enemy's sandcastle when they were not looking.

These sandcastles were six feet high and intricately decorated with shells, sticks, stones, and beautiful carvings.

My mother would help with this part. At the end of an epic sandcastle building day, each sibling pair would devise a military-like sneak attack to destroy the competition's beautiful display that a rising tide would have taken anyway. When my sister and I were brats, my brothers would bury us vertically in the sand. We cried and Mom would come running to our rescue. My brothers never let us get what they thought was too "girlie" because they wanted us to grow up with practical skills and grit and be able to take care of ourselves.

In later life, even when my brothers, sister, and I would be scattered around the planet, we would make time to meet on Cat Island several times a year. We always made it to The Bahamas for Christmas until my brothers got married. I can't recall who started this tradition, but every Christmas during these years, we would pack up our outboard boat with food and Christmas gifts and set off on a journey to an uninhabited Bahamian island called a "cay" (pronounced "key").

There are nearly 700 islands in The Bahamas, so we had plenty to choose from to explore. We would pack food and water, plan out a possible route for the short December day, and my mother would go so far as even wrapping presents so we would have them Christmas Day on an uninhabited cay. She even brought along battery-operated Christmas lights to decorate beachside bushes!

These were Robinson Crusoe trips where we would scout out an uninhabited island on a nautical chart and then chart a course to explore it. It's fortuitous that we enjoyed each other's company because we were stuck with each other for ten to 14 days with only a VHF radio for true emergencies, albeit there was no guarantee the Coast Guard could even hear us if we called.

Though we would spearfish for our food, Mom packed these epic coolers that none of us were allowed to sneak into for fear the ice would melt too soon. Of course, my sister and I would sneak in to swipe a bite of salami with an ice cube every chance we got. There's a Bahamian expression, "If Mama ain't happy, ain't nobody happy." So my eventual conclusion was not to mess with a German mother's perfectly packed cooler when you're in the middle of the ocean!

We took a very limited supply of water for occasional showers, so we had to wash our hair in the ocean and rinse it off for five seconds with the sun-heated water bags. And speaking of supplies, we always had a plentiful supply of cigars plus dirty joke books for the campfire at night.

My brothers would set up the tents at the camping ground while Mom decorated sea grape bushes or whatever was available for our Christmas tree. This always seemed so beautiful to us.

Being little munchkins, my sister and I had a very important job. We had to walk around whatever island we were on to collect firewood for our nightly bonfires. That was a more daunting task than it sounds like, because much of the dead wood was crawling with scorpions. Fortunately, there are not too many other dangerous creatures in The Bahamas, though scorpions certainly deliver quite a sting. I don't know why the universe of scorpions had it in for one of my brothers, but he always took it in stride.

Our days were filled with water gun fights, sandcastle building, real conversations that seem to be lost nowadays in most families, lessons on tying nautical knots, spear-fishing for fresh food, smoking cigars, and, of course, the adventure of exploring uncharted islands like Christopher Columbus did.

My fondest memories are of the nighttime fires on the beach. My mother, who really could've been a five-star chef, would cook over these fires, but she also brought smoked salmon, caviar, bagels, cream cheese, and capers (you can't forget the capers!) in those packed coolers and set out an elaborate, beautifully crafted platter that we would nibble on at the end of each epic day. It was a crazy contrast between Mom preparing gourmet food at our campsite and us not showering for days. I'm not complaining! Being the youngest in the family, I would always maneuver my way in for a secret nibble while Mom was preparing the food and the others were not looking. I was always hungry. Always!

My brothers and Dad are generally a little bit more serious in life, but on these camping trips they would put on reindeer antlers, light their cigars from the ashes of the campfire, pull out the joke books, and just forget for a while that they were grown-ups. They would laugh uproariously at the jokes. My sister and I had no grasp of the underlying meaning of some of the jokes, but we laughed anyway to join in the fun.

There was one particularly unforgettable Christmas trip where my dad charted a course to an island named No Bush Cay. Upon arrival at December dusk, we found there was a reason for its name. It was just a rock! So, we made haste in the fading daylight to the next nearest cay, where we set up camp after sundown. We woke up in the wee hours of the morning to find our campsite under water—salt water!

Our sleeping bags were soaked and much of our gear was floating. We had not realized in the dark that this island had a rise on the beach side where we alighted, but we had pitched tents in the dark on the half that was below the high tide line. Half of our gear was gone, my brothers were scrambling to grab everything that was drifting out to sea, and my sister and I were probably laughing our butts off. You can't win them all! At least Mom's Christmas presents that year were still tucked safely away on the boat. A kid has priorities you know!

We continued with the tradition of these camping trips until I was about fourteen when my brothers started to bring girlfriends and eventually wives into their lives. While all of us would still venture to our home on Cat Island multiple times a year for holidays, it is to these family camping trips that I attribute my understanding of the concept of family.

CHAPTER 2

Innocent Munchkin to
Troublesome Teenager

MY DAD IS A private person, so I can't tell you much about his life. I do know my granddad, my dad's father, was quite famous in the publishing world, having started *Life* magazine and run *Time* magazine as well as writing several books. The early years of Dad's adult life were spent in the publishing industry, whereas later he learned a lot about electrical and mechanical engineering to help my brothers in their business. His work frequently took him away from home and family for much of the year while I was growing up. He is also a very experienced pilot with thousands of hours in all weather conditions.

My mom grew up in a very loving family in a small town near Nürnberg, Germany. Her dad owned a dairy, making butter and yogurt for sale throughout Bavaria. This village transports you back to what I imagine the 1950s in post-war Germany might have looked like.

My parents met in New York when Mom came over

for the summer to study at New York University, where my father was an undergraduate student.

Dad has always worked hard, and Mom worked equally as hard, devoting her life to helping Dad in his business and raising a family. Over time, they began to build the most incredible life for all of us.

Growing up, my siblings and I benefited from our parents' eclectic lifestyles. We bounced around to different boarding schools on the East Coast in the US as well as in England. We grew up in a very different world than most kids we knew and were always taught to appreciate other cultures and every experience. I remember spending summers in the South of France mingling with people I assumed were important to my dad's business. Everyone sipped champagne. I smoked my first baby cigar at eight years old. The era of the 1980s was certainly a different time!

Once when we were in New York, I remember we were at a business event with my dad, attending a circus. My sister and I spent the entire evening in the company of Michael Jackson. Oh yes, *the* Michael Jackson, though I had no realization of who he was at the time. He was a very odd gentleman as I recall. He did not talk, but he liked to play tic-tac-toe with us. We had so many extraordinary experiences of this nature. I was half convinced as a child that Dad was some kind of secret agent.

When we visited Mom's hometown in Germany, we would feast on bratwurst, sauerkraut, and dumplings and explore fields of wildflowers. When I was older, my parents allowed me to bring friends when we went to Europe. In Germany, we consumed giant mugs of beer and pretzels the size of our head that we could wear as necklaces and got into trouble with boys at Oktoberfest.

In the winters, we would meet family and friends in the Italian Alps for ski trips where all the adults would ski from little hut to little hut, eventually getting smashed on a mulled wine called Glühwein. On one tipsy ski run, I distinctly remember my mother topless on her skis in true German party fashion, while my brother had lost his pants, and who knew what the hell the other adults were up to. They were all very good skiers, I have to say, but certainly too inebriated to find their way back down to the lodge, so this day everyone formed a train and the first in line held onto the ten-year-old's waist (me) as I guided them safely back down without running into a tree or going off the side of the mountain.

Later, while we were living in England, I recall my dad inviting me one day to accompany him to a party at a prince's house. I remember seeing security guards when we entered the home, and I was captivated by a photo of Fergie on a foyer table. I'd read about her in the London tabloids and couldn't believe I was maybe in her house. Then I looked at the guy next to her in the photo and asked my dad, "Who is that weird guy?" I distinctly remember my dad laughing out loud and telling me the fellow in the photo was Prince Andrew, who turned out to be our host that evening. How was I to know? Anyway, Fergie was so much more interesting to me at that age.

The dinner party was filled with dignitaries, sheiks, royalty, and such. I sat next to a Saudi prince, who asked my dad if I was married. It was an odd question to me, as I could not even imagine having a boyfriend. He offered quite a sum for me, and Dad joked he might sell me off for the right price! I also remember staying very close to my dad's side for the rest of the night.

One summer my entire family met up in the south of France for a few weeks. We boarded a beautiful antique powerboat and headed toward what looked to me like a rock in the far-off distance. I think I was only eight or nine at the time. When we arrived to meet with friends at what looked like a run-down shack, I discovered it was actually a crazy Greek restaurant called Le Pirate. All the staff were dressed as pirates, who explained the house customs. I was very confused. Apparently, people would pay a good sum of money to eat Greek specialties and drink quite a lot and then break the plates and wine glasses either by throwing them out the window or onto the floor. Seems this is a Greek custom!

My sister and I had a ball while the adults got into their own mischief. Kids gone wild. My sister smeared ketchup on my face while I force-fed her butter. We were two little butterballs ourselves, running around with food in both hands and having food fights. It felt as if the parents had flown the coop.

The tricky part when we left this strange restaurant was that we had to step carefully over all of the smashed crockery and wine glasses. To this day I still don't quite understand how Le Pirate offered such an amusement for at least some of the adults. Maybe it's because adults get to act like kids for the day.

The family stories could go on, but the memories in The Bahamas are the most special to me because it was a time when we could be together as an immediate family and be present with and for each other. I'm sure my siblings have different memories of aspects of our childhood, so I can only speak from my perspective, but I have wonderful memories of these times.

We had many exotic family trips. I suppose at a young age I started to live by the philosophy that I didn't articulate until a handful of years ago, in my late thirties, with the motto: "Do it for the story."

I have always loved adventure. I've come to thrive on the unexpected. I just am not built for boring. I've learned how to adapt to ever-changing circumstances and uncertainty, in part because of the way I was raised and maybe because of my genetics. However, I've changed my motto to "Live your story responsibly," because these days I realize when I embark on a riskier journey now, I do weigh the pros and cons first. So, I say live your story responsibly with a dash of irresponsibility for a little spice. This is a personal life choice.

Sizzling Bahamian Summers

MY SUMMER HOLIDAYS SOMETIMES offered exotic global trips, but each summer my sister and I were allowed to invite five or six friends to Cat Island for a few weeks of fun in the sun.

As I reflect back on those summers, I owe a huge shout out to Mom, who pretty much wrangled a houseful of teenagers on a daily basis. She chased us on and off the beach to get us to clean up the house, stop throwing our wet towels on the sand, stop dying the porch stones with Kool-Aid because that's how we dyed our hair, and, in general, acted as our group therapist for weeks of what I can only describe as 90210 teenage drama and so much more.

These summers were so magical for my friends that decades later they look back at the summers at my home on Cat Island as some of their fondest times. My mother was a mom to everyone. She didn't pick favorites.

We spent our days gallivanting around the island, sneaking beers, jet skiing, having tube wars with the speedboat to see who could kick another one off the speeding tube, snorkeling, building sandcastles, and sitting down to homemade meals Mom made every single night. Yes, every single night she cooked for us. Some of my friends still recall that these were the only consistent family meals they had throughout their childhood.

Remember that back in the mid-90s we didn't have a television, movie theaters to go to, or malls to shop on the island. We had to make our own fun and, thereby, created many lasting happy childhood memories.

Let the Bullying Begin

BEGINNING AT THE AGES of ten and eight years old, my sister and I moved every few years of our life, attending different boarding schools. Some people may think I was sent to boarding school because I was a bad kid. Nope, not at that point in my life anyway. It was a family tradition. Both my parents went to boarding schools as did both my brothers, and then my sister and I did as well. There are many benefits to boarding school in that it teaches you independence at a very young age, but there can be drawbacks, too, with respect to moving around a lot and not developing a sense of community.

The ages of seven to fourteen were particularly challenging for me. I was not only an overweight kid, I had glasses and braces with headgear, which made it quite difficult for me to fit in anywhere. Honestly, kids can be little shits. If you do not fit into the norm of what other kids think you should look like, talk like, and act like, you become a social pariah, and you don't have many friends. Add to that, I was kind of a global nomad if you will, so I didn't sound the same as my peers or use the same expressions. Just another tick on the list of not fitting in very well.

I didn't realize it at the time, but learning to become a chameleon in my effort to fit in with different groups of kids would become one of my superpowers, because in that phase of my life, that's all I wanted—to fit in.

So, can you guess what happened next? Let the bullying begin! Oh yes. Young girls especially can be so cruel. The bullying got so intense that I had to change schools a couple of times because kids were throwing balls at my head, pushing me down the stairs, reading my diary, posting it around school, and I even woke up in the middle of the night, wearing my headgear of course, with girls throwing popcorn at my head. Why popcorn? I have no idea. They could've been more original, but I don't think they had perfected the art of bullying quite yet.

Then there was Catholic boarding school in England. An all-girls school, I might add, run by Catholic nuns. Oh, those nuns. I had left my previous school in Central London because the bulling was so intense and transferred to this boarding school in the Surrey suburbs of London that was full of bratty kids and strict nuns. I was ten years old and had no idea what I was in for.

I remember constantly getting in trouble. One time it was because I questioned the concept of God. I just couldn't understand that if God was supposed to be this all-loving being why I had to pray to him while I was sitting on a hard church bench or on my knees in a church when I could be outside lying on the grass praying to him. The nuns did not like this very much. Punishment was often a ruler smack on the knuckles or behind. Of course, nothing was ever said about these smacks. It was one of those unspoken things that we just endured.

I watched the older girls sneak out in their risqué outfits to see boys from the school next door and sneak back in through the bathroom window, smelling like alcohol. I was the youngest one in the school at that time. I was the runt. I was still overweight, wore glasses and braces with headgear, and I had a giant space between my two front teeth from sucking my thumb. As you can guess, I was not popular, and I was an outcast right away because I was not English.

During my boarding school years, I called my mom in tears when things were bad, and she would somehow make her way to me at least once a month to comfort me. I wouldn't know where she was in the world, but she would always stop everything to come support me.

Later, in school back in Connecticut, the bullying became so intense that I had Mom bring me food so I could bribe the girls to be nice to me. This went on for years. I didn't appreciate the impact of the mental and physical abuse at the time, because, yes, I was still just trying to fit in.

Mom would always tell me as I was crying to her, "Sweetheart, one day this will all stop. I promise. I love you." Of course, I didn't believe her at the time, but the experience of being severely bullied taught me kindness and empathy for others at a very young age. The problem for me was that no group wanted to hang out with me— not the cool kids, the band geeks, or the dorks. I was on my own, bouncing around the world from new group to new group.

I think about kids today and the cyber bullying that happens. I'm not sure I would've made it through that world to be honest. I distinctly remember at eleven years old saying to my mom that I never wanted to have children. I think the bullying probably had something to do with me not having a maternal bone in my body. As I write this, I'm now in my forties and have no children. I'm divorced and have a cat. Yes, I may be that "cat lady" we used to make fun of in our teenage years. Honestly, though, I love my life today, even with all its myriad challenges.

Okay, this is not a sob story about my life, so I'm not going to dwell further on such things, but I will say that, when I was older, these experiences did shape my ability to empathize with others in their life struggles.

The Galapagos Transformation

THERE HAVE BEEN MANY pivotal moments in my life. One happened when I was thirteen and a half. We were off for summer break, and I was tired of being picked on all the time. I'm not sure if I was just growing up or if I started exercising and eating right, but I lost a lot of weight, got contacts, dyed my hair for the first time, shaved my legs (over my father's objection), and purchased a new wardrobe.

Now that I think about it, I did conform to society social norms for a few years. The change started when we took this particular family trip to the Galapagos.

My dad planned this family trip for our immediate family of six. We set out on this epic adventure where we hired a private guide and wended our way throughout the Galapagos Islands. We swam with iguanas, seals, penguins, and blue footed booby birds. Later, in Ecuador, we trekked through the Amazonian rain forest while learning about rain forest medicine from tribes deep in the jungle.

On one Galapagos island we were in search of flamingos. We found ourselves wading deep in what we thought was mud but turned out to be a combination of mud and flamingo poop. We had to trek about a quarter of a mile through this stuff to get to those flamingos. I remember watching my brothers step so gingerly as they pulled their feet out of this mud, which was only up to their kneecaps. My sister and I were not so lucky. The mud was up to our thighs as I recall. I could barely take a step. Each time we lifted our legs, we would face-plant right into flamingo poop.

We finally reached the flamingos. I was expecting some kind of miraculous feeling. Nope. Just flamingos, eating their own poop, not moving, standing on one leg, the other tucked up. So memorably anticlimactic, but we lived that story and still reminisce about it today.

Perhaps the more interesting and accidentally

irresponsible adventure in the Amazonian rainforest happened while we were spending some time with a local tribe. My sister and I wandered off together and saw that we could swim in the river. We were told not to swallow the water or pee in the river because of these tiny Amazonian fish that can swim up your urethra. No problem. We could follow these directions quite easily.

So, we stripped off and jumped in wearing just our underwear. We were swimming around, splashing, and just generally enjoying the fact that we were in the middle of nowhere having some quality sister time together. One of the guides came over to us and told us to be careful because there were piranhas. That got our attention and shocked the living hell out of us! He said not to worry because in the summertime (which it was), the fruits fall from the trees, and the piranhas tended to like the fruits and vegetables more than human flesh. Tended to like? Right?!?

I'm not sure at thirteen years old how you're supposed to interpret that, but we took it as a signal to get out of the water right away. We couldn't get up on land, so we made a straight line to one of the little canoe boats. The boat was very narrow. It kept tipping over as we were trying to get in. I was envisioning going back to school with no toes. Thankfully, there was a happy ending. My sister and I both still have ten toes each. That swim is yet another memory I share with my sister.

The adventures over the few weeks we were in South America are so clear in my mind even today. At the end of the trip, something interesting happened to me. Yes, superficially I lost weight, got rid of the glasses, braces, and so forth, but I also became a little bit braver. I can't pinpoint the exact moment it happened, but I realized that I was not going to let bullying hold me back anymore. When I returned to school, I was going to fight back. I wasn't sure yet if this was to be metaphorically or physically, and I don't even think I knew what the word metaphorically meant at the time anyway.

A Different Kind of Teenage Life

WHEN I WENT BACK to school in the fall after returning from the Galapagos, suddenly the mean girls and cute boys started to talk to me. I was dumbfounded. I couldn't understand what was happening. These cruel little humans wanted to be friends with me now? What? Should I have been grateful?

My dad always tells people that he knew I was different at a very young age. Three years old to be exact. I still don't know what he means by that precisely, but he often comments that I seemed to march to the beat of my own drum before I even knew what a drum was. Whatever he means, I'll take it. He said sometimes I was preternaturally bright at a very early age, as if I'd lived before. Maybe that was just the youngest sibling striving for attention.

So, what did I do next? Against every instinct and desire to be popular, I rejected the popular kids. I could not stand by and watch them bully other kids as I had been bullied. Bullying was especially prevalent in high school. I bounced from group to group, whichever one would take me or hang out with me.

There are certain things in life you are taught not to

talk about, especially in "polite society." Sex. Politics. Religion. You need to remember that I grew up with a very global mindset, so to me no topic was off limits. I wish somebody would've given me social pointers on this early on.

Are you ready for it? After I turned fourteen and the summer before transferring to a new private school, I met a boy. Oh, what a gorgeous human he was. His name was George, and he was my sister's friend. He was about five foot eight, sandy blonde hair, blue eyes that could pierce your soul and make you fall in love, and a great physique.

At the time we had a home in the northwest corner of Connecticut, and I was to attend high school in Rhode Island that fall. George would sneak onto our property at night with his friend, and I would slip out with my sister or a friend to go see him. I had smoked pot a few times when I was thirteen in The Bahamas, but this was my first adventure with a two-foot-tall purple bong in the middle of the night.

I wore blue plastic zip-up pants I had purchased in London that summer, a chain ball necklace, and a tight little Mr. Bubble T-shirt for those of you old enough to remember that fad. And I had purple-dyed hair. Apparently, I thought I was a skater with a little Spice Girl thrown in because I certainly dressed like it, but I was never either one. My generation calls this being a "poser." I'll just say I went through many fashion phases.

Not long before I left to start this new boarding prep school, George and I snuck out to our pool house one night. I drank a few sips of beer while doing my best to flirt, and George offered me a hit of marijuana through this giant bong. I had no idea what I was doing, but I accepted because I was trying to be cool. Who doesn't want to be cool at fourteen? So, I'm high as a kite and George advanced on me. He came in for a kiss. I wasn't very experienced at the time.

We proceeded to have an epic make out session in one of the bathrooms in the pool house. He lay me down on the floor and started undressing me. I started getting a little bit nervous. When we were both stark naked, he asked me if I had had sex before. I told him I had not. I think that naturally got his teenage boy's attention as he was a few years older than I.

He had the balls to tell me that no girl goes to high school as a virgin. I would be uncool, and I wouldn't have a lot of friends. I instantly was transported back to my younger days of being bullied and said, "Okay, let's do it." He was a teenage boy, so he wasn't experienced. The sex lasted the classic thirty seconds or so, and then he got up and left. I never saw him again. So that's the short story for my first experience with sex!

I'm sharing this story because the first day I started at my new school I thought I would be super popular and cool as I went around telling all the girls I wasn't a virgin. Yeah, nope, not a great idea. That wasn't all. My dad had offered me a piece of advice that I willfully ignored. He told me that this was a conservative New England boarding school where I should probably have at least one gray skirt, knee high socks, and a blue blazer. So, how did I roll up to this new school on the first day? I wore red leather pants, eyeliner that looked like a clown drew my face, and my hair was blue. I quickly found out blue hair (or whatever) wasn't "allowed." Oh yeah, social pariah right from the start.

I purchased a new wardrobe and tried to fit in the best I could, but I was already labeled the slut. Definitely more unkind than being labeled a band geek or a dork.

After my initial shock therapy transition into this new high school, I thought about transferring schools again, but I stuck it out for one reason. This school had an incredible, semester-long program on a beautiful 70-foot sailing vessel with six students to go tag sharks and turtles. I knew this because growing up I had seen this yacht stop at Cat Island, where I'd met the leading faculty member. That's how I came to go to this school. I was the kind of kid who only applied to one school and was determined I would get in. Surprisingly, the targeted approach worked most of my life—until the job market after college, a story for later.

It was such a welcome relief when we set sail. We sailed to different islands and tagged sharks and turtles for marine research. For days on end, we would wake up at six a.m., scrub the boat, complete our schoolwork, tag marine animals, input the data, and take turns at the helm sailing the boat. I much preferred being out on the open ocean with a few individuals getting my butt kicked with work and not showering for days than being back at school. It was on that trip I knew I was going to chart my own course in life, wherever that would take me. I was never going to fit in. I remember thinking that precise thought while watching dolphins off the bow of the boat at dusk in the middle of the ocean in The Bahamas.

Even today, though I have amazing groups of people I work with, socialize with, and even a very select few

I trust my life with, I'm a bouncer. I just bounce from group to group. I used to get jealous of those kids who grew up in one neighborhood and had friends they've known for decades. I didn't know what that felt like, so I stopped trying. It's quite liberating to realize at a young age that you're just going to be who you are. I think it takes some folks well into their middle years to figure that out, if they ever do.

Trinidad & Tobago

ANOTHER MEMORABLE EARLY LIFE adventure was going to Trinidad & Tobago with my mom, dad, and sister. My dad sure can plan a trip. He is meticulous. He researches thoroughly the offerings of each country on his itinerary. My brothers are sixteen and thirteen years older than I am, so at this point in my teenage years, they were often off in the world on their own. My sister is only two years older than I am, so we grew up experiencing many of the same family trips.

Trinidad & Tobago is an island country in the southeastern West Indies, located near the northern coast of South America. It's beautiful. Trinidad is known for its rain forests and rich music culture, while Tobago draws tourists and scuba divers.

My dad arranged numerous adventures for this family trip. Riding horses bareback on the beach, watching leatherback turtles lay eggs on the beach, scuba diving with manta rays, going on rain forest adventures, and enjoying private resorts where few other tourists would be found were all in his plan.

On one of the adventures, we hiked deep into the rain forest of Trinidad. We had a guide and about a four-hour hike to a location where we would then use bamboo strands to tie up hammocks about 20 feet above the ground. We were planning to stay the night. The hike into the rain forest was magical with waterfalls on our left and right and wild animals approaching us out of curiosity. We learned lots about the flora and fauna from our guide.

When we arrived at our designated camping area, our guide made quick work of climbing up trees to build a ladder for each of us to get up to our hammock that he had strung. I would say bravery and an adventuresome spirit were required as we were well off the ground and the hammocks were tippy. I wondered how I was going to pee, and the guide told me to hang my butt over the hammock. I had to pee a lot, so I became skilled at hanging my little tush over the hammock and peeing on the creatures below.

As sunset approached, we were instructed not to leave our hammocks for any reason during the night because jaguars and other jungle animals could devour us. Well, okay.

The problem was, it started raining. A torrential downpouring rain. Naturally, it rains in the rain forest, but this was like a monsoon. The guide urgently informed us that we had to risk getting back down the mountain in the middle of the night. We climbed down to the ground. It was raining so hard we could barely see ten feet in front of us as we started hiking back down the mountain in the dark. The rain continued to come down, the mud was piling up, and each time I would take a step, the mud would go higher and higher from my knees to my thighs until it became virtually impossible to move.

I'm not sure how many hours we were into our descent from the mountain when I suddenly lost my footing. We were on a very narrow trail on the side of the mountain and one thing led to another. I slipped. I fell off the trail and held onto a tree. I yelled, and everyone stopped. They tried to pull me back up, but I kept sliding. My body smashed from one tree to another until I finally got a grip on one of them and hung on tight. I think I had slid several hundred feet or so. I could still see the flashlights above me and hear my mother's frantic shouts to me.

Our guide built a pulley system to rescue me. It took the better part of an hour to winch me back up to safety. Everyone was covered in mud from head to toe and looked slightly terrified. My sister and I started laughing. The grown-ups were not laughing, but my sister and I thought it was a great adventure.

Bruised and battered, we made it down the mountain by dawn. We later learned that the part of the rain forest where we had been had flooded beyond recognition. Now it made sense that the guide insisted we leave the mountain and take the chance of being eaten by jaguars that fortunately had the good sense to stay out of the rain.

Most of our family trips had some kind of adventure we could never have predicted, but you know what they created for me? Memories. Experiences. Stories I will keep in my memory bank about my childhood. I always thank my parents for these incredible opportunities and experiences they shared with us growing up.

In Trinidad I even had a boy fall in love with me. He

was a local islander, and he built me a raft out of bamboo and carved a piece of bamboo for me. He carved my name, his name "Rafy," and that he loved me on the piece. I still have it in my room. I love memories. I don't dwell on the past, but I reminisce in the most beautiful of ways.

College Almost

I COPED THROUGHOUT HIGH school the only way I knew how—I flirted with the boyfriends of the mean girls. Oh yes, my misadventures snowballed into high school being an epic wipeout for me. I had a few friends here and there, but I pretty much drifted through high school. I survived the experience as most of us do even when we don't think we will, although I survived with a twist. I graduated sooner than I was supposed to due to the higher education system in Europe before transferring to New England. I remember that when it was time to apply to colleges, I only applied to one, Occidental College in Los Angeles, because they had an amazing marine research program. I was determined to go there to become a marine biologist. Admittedly, this was cocky because you're supposed to have backup schools.

My SAT scores were just crap. I took the ACT sober, drunk, and high to no avail. I didn't even send in my standardized test scores to Occidental. I wrote a nine-page paper about why they should not look at standardized scores and instead look at me as a human being. I couldn't believe it worked, but it did.

Upon my acceptance by Occidental, I realized I was not quite ready yet to attend college. Why? I'd been in school most of my life. I wanted to experience life before diving back into the academic scene. Also, truthfully, I wanted to be able to legally drink in college, and I wasn't old enough yet. Priorities, right? I wish I had a better reason for wanting to defer from college, but that was it.

I closed my eyes and spun one of those old-school globes, and my finger landed on Beijing. So, Beijing is where I decided to go with no plan, no idea what I was going to do, or how I was going to get by, but I was pretty independent by sixteen, almost seventeen. Before I embarked on moving to a country that none of my family had ever explored, I needed to have some time with nature.

My life was always on the go and whenever I needed to sit still or recenter myself, I would do one of two things: I would go off into the wilderness for a life-or-death survival trip or head back down to The Bahamas. This time I went for a survival trip.

My sister and I discovered a really interesting adventure travel company that offered various three-week trips to locations around the world where you would do things like scuba dive, hike in the rain forest, learn survival skills, and sail a catamaran. I took many of these trips. My sister and I went scuba diving together in Sharm el-Sheikh in Egypt. I went to the outback in Australia, the rain forest, rock climbing, and every other nature adventure you can think of. I also lived aboard a research vessel studying chambered nautilus.

I wanted to get back to nature before my next step in life, so I signed up for a six-week Outward Bound adventure in New Zealand. I didn't know this at the time, but in the late nineties, most of the kids on this particular Outward Bound trip were troubled kids and were sent there as punishment. After I flew twenty-five hours to reach New Zealand, one of the first questions the Kiwi kids asked me was why I voluntarily flew across the world to get my butt kicked. It was a great question. I still don't have the answer.

These Outward Bound trips were designed to be pretty grueling. We woke up around four thirty in the morning to run several miles, swim in frigid water, do push-ups in a cold outdoor shower, get changed in five minutes at base camp, eat breakfast, and then we were off for adventures for the day. Later, we embarked on longer adventures like hiking for a week or rowing a Viking style boat.

What I didn't take into account was that while it was summer in the US, it was winter in New Zealand. I love warmth. I need warmth. I did not pack for the cold in New Zealand and had to suck it up. This trip tested my endurance limits like I had never been tested before.

The hardest part of the journey was dealing with the people. It didn't bother me after a while to be soaking wet and cold to the bone on the side of a mountain with sideways wind and rain cutting my face, but trying to get along with six other kids in a group twenty-four seven was really hard. You got to know each other intimately and quickly. You had to build trust with one another because you were literally in life-or-death situations trying to navigate the side of a mountain with an old-fashioned topographical map and a compass. No GPS for us back then. You were only as strong as your weakest link because you had to wait for the slowest one in the pack. Each of us had to succeed for all of us to succeed. It was a great life lesson that I think many adults still need to learn.

Toward the end of the trip, the senior leaders walked us up the side of a mountain and dropped us off one by one in our own very small area for something called a solo experience. We weren't supposed to leave our assigned territory during the three days of our experience. They provided each of us with three carrots, four apples, and three stale oat cakes. We didn't even have a tent. They gave us a tarp, a mat, a pen, a journal, and the bare minimum essentials. We were supposed to commune with nature, contemplate life, sit with our thoughts, meditate, and appreciate our life.

I was 16 years old. I would say I wasn't particularly in tune with my inner meditative thoughts yet. When they dropped me off, I was immediately bored. Never a good thing for me. I knew I wasn't supposed to leave the area, but I couldn't help myself. I kept poking around and walking ten feet further to the left and then another twenty feet, and so on. I know why they told us not to leave our area, because I got lost. I finally found my way back around dusk and opened my little snack pack. I was famished. It had gotten quite dark, and I only had a small lantern.

When I tried to open the bag of food, it just ripped. All of my food went rolling down the side of the steep mountain. I was stunned. What would I eat for the next three days? Yes, I know you can survive without food for a month, and I probably knew that then, but that is not the immediate thought that runs through your head as a hangry teenager.

Since I couldn't do much about the food situation, I threw the tarp over a tree in case it rained and wrapped my thin blanket around my shivering body. I went to bed hungry, cranky, and then it got worse.

I woke up to creatures with beady red eyes nibbling my toes. I let out a toe-curling scream with no one to hear me. Possums! Those little fuckers were trying to eat my toes. I shooed them away with a stick and slept curled up in a ball for the rest of the night. I woke up to pouring rain and my stomach growling something fierce. I huddled under the tarp and tried to journal my thoughts. Every thought was completely negative. I hated every moment.

Why did I go on this stupid trip? What was wrong with me? Why couldn't I just be normal and go to the beach like everyone else?

The rain stopped, and a little bit of sunshine peeked through the trees. I heard the cry of what sounded like some kind of seagull, so I figured I must be near the ocean. In true Ali fashion, I left my area and started a trek down the steep mountainside. I figured how bad could it be? I really should never ask myself that kind of question!

I tripped over my own foot while trying to climb over a downed tree, and I started tumbling. I can't tell you how far I tumbled, but I ended up rolling right into a rock. Thank God my gluteus maximus hit the rock first. I was covered head to toe in cold, wet mud and bruised on what felt like every part of my body. But, you know what? I looked around. I made it. I was at the ocean. I don't know what I was looking for or why I decided I had to go to the ocean, but then I noticed on the sides of the rocks there were hundreds of little mussels. Food. Glorious food!

I pulled little mussels off the rock, cracked them open, ate them raw, and filled my belly. I fit as many as I could in the side pockets of my pants and started to make my way back up the mountain. I didn't know how I was going to find my little campground. If I didn't, how would I be found when my "solo" was over? Would I become one of those lost-in-the-wilderness-never-to-be-seen-again stories? Probably eaten by possums. Ah, the inner dialogue of a teenager.

As I was climbing back up the mountain, I was so grateful that I grew up in The Bahamas roughing it, because I just dug in, pushed deep, and engaged every core muscle I had to pull myself up the mountain, step-by-step, retracing the slide marks from when I had fallen earlier. I didn't have a watch, so I could only assume it was several hours later, but I made it to camp! *I'm alive*, I thought, *and I am a freaking rock star.*

I sat down at my meager campsite, and I cried. I cried for what felt like the entire rest of the day. I didn't cry because I fell down a mountain or got attacked by possums or lost my food. I cried for my younger self. It took me almost a decade to come to the realization that I had not grieved over all the trauma from being bullied as a kid. I felt so light afterward even though I was shivering, had two days to go with no food except the mussels in my pockets, very little water, and had cuts all over my body.

There is something to be said for kids going to nature to deal with some of their trauma. It was in that moment after making it back up the mountain that I let go of so much of my childhood trauma. I was no longer going to hold onto it. I did not intentionally set out to come to this realization, nor had I realized I was still holding so much trauma inside, but it felt so good to let it go.

Having shared that experience with you, I have to say, when I look back at my childhood, I really only remember joy. I'm fortunate and grateful because I know there's so much trauma for so many other kids. I can honestly and authentically say I don't hold onto the experiences of being bullied as a kid anymore.

After three days I was collected and brought back to base camp. We ended the trip with a marathon run through the woods. Oh God, it was awful. I had terrible shin splints, and tears ran down my face. Everyone was passing me. I think I was the last to finish. But, dammit, I did it!

On a lighter note, there was this gorgeous Brazilian man in one of the other programs who was probably ten years older than I was. We had the most romantic get-together that night at a hotel in Wellington, New Zealand. You think it ends there? Oh, no no, not with me. He was headed back to Brazil and asked me to come along for a few days. I had nothing to do, nowhere to go, and could go to China whenever I felt like it. We flew to Brazil together and had a lovely time. There was not much talking, and the excursion could probably be written as one of those bare-chested-men-on-the-cover romance novels. It was a great way to end such a butt-kicking trip and a beautiful beginning to the start of the next chapter in my life.

CHAPTER 3

Preparing for a New Life

AFTER RETURNING FROM BRAZIL, I decided to catch a ride on a cargo plane to The Bahamas for a month before departing for Beijing.

My mother was living full-time on Cat Island at that time. I can't recall where my dad was. Mom and I had the most beautiful bonding time together cooking, sunbathing, having dance parties, drinking, and having hours of conversation. We knew we might not see each other for quite a while, so we made the most of our time.

I really didn't know what to expect from my decision to move to China, but I wasn't nervous about it. I felt fearless at this point in my life, as teenagers often do, which was probably a sign I was getting a little bit too cocky, and Murphy would strike soon. I was not concerned about this or fully appreciative of what this might mean. I was just having a blast. Most of my friends were preparing for college, checking off books on an exhaustive mandatory reading list, and taking the "normal" track of life. Not me. Never.

About a month before departing for China, I fell in love, well, teenage love. I still remember teenage love being so powerful because you don't know how to control your emotions. This boy, who was twenty-one or twenty-two years old, came down to Cat Island with his family. I was at a local resort clubhouse that night. He turned the corner, and I couldn't breathe. He was tall, six-pack ripped abs, beautiful blue eyes, and this really sexy strut. My devilish Ali flipped the switch and was on a mission. The mission? Get the boy! I still have one photo of him in one of my scrapbooks.

To be fair, it wasn't that hard. There's not that many places to run on a small island, and there were only about twenty folks at the resort at the time. We hit it off instantly. There was electric passion. We sat on a swing set by a bonfire, drinking and listening to someone play the guitar, flirting the night away. Later, he walked me down the beach to my home. You can guess what was going to happen next. I remember that kiss to this day. There are a few kisses in your life you never forget.

I went back to his room and after we were done with hours of naughtiness shall we say, he asked me where I had learned some of my bedroom skills. I said I had a little experience although naturally I hadn't had that much practice at sixteen. He proceeded to tell me that there were some things that I could work on, and he would be happy to show me over the next few weeks. No, I'm not kidding! I was mortified. Who wouldn't be? I was just told I was bad in bed, not something anyone wants to hear even at a young age.

Maybe not surprisingly, I said yes, and he told me to

bring a notepad and a pen the next time. I should mention that he had no idea I was sixteen. I told him I was eighteen. Furthermore, we were in The Bahamas, so I don't know if there's an age for what's appropriate and what's not.

As the weeks rolled by, we went kayaking, swimming, spearfishing, took long walks on the beach like in the movies, and I found myself falling head over heels for him. I had not told him I was leaving the island soon as he was on break from the University of Florida and would himself be leaving before long. He certainly had no idea I was moving to China. I didn't see any reason to ruin the romance.

About a week before I was to leave the island, we were snuggled up in his room one night, and I told him I would soon be leaving for China. He was gutted when I told him. It was one of those summer romances you take with you. I never saw him again.

For a brief moment I debated postponing my trip for him. My adventurous nature won out, and I packed my duffel bag, ready to take on an entirely new adventure that resulted in experiences I could never have imagined, except that I actually lived them. Away we go.

CHAPTER 4

China—Navigating Uncharted Territory

As WE WERE LINING up on the final approach for landing in Beijing, I looked out my window and suddenly had this overwhelming feeling of complete dread. What am I doing? I don't speak Chinese. Am I crazy? Where am I going to go?

I had made a mistake by packing my oversized, beat-up duffel bag with no wheels, one that looked like it could carry a dead body. There were no carts anywhere to be seen. Being young and spry, I engaged my core and put the duffel bag on my back as I cleared customs without having a clue what the customs agent was saying to me.

I walked outside, sat down on the sidewalk, and cried. Remember, this wasn't in the modern technology era where I could call my parents on my smart phone. This was back in the late nineties. I was going to have to find one of those Nokia brick cell phones and purchase an exorbitantly expensive phone card to call my parents to tell them I had arrived.

A kind-eyed taxi driver, who could not have been much over five feet tall saw me. He stepped out of his taxi and mumbled something to me in Chinese. All I knew how to say in Chinese was "I don't speak Chinese." He immediately scuffled away, and I was convinced I was just going to have to stay there until something happened. I did not know what, but surely something would happen.

The taxi driver came back with a map and started pointing feverishly to a location I couldn't quite decipher because his finger was in the way. Eventually, I could see that he was pointing to what looked like little school or church symbols. Either way, I think he noticed I was in distress, and I nodded my head okay.

Off we went. Wow! There was so much traffic. There didn't seem to be any rules or laws about traffic lanes. (There still aren't any that I have discovered the many times I've been back to China since then.) The road we were on had eight lanes. The city is surrounded by something called ring roads. The inner ring road denotes the center of the city and as the rings expand, you get further and further out of the city center. I didn't have a watch. I had no idea how long we were in the taxi, because I was just holding on for dear life as this man was talking to me in Chinese that I still could not understand and weaving his way through all this traffic.

I'm guessing it was about an hour later when we arrived at our destination. I pulled out my American dollars because it was illegal to exchange money at that time in the country. I knew I was going to have to find a black-market currency guy. I'm sure I paid triple or quadruple what the normal taxi fare was, but I was thankful for his help.

I crossed from one curb to another and sat down on the sidewalk by a bench not knowing what to do next.

I saw only Chinese people, no foreigners in sight. I was five feet nine with blonde hair, green eyes, and an athletic physique. I stood out in the crowd. After some time passed, this beautiful man approached and spoke to me in broken English. I found out he was French. I could speak a little French, but his English sufficed for the purpose of our conversation.

I explained my situation. He found a hotel for the night for me and said he would help me sign up to a language school in the morning. After he set me up at the hotel, I realized I was famished. I hadn't eaten in over fifteen hours. We went out to dinner together. I was introduced to something called "Bai Jiu." It's similar to grain alcohol or moonshine. I can't quite remember what happened next. I think I accidentally roofied myself.

I woke up with this beautiful gentleman in my bed, and I had not been in China twenty-four hours yet. My immediate thought was, *Great, Ali. Really? You can't even wait a few days before you find another beautiful man to sleep with?* The problem was I needed him. I needed him to introduce me to people, anyone really.

I impatiently waited for him to wake-up. I wanted to start figuring out what my next step was going to be. I've always been a planner. I may sometimes engage in risky activities, but I usually have backup plans. Not this time though.

After he got dressed, we went out and he introduced me to a few folks. Multiple broken English conversations led to chatting with some folks at the university next door, and I found a program that sounded right for me. It was a program for foreigners to spend a semester in Beijing attending classes and immersing in the Chinese culture. Great! I signed up. I paid. I didn't hesitate.

I was assigned a room with a German girl and felt right at home as my mother is German. We hit it off right away. She introduced me to all of the other foreigners in the program. I was off to a great start after just forty-eight hours.

On my third day in China, I started university classes. The students were a mix of nationalities—Russian, Australian, European, American, African, you name it. I had taken a semester of Chinese in high school, but I didn't remember a single useful sentence. For the first month or two, life seemed pretty monotonous. I would wake up, go to class, and socialize with all the foreigners. I did not practice speaking Chinese. I was embarrassed that I spoke it so poorly. I did spend a lot of time at bars. I was only in my late teens, so this seemed to me like a good way to spend time then.

I really just wanted to have fun and experience the culture in the beginning, but after so many barhopping experiences, partying with foreign men, and diligently practicing my ten Chinese characters per day while memorizing sentence structures, I started to get bored. I got bored easily back then. I realized I wasn't really going to immerse myself in a cultural experience if I didn't stop surrounding myself with foreigners. I had even started teaching English to Chinese schoolkids as that was commonplace back then. However, the school didn't want me to speak Chinese, only English. That was a problem. I was not there to practice my own native tongue.

Change of Course

I MADE A PROBABLY risky decision. I would like to say it was calculated, but it wasn't. I found a Chinese family who would take me in and went to live with them. They did not know one word of English. The rent was incredibly cheap. I made a plan.

Each morning when I ate breakfast with my Chinese family, I would make it a point to try to jot down at least three characters in something called pinyin (the English spelling for Chinese characters) for what I thought I heard them say, research the characters, and then talk about them in class. I would try to learn what the character meant, how to use it, and how to put it in a sentence.

My family had a very strong Beijing accent. There are fifty-three or so dialects in the Chinese language. I speak Mandarin Chinese. Language is a tricky thing. Think about how different it can sound listening to an American Southerner and a New Yorker with their accents and their own "vocabulary."

After classes, I would then spend time bargaining in the streets for fake Armani, Gucci, and Ralph Lauren clothing. I had to wear knockoff foreign brands since all the Chinese brands were so teeny tiny. I was in incredible shape, but still the size of a cow compared to the standard Chinese female physique. I was often asked if I ate meat because I was so big. Oh joy. I respected and understood it was not a rude comment in China. They were saying I was healthy and had money to eat.

A few more months passed. Surprisingly, I found that my Chinese was not getting better. I was trying to learn in a structured school environment, but I still wasn't speaking Chinese very often. I also was still primarily hanging out with foreigners. So, I made another pivotal decision. I quit school. No idea why, I just felt like it was the right thing to do.

I had been partying since I was fourteen years old. I loved to have fun. If it were possible to make a living on just having fun, I would've figured out a way to do it. I started going out late night to bars, drinking, arm wrestling, watching cockfights, and found myself so relaxed with some level of inebriation that I started practicing my Chinese. Don't get me wrong, I studied every day from my textbooks with respect to the characters, but I allowed the locals to help me with sentence structures and how to use the words properly.

I was also starting to gain weight, about twenty pounds. That should not have been a big surprise. I was eating Chinese fried dough for breakfast followed by greasy chicken with rice at lunch, and considerable alcohol at dinner followed by late night street vendor snacks at the night market.

Night Market

OH, THE NIGHT MARKET. Beijing and other Asian cities have these night markets that sell food that you probably have only seen in movies or read about in books, if you have heard of them at all. There were hundreds upon hundreds of vendors selling peculiar culinary oddities. Remember COVID-19 in the Wuhan market? People were eating whale's blood, baby birds, silkworm pupae, duck intestines, camel foot, and pig brains. You get the idea. I love to immerse myself in different cultures and will never judge something until I try it. I completely respect those who do not have a desire to do that.

From the corner of my eye, I spied a snack I couldn't resist. I rushed over and told the vendor in broken Chinese, "I want that one," as I pointed to three small deep-fried scorpions on a stick. It cost me one dollar.

I crunched into the stinging spine of one of them, not quite sure what happened to the poison in the tail when it got fried. I was elated because fried scorpion tasted like an over-fried French fry. It was delicious and nutritious! No poison. Payback at last for those years of being stung by scorpions as a kid in The Bahamas!

Fully pleased with myself, I continued making my way alone in the middle of the night market in Beijing as a teenager while my peers were no doubt having a keg party on a beach in college back in the US. I concluded I had made the better trade.

Back to becoming an Oompa Loompa with my weight gain. I had exercised and been active my entire life, and since I lost the weight as a young teenager, I was determined to keep it off. I could barely fit in my pants anymore. I couldn't purchase a larger size because I already had the largest size they offered at the fake goods market.

I needed to add some form of exercise into my regimen. I started taking Wushu classes, a type of martial art defensive dance you could say, with some of my Chinese and foreign friends. I did not find it a particularly interesting or rigorous workout other than I had a mild crush on my Chinese instructor, but I decided to leave that alone.

I searched around and found a broken-down kickboxing gym. I love kickboxing, but I had only been exposed to the foreign cardio type of kickboxing they offer in American gyms. This was Muay Thai, Thai kickboxing, where pretty much anything goes. You can strike with your hands and your feet, and you don't wear big boxing gloves. It's hard core. You can look it up.

When I tell you the moment I turned the corner for my first class and quite literally ran into the side post of the door because I was speechless, I'm not exaggerating. The most beautiful specimen of a human being was standing right in front of me with not an ounce of fat on him and me with my little muffin tops hanging over my stretchy yoga pants. I wasn't overweight, but I definitely had to get my butt in gear to lose my morning Chinese fried dough love handles. Let's call this beautiful character Stephane.

Stephane had long dark hair, seductive brown eyes, just a little bit of chin hair, every muscle was just popping out of his body, but not so much that it was unattractive. His voice was soft and beautiful as he started to teach the class in Chinese. Wait? What? Oh dear! He didn't speak English. He was a beautiful Italian stallion who moved with the grace of a ballerina. I had no idea what the hell he was saying for the first few weeks while I stayed in the back of the class trying to burn off some of those calories, get in a workout, and just stare at him. I did learn he was ten years older than I was.

I decided to trade morning fried dough for sushi and tried to find healthy snacks. I compromised with those choices because I certainly wasn't going to give up drinking at the bars. That was just too much fun, and my Chinese was improving every single day or rather every single night.

I looked forward to my kickboxing classes with Stephane three times a week. After about three weeks, I noticed that he kept looking at me. I thought he was checking out my love handles in complete disgust, but he kept smiling at me, winking at me, and trying to fix my form while gently caressing my backside. I was friends with one of the Chinese students in the class who was able to speak English. This friend told me after class one day that Stephane would like to ask me on a date.

I laughed out loud. There was no possible way. Whatever number you may think I am on a scale of 1 to 10, this guy, at least in my mind, was definitely a 9/10. I've always been quite realistic in understanding the type of men I was able to attract. Of course, I said yes, and with the help of my third-party translator friend, we agreed on a location for dinner that night.

I think I must've tried on ten different outfits, but perhaps more impressively, I wrote down and memorized twenty questions to ask him on our date. I cannot recall what type of restaurant he took me to, but it had chairs, so that was good enough for me. I was so confident in my ability to deliver these memorized questions that I started firing them off. About four questions in, I realized I had no idea what he was saying when he answered. I think he understood that I was perhaps a little bit over my head. When you can't converse with someone with words, you can find small gestures that relax the mood and can help you enjoy a pleasant dinner.

After dinner, he slipped his hand into mine and walked me back to my place. I wished him a good night, still acting like a shy schoolgirl. He grabbed my hand and gave me an intensely passionate kiss. He tried to tell me something in Chinese, but I still couldn't understand his sexy accent. We popped into a taxi. I had no clue where we were off to. I'm not sure why my brain didn't compute that he was taking me to his place, but that's what happened. It was an amazing night where we stayed up until dawn drinking terrible Chinese wine in his apartment, and playing around as if we had been together for ages. No words were necessary.

These romantic encounters with weekly dinners and me trying feverishly to become more fluent in Chinese while practicing with Stephane lasted for months. The language of love, which will only get you so far, I might add, made me double down on my effort to learn Chinese. Within six months, I had gained enough language proficiency that I could speak Chinese well enough to communicate about practical things like opening up a bank account.

My life was flourishing. I was basically fluent in Chinese, my rocking body returned, and I started to compete in small competitions in kickboxing. I found a new job as a Chinese food taster where I wrote reviews for a Chinese newspaper and got paid for plastering my foreign face in the local paper. And I had an Italian boyfriend with whom I conversed in Chinese, who told me he was madly in love with me after only a month. (Yes, I know. And, yes, I believed him.) I remember thinking that life could not get any better.

We traveled around with friends to different parts of the country where we drank grain alcohol on the beach, watched fireworks, tried the most unusual culinary delicacies, checked out local villages, and really dived into the cultural history of China.

I'm not saying life was all smooth sailing. There were some pretty intense moments where I had to adapt to circumstances very quickly. Once I went on a solo trip, not a smart idea. I was in a very rural town. A man was shot by another man. The dead man's body fell on me. I was stunned and covered in blood. The man who shot him picked me up off the floor and told me to go away and don't say a word. I went away, and I did not tell anyone what happened. I will never disclose the name of the town, but when a human falls on you after being shot dead in front of you, it's not something you forget.

The experience did make me appreciate the many rights we have in first-world countries. I would offer more details, but I really don't have any. The event happened. I walked away. I was probably in shock. Other than telling my immediate family members, this is the first time I've talked about this experience. I know that was heavy, but it is part of my lived experiences.

On a lighter note, on a trip to Qing Dao, a city where they brew a famous beer, a group of friends and I were on the beach one night, drinking grain alcohol, and the fireworks started going off. The next thing I remember was waking up buried in sand. It was as if someone built a sandcastle over me. All my friends were laughing. They pulled out a camcorder to show me what had happened.

I started acting like a dog or cat when I heard the fireworks and began to dig a hole. Oh yes. Classic Ali I suppose. What they didn't know was that when I was a teenager on Cat Island, I was burned pretty severely by fireworks that fell sideways, and I dove headfirst into the sand for protection. The deep recesses of my memory apparently kicked into survival mode—flight or fight to protect myself. I mean who digs a hole in the sand on a Chinese beach (admittedly while completely intoxicated) during a fireworks display? It's a good thing I'm okay being eccentric.

Not an Experience I Would Advocate Trying

I DECIDED I WAS never leaving China. I hadn't quite built up the nerve yet to tell my parents. That was my plan though. I would marry Stephane, we would be kickboxing champions, and we would live happily ever after. I really wish I could have a conversation with my younger self and offer just a little bit of wisdom.

We both saved some money. Well, honestly, I saved up most of the money because he was pretty much a broke kickboxing instructor. I didn't appreciate at the time how absurd it was that a teenager was supporting a man in his late twenties. It's a pattern that took me nearly forty years to break. Again, a conversation from my wiser self to my younger self would have been good.

I wanted to visit this beautiful island called Hainan in southern China. Why wouldn't I? I'm a beach girl. Oh no, young and dumb Ali. I agreed to go to a city in northern China called Harbin, where temperatures averaged minus 35 degrees Fahrenheit in the winter, because that's where Stephane wanted to go.

This was near the Mongolian and Russian border. We didn't have the money to fly, so we decided to ride the train. He was so cheap he didn't even purchase middle car seats. It was the back of the train for us. The dirtiest of the dirty. I really should've started picking up on these red flags now that I think about it, but when hormones and pheromones rule your life at that age, you are blissfully unaware.

We boarded the train. There were six stacked beds in a car. I didn't know at the time, but you always want to get there early to get a top bunk. Why? Because when you wake up and you are on the bottom bunk, you will very likely be covered in sunflower seed hulls that were spat out overnight by your fellow passengers. It's a thing. It was disgusting. It was a twelve-hour journey from hell, but we made it.

We traveled past the famous Harbin ice city, a major tourist attraction where in the winter they build a city out of ice and lights. In Harbin, you can climb up a castle, bobsled down a hill, and climb the giant stairs, all made of ice blocks. It's beautiful and, as you would expect, bloody freezing.

I wanted to go there, but Stephane insisted that we push north a bit farther, closer to the Russian border to this snowboarding resort. I had been snowboarding before, so I just went with it.

We arrived at this stunning hotel that looked like it had been commissioned by Russian Czars in the 1800s. There were so many Russians, in fact, that I could not find a Chinese person within sight at first. It looked way too expensive for what we could afford. Of course, I was right. Stephane didn't call ahead for prices. He heard about the place from a friend. I trusted his judgment and did not utilize the important wisdom my father taught me when I was young: trust but verify.

At the check-in counter we found the room prices were double what we had anticipated. I did have enough cash, so, again, I just decided to go with the flow. The rooms were amazing, and it was such a beautiful winter wonderland that I was swept away once again. The next day ended up being a complete disaster because there was ice rather than snow on the slopes. I was not happy. Stephane knew I was not happy. He and I just couldn't stop arguing, and we were stuck together in this place.

We tried to walk to a small town that night, but there was so much snow that we had to use the tunnel system. What pray tell, you may ask, is a tunnel system doing in the middle of nowhere? Tunnels were carved out of hardpacked snow and lights were installed inside them. You could walk outside the hotel and enter a barely lit cavern not knowing how long you would be walking through it or if the snow was going to cave in on you while trying to make your way out of town. I think the snow must've been at least nine or ten feet high. I would say it wasn't brilliant fun, but it did lighten the mood a bit when we were laughing and having snowball fights.

We could only afford three days at this hotel before we had to head back to Beijing. As we were on the train, Stephane begged me for another night or two to go see the ice city in Harbin as I had originally asked. I was such a pushover back in those teenage days that I said yes.

We checked into our new hotel and immediately went out to explore the ice city. Our outside escapades only lasted about thirty minutes because at those freezing temperatures, I didn't have clothes warm enough to account for the wind chill factor. Tears would turn to ice when you walked outside. It was miserable. No amount of the Chinese version of hot cider helped. I just wanted to be on that beach in southern China, sipping a cocktail. I really did try to make the best of where we were though.

On our last day I decided to check us out early and proceeded to give the hotel reception my credit card, as I'd run out of cash. They said they needed a photo ID. No problem, I handed them my driver's license. Nope. This was unacceptable. They needed my passport. I went up to the room to fetch it from Stephane. The only job this oversized child had was to bring our damn passports, and he had forgotten to bring them.

Unbeknownst to me, in the early 2000s, only a handful of cities would accept foreign credit cards without a passport. I was mortified. I managed to get ahold of the US consulate and, it's hard to write this with a straight face, but the person on the other end of the phone told me that they could not identify me and therefore could not help me. I still can't make heads or tails of that today, but a 17-year-old American citizen was about to go to jail in northern China for non-payment of a hotel bill, and our embassy said they were not able to help.

Stephane was terrified too. I used a few of the minutes left on my phone card to tell my mother I was going to jail and please give me a week to get out on my own, but if that didn't work, please call Henry Kissinger (a family friend) at the State Department to help me. I then used the remaining minutes to call a friend in southern China with a request to fly up with money and our passports.

That's all the information I gave before being thrown into a jail cell that already housed five women. I didn't know what happened to Stephane. I guess he went to the men's jail. He never talked about it. You would think I would have been terrified of going to jail in China. Strangely, I wasn't. I wasn't even nervous when they closed the cell door behind me despite being terrified when they took me from the hotel. I was eerily calm. I looked at the women. They were dressed in rags and sleeping on hay and ripped sheets. I could see buckets with chicken bones in them, and I recall the hardened sadness in their eyes. I kept to myself for the first few hours, but they kept giggling and pointing at me. I imagine it's because they'd never seen a foreigner in jail before. Never mind the blonde hair, which fascinates many Chinese.

They were probably wondering what idiotic thing I had done to get myself in here. China is a communist country without rule of law as Americans know it. There is no due process. You can speak poorly against the government or steal vegetables and get thrown in jail for an unspecified amount of time. You're on your own, baby.

I finally mustered up the courage to ask them in Chinese what they were looking at. They couldn't quite understand me. When I listened to them, I could detect hints of Mandarin, but it was definitely a different dialect. I could understand enough though. We were allowed to take walks and go to the bathroom at specified times. We were served rice and chicken bones or some iteration of that for meals, but most of the time we were just in our cell. There were no real beds, only hay beds.

The days passed very quickly. I was getting the hang

of their broken Mandarin and whatever dialect they were speaking, and we started talking about why they were in prison. One woman didn't have enough money to buy food, so she stole food. One woman cheated her uncle for money because he was a lousy person, but she got caught. I should've been feeling sorry for myself, but I knew eventually I would get out. Either my friend would come up or my parents would make the trek over here weeks or months later to come find me. These women did not know when or even if they would ever be released.

There was no egregious mistreatment of any of the women that I could see. It was freezing though. No heat. Lots of huddling together. The experience was not what I expected, thankfully. I think I'd watched too many movies when I was a kid. This was not a maximum security jail for sure.

About five days later, my Australian girl friend from Beijing did arrive with the five hundred dollars I had asked for and our passports, and I bribed the prison guards to let us go.

Stephane and I were out. Just like that. No fuss, no muss. Money will usually talk in China. Yes, I got the Italian out. I did debate leaving him for another day, but I was trying to be my best self and not be a complete bitch despite a momentary inclination in that direction. I called my mother on the way back down to Beijing to tell her I was alive, safe, and out of jail. Nothing to worry about. We really don't talk about this experience much, but I suppose she trusted my street skills. At least I like to think so. I figured it out, which I always seem to do.

Now, as for my relationship with Stephane, yeah,

I wouldn't say things went smoothly after that. He tried to salvage the relationship and somehow convinced me to move from Beijing to Shanghai with him. Shanghai was even more expensive than Beijing. We rented a gorgeous apartment we really couldn't afford. While I was working and going to advanced level Chinese classes, he did nothing. Well, not nothing. I would catch him sitting cross-legged with his eyes closed meditating. He said he was trying to convene with some kind of god. Who the hell knows? I pretty much just ignored him for three months straight unless we were arguing ferociously.

Stephane would call his mommy and repeatedly yell the words, "Va Fan Culo." I knew he wasn't telling his mother he loved me. I think it was something along the lines of "go stick yourself up your own butt" I later learned.

Still, I wasn't ready yet to head back to the United States and a "normal" life. So, I did what came natural to my 18-year-old self. I left him in a pre-paid apartment and went to Southeast Asia and Australia for several months.

A Romance with Southeast Asia

WHEN I WAS IN China, I became friends with a girl who was born on the Gold Coast in Australia. Think of it like the South Beach of Miami. Beautiful humans, gorgeous beaches, beach bums, and surf bums. It was a backpacker haven. I decided to go visit her.

On my way, I stopped in so many different places in Southeast Asia. I bounced around Cambodia, Thailand, Laos, the Philippines, and a few other countries I honestly can't recall. I didn't have a plan. I had a *Lonely Planet*

Guide, a map, and my own intuition. Recently, in 2023, my niece spent a year traveling Southeast Asia after graduating college. She told me she didn't know how she could have traveled without her smart phone like her own mother and I did. I giggled. What do you say to that?

Though I have many stories about Southeast Asia, I'll mention just one I recall in vivid detail—the full moon parties on a small island called Koh Phangan off the Thailand town of Phuket. I have heard many visitors there spiraled out of control into addiction in the 2020s, but back then when I was there, it was just free love, ecstasy, lots of bands playing, independent thinkers, and obviously crowds of young, naive kids.

I finally made my way down to Australia. I stopped in Darwin (northern Australia) first, where I went on walkabouts with local guides and crocodiles (think the backdrop associated with a Crocodile Dundee movie). I also trekked up rain forest mountains over on the East Coast in Caines, where I stripped down to my underwear and pretended I was a Victoria's Secret model while washing my hair under this pristine waterfall.

I weaved my way up and down the east coast of Australia, went scuba diving every chance I got, hitched rides with numerous strangers, and I just generally got lost in the world to numb out the reality of what was waiting for me back in China.

When I arrived on the Gold Coast, my friend and I talked at length. She advised me to leave Stephane. I spent a few weeks with her and had a beautiful but short romance with her brother. She wasn't really happy about that last part, but he was just too lovely to pass up. Her mother cooked for us, we took long walks, and then one morning I woke up and realized I was ready to start the next chapter of my life.

I've long been quite adept at realizing when something is over and it's time to begin something new. I think of it as a superpower now, but back then I just looked at it this way—if the fun had run out, it was time to move on.

I called my parents and told them I would be starting Occidental College in Old Pasadena, Los Angeles, in the fall. Then I called Stephane in China, told him I had paid for his apartment for two extra months, and wished him the best. We did end up talking on the phone when I got back to the US, but our relationship simply fizzled out. I can't recall the exact details.

China was an experience of a lifetime, but it was now in my rearview mirror. I had no plans to return. Little did I know that China would constantly be woven into my life for the next twenty years.

CHAPTER 5

Normality Begins?

Back in California at Occidental College, I felt like a zebra in a pack of peacocks. The moment I walked through the orientation doors my freshman year, I knew I was not going to enjoy college. Within several hours I realized I couldn't relate with any of the kids on campus. They were talking about their high school experiences, the scores they got on their SATs, what they intended to major in, and rumors of the first keg party at the fraternity house.

Oh my God, what have I done? How was I going to survive several years of this? I had become accustomed to living a life filled with unexpected adventure, and now I had to make another attempt to fit in. I felt like that high school kid all over again. I didn't have trouble as I did in high school with respect to looking or acting any different though. I had blonde hair, an amazing physique from exercise, and cool clothes, but inside I was still an outsider.

I tried to make the best of it. I wandered from group to group for the first few months, attended the standard keg parties, engaged in the small talk you're supposed to with girls at that age, attended classes diligently with a double major in marine biology and economics, made straight A's, yada yada yada. I was behaving. Well, mostly. Of course, I had my dalliances with guys here and there, but I was much better at keeping my extra-curricular activities under the radar this time. I didn't want a relationship. I just wanted to have a couple of drinks, a little fun, and move on. Of course, college boys loved that.

I was fortunate that my dad paid for me to attend school. He said I had one job in college. Get straight A's. That's it. He didn't put any other restrictions on my social activities, which I think was an error in judgment because there were lots of loopholes in that proverbial father-daughter contract that I seemed to exploit quite well.

I even went so far as to join a sorority for about six months, but that was a complete disaster. I didn't fit in. I didn't follow the rules and eventually most of us from that sorority house dropped out together, got ourselves a house across the street, and held competing parties with those sorority girls, who treated women quite poorly in my opinion. I appreciate the values of sororities and fraternities and that some people have the most amazing experiences with them, but that life was just not me.

A Family Trip to Belize.

DAD WAS AWAY FOR work quite a lot when I was growing up. My mother always told us that "Daddy has to work to help the family." My sister and I would generally see him from time to time once we were in college in California, but he always made special time for family when it mattered, like at Christmas or birthdays. During this period, when I was about nineteen, my dad planned an exotic trip for us to Belize during the winter.

For the rain forest part of our adventure, we hopped on a little single engine Cessna plane and landed on a dirt runway in the middle of the rain forest to reach a resort that Francis Ford Coppola had built. There was no other sign of civilization in this amazing tropical resort. We spent our days riding horseback and pretending we were doing an exotic shoot as we splashed around in the pools and explored the deep jungle with the most exotic (and poisonous) creatures. I was at breakfast one morning with my father in his villa when he pulled out this 1990 style satellite telephone. Even then he was a man always working.

Then we returned to the coast of Belize, where Dad rented a beautiful catamaran sailboat. A husband-and-wife couple sailed us around to picturesque islands with dirt roads and local fish markets. Finally, we visited the main island off Belize called San Pedro. We were planning to spend New Year's there. My parents had returned to the boat before midnight, but I dragged my sister out for a night of party fun. I was in full swing of my younger self, but my sister, well, let's say she was the more reserved one. I was always bugging her to have more fun, come play with me, and do naughty things. But I succeeded only about 20 percent of the time getting her to come out with me.

This New Year's night was one of those nights when

she agreed to come out with me. We were drinking and dancing on stage in sexy little white linen skirts, no bras, skimpy tank tops, and we were loving it, bouncing around from tiki bar to tiki bar. We met some locals and caught a ride on the back of their pickup truck deep into the jungle off a very bouncy, pothole-filled dirt road. They told us we were going to a jungle party. My sister was rather hesitant to jump into a truck with strangers, but I convinced her we would be all right.

When we turned the final corner on this dark road about ten o'clock, I couldn't believe my eyes. There was a two-story jungle club with disco lights and lots of music coming out of it. I don't know how they built that nightclub in the middle of the jungle, but we ran in ready to rock it out. When we entered the club, we encountered a giant foam party. There were huge foam machines spewing out sparkly white foam. We were soaked in bubbles and downing tequila shots like they were water, having the time of our lives. And boy did we dance.

I nearly choked to death when I inhaled too much foam. My sister tried to convince me in my moment of weakness when I could not breathe that we should leave. I almost listened to her. Almost. With irritated hesitation, she acquiesced to my request to stay for another thirty minutes. I'd met this gorgeous foreigner who was living on the island at the time. I didn't know his name, nor did I care to, but he was beautiful. Tall, blonde, blue eyes, and very muscular. In my journal I have him recorded as "Sexy jungle foam party man."

I was pretty inebriated at this point and fell asleep. I only remember waking up at the crack of dawn knowing that I had to get back to the dock because the captain said he would pick up my sister and me at six a.m. sharp. I ran down the only road in sight and just kept running. Thankfully the karmic gods had my back, as I was running in the right direction.

I found my sister curled up like a little kitty cat at the end of the dock. I was so furious with her. I couldn't believe she left me, and she couldn't believe I'd kept partying. I cuddled up next to her and passed out until the captain came to get us with a very disapproving look on his face.

Our parents asked me what kind of night we had, probably with a pretty good idea of what we had been up to, but they were pretty cool. They didn't say a word, and we went on to spend the day on a deserted private island, cracking coconuts, sunbathing, and having a family picnic.

The Belize trip was incredibly special for me, as all our family trips were, but I knew this would be one of the last trips because my sister would soon be graduating college and going in a different direction. When we went to visit the Mayan temples, I had no idea that the next time I would see them would be from a wheelchair.

I'd always been fascinated by the Mayans, who had one of the most advanced technological civilizations in the world at the time. Then, suddenly, the Mayans were wiped out by disease, apparently due to lack of urban planning for a sewer system. I was stepping back into a piece of history thousands of years old. I climbed up one Mayan temple to the level where they would observe the stars over the rain forest canopy. I appreciated their ingenuity. The experience was unforgettable.

Cocaine Cowgirls

ON EITHER MY NINETEENTH or twentieth birthday, I rented a limo for a bunch of friends. We ventured to downtown LA, dressed half naked, and rocked it out at the hottest bar in town. My sister was just an hour north of me at a college full of women. I was my sister's devil on her shoulder. She was quite innocent, and I found it wildly amusing to attempt to corrupt her all the time.

We were wearing cowboy hats and shirts that barely covered our nipples. One of my friends and I went to the restroom. A woman in there pulled out a white bag and offered us a line of cocaine. I knew what cocaine was because a lot of kids in my high school partook, but it never interested me. Oh dear God. This was the beginning of the end of the next several years of my life.

When I took this little spoon with a giant, white, silky, powdery bump on it by simultaneously closing one nostril to sniff in with the other, the world stopped. In an instant. I looked in the mirror and genuinely felt like the most hot, sexy, and desirable woman on the planet. The woman told me that I needed a "gummy." I thought she was referring to gummy bears. She meant I had to put my finger on the cocaine and rub it against my gums as that added to the high of cocaine. She was right!

We rocked the night away, dancing, drinking, and winding down at the bar as if we were in our own private club. My sister didn't do drugs, but she did get quite inebriated. We had to save her from crawling across the street because she swore that she saw Tom Cruise. She didn't. She would have been roadkill, but we had reflexes like a cat on the cocaine consumed that night.

From this occasion, cocaine would be a recurrent theme on and off in my life for the next several years.

On my birthday night we met a bunch of Hollywood socialites. I grew up in a world of socialites with my father's business, but I was accustomed to backpacking in Southeast Asia and not living the high life. We tagged along with the socialites to the hottest bars in town over the course of the year, met one wealthier person than the next, bottle service everywhere, and red carpet was laid out for us. We were a bunch of young and hot blonde college kids. That's what you did in LA at the time.

I developed two personas. I was the diligent schoolgirl by day and naughty porn star by night. I continued to get straight A's in school, pretended I was interested in all of the regular college activities, but the moment classes were over, I was back down in LA living my alter ego. A chameleon lifestyle.

I met billionaires, drug dealers, finance guys, movie directors, and all with their own jets where we would pop off to the south of France or down to Rio de Janeiro for the weekend. I'm certainly not writing a book about the wild adventures of Ali on cocaine in college, but suffice to say, I was living yet another life most could not envision. Yes, I know, not a healthy lifestyle, but it was a different one, which is all I cared about at that moment.

On one such night when we were partying in downtown LA, my stripper friend spotted Hugh Hefner across the way, snuck under the rope, sat on his lap, and got an invite to the Playboy mansion. I had arrived! We not only were invited to the Playboy mansion that night but other times as well. A few of us frequented more often, but kept it a secret from the others for fear of judgment or jealousy.

Back in the early 2000s, Hugh Hefner still had about seven girlfriends before he "settled down" to three. There was a reality TV show aired about this. I developed a friendship with the seventh girlfriend and received all the gossip about what went on in the Playboy mansion. I pretty much stayed out of sight while I was there. Why? First, I was probably a four out of ten compared to all these girls who had more plastic surgery than Joan Rivers. Second, I still had to do my school life. Then I would quietly return to the Playboy mansion, where I had made friends with some of the staff.

I would spend my days doing my marine biology homework on trampolines with monkeys jumping all over me. I would then spend time in the pool and warm up in a jacuzzi in the underground grotto, the site of all those orgies reported in the tabloids. Yes, there were many of them. I'd also go to the tanning salon underground. My life was surreal. I couldn't believe I was living this life. I was still getting straight A's, and no one was bothering me, so what was the problem?

I even had the façade of dating a very nice, innocent guy back in college, and I think this is probably my bad karma for life, but he had no idea the double life I was living. He was a very kind human being. I took his virginity against my better judgment, he fell in love, and I led him on. There's not much more to that story, but I still do feel like I paid in spades karmically later on in life.

I attended the Midsummer Night's Dream parties at the Playboy mansion where everyone was dressed up like characters from Shakespeare's *Midsummer Night's Dream*. You could walk into the underground grotto and find orgies left and right, drugs on silver platters, and famous people who would have been destroyed if it became known they were there. I saw many of them. I will always keep the names of those I saw at the Playboy mansion to myself. It was not my business.

I was in this for a good time, not a long time. I know there have been exposés on happenings at the Playboy mansion, but I'm not going to be one to add to all that. I have no judgment. Each to their own. You make your decisions. So do I. Some of my experiences remind me of Molly Bloom's book and movie. I have a deep respect that she kept the names of many of those famous poker players out of the media.

The Last Dance in Hollywood

IT ALWAYS HAS INTRIGUED me how some of us are able to destroy our own lives, sometimes quickly, sometimes slowly. And I would say that by now I was on the way to destroying the life I had built as my cocaine addiction was running rampant. I was lying to my family, I was calling my sister in the middle of the night because I thought I was in cardiac arrest, and I knew I couldn't keep this up for much longer.

I think if I had kept it up, my family would've intervened, but I've always been pretty good at knowing when I am about to hit bottom. Then I stop and reassess.

I redirect. And that's what I did this time. I told my parents that I needed to transfer to be closer to the East Coast and near my home on Cat Island. I think they knew what was going on, but they had the grace to just let me fill out the transfer paperwork and support me.

I filled out a transfer application to the University of Miami and was quickly accepted. And, just like that, another chapter of my now sadly shambolic life ended as I headed back across the country to begin anew.

CHAPTER 6

Second Attempt at Normality

THE MOMENT I TOUCHED down in Miami in the mid-2000s after transferring from Los Angeles, it wasn't even a thought in my mind to pick up cocaine again. I had quit. Cold turkey. In my mind, I had work to do, so I didn't have time for drugs anymore. I don't know if I was addicted to cocaine or if I was just bored. Either way, I thought my story with cocaine was history, but I still had a little way to go. I didn't know that yet.

Once again, I was in a new school with new people in a new location. Transferring as a junior in college is quite tricky because everyone has already developed their friendships. I lived off campus. I didn't know anyone. I attended classes and decided to switch my major to entrepreneurship, learning how to start and run a business. I found it fascinating and fell in love with business. My dreams of being a marine biologist simply melted away. I'm not quite sure where they went or why. But I was diligent with my studies, continuing to get straight A's at the University of Miami.

I lived off campus and was hanging out at Monty's, my favorite beach bar in Coconut Grove, when I met an interesting guy. Yes, another one. He was different though. We ended up more friends than anything. He introduced me to his friends and some of the girls on campus. I thought one girl he introduced me to was a complete bitch. She was so prissy, a sorority girl, and she seemed so full of herself. Ironically, six months later she became my best friend, moved in with me, and dropped out of the sorority. I guess I might have that influence on some people. I'm simplifying the story, but you get the idea. I would go to class, study hard, we would go out to the standard college bars and drink like normal college kids. I felt like I was finally starting to have it together. Until . . .

Falling in Love

I REALLY DID FALL in love for the first time as a young adult. My roommate and I were invited to a party. I believe I was twenty-one or twenty-two at the time. I'm not trying to toot my own horn, but I was super tan, in the best shape of my life with a rocking body and flat abs you could bounce a penny off of. A group of lawyers in their young thirties was at the party.

The moment I walked into the party apartment in South Beach, I was greeted at the door by a young woman with a silver platter filled with an array of drugs spiraled in a circle. It was beautiful. Not the drugs, the artistic representation on the platter. Surprisingly, I did not take any drugs. I was very proud of myself.

These people, men and women, were South Beach

gorgeous. They were the kind of people you see in movies and on TV shows. I didn't think I was in trouble yet as I was behaving. The moment, let's call him Jared, turned the corner and introduced himself to me as the host, I knew I was done. Later Jared, his friend, my best friend, and I went to some ritzy Miami Beach clubs where they knew the bouncers or the owners. This didn't faze me, because I had just come from that life in Los Angeles.

Jared and I talked all night. I remember the first kiss he gave me felt like the last one I ever wanted to receive. It was the type of kiss that you watch in romantic comedies where your foot lifts off the ground and nothing else matters in the moment. He took me back to my place, and we slept next to each other. Admittedly, I did try to make out with him the next morning, but he told me he liked me too much and that I was the most unusual woman he had ever met. He wanted to wait. My concept of time may have been slightly warped at that age. Honestly, within one month we were madly in love.

Hindsight 20 Years Later

NONE. NO HINDSIGHT. I really did feel like I was in love, and in my mind, he is still the one who got away. It was probably the drugs that came later on in our relationship, but he still holds a place in my heart. He was the first man to ever teach me about being in a real relationship.

We dated for about two years. Unfortunately, cocaine did eventually work its way back into my life because of the lifestyle we were living, but I was a little bit more responsible for quite a long time with the drug. I would only engage on the weekends, as weekdays I was a studious college student. I even joined a business fraternity to start networking locally. I was very proud of myself for being able to live a "responsible" double life.

Jared and I were the leaders of the pack, you could say. I may or may not have been quite cocky at that point in my life, but when you hang out with ridiculously wealthy people on exotic yachts, getting into the hottest clubs, flying to different islands on the weekends, it leads to a warped sense of reality. We continued on like this successfully for eighteen months of the two years we dated. I even helped Jared switch careers as I wrote his business plan for him.

College Summers—China Continues

THROUGHOUT MY COLLEGE YEARS, I ended up going back to China multiple times to work for outsourcing companies. I also wrote business plans for pharmaceutical companies who wanted to start marketing their products in China, and I traveled all around the country. I left my college persona at the door on the last day of school and pretended to be a grown-up during the summers.

I visited Chinese factories and met with foreign businessmen at five-star hotels over high tea service during the weekdays. On the weekends I would climb the Great Wall of China or fly to a different city to visit a friend I had kept in touch with from when I lived in China during my teens.

One summer when I was in Beijing, I develop friendships with a whole host of Swedish folks who worked for IKEA. We went out every night. Once we came upon a very long street of tall buildings with rooftop bars. You had to climb up an obnoxious set of stairs (in stiletto heels for the girls) to get to the rooftop bar. The problem was the rooftops of adjoining buildings were not constructed to connect. That problem was solved with rope bridges someone added to connect the rooftops. You could have a drink in one bar and then take the rope bridge across to the next rooftop.

Thinking back on walking across a rope bridge many stories above street level in stilettos and pretending to be a tight rope walker while semi-inebriated, I'm surprised I didn't become disabled earlier. We finished up many nights with long sticks of street vendor chicken or beef only to meet up again the next night. In those days, there truly was never a dull moment in my life. I thrived on the excitement of what would come next.

Business Plan Competition Time

ON THE ACADEMIC SIDE of life at the University of Miami, I was thriving. I was nailing it in my entrepreneurship and consulting classes. I learned about a prestigious business plan competition held each year at the university. There were two categories: high potential ventures for business ideas over ten million dollars and small business ventures for under two million dollars.

In my school life, I built a relationship with a guy named Aaron who became my best friend for years. We were almost like brother and sister, and we worked very well together in school. We decided to take this challenge head on. It was my hardest intellectual and academic challenge so far.

We worked tirelessly after school for months to perfect this business plan, writing it, practicing it, submitting our application, and eventually being invited to compete in the competition.

We devised a real estate development idea for communities called "cohousing." This is a concept created in the 1980s in Denmark. We proposed to commercialize it. Essentially, the idea is that like-minded individuals would come together and hire a developer to build a community around their shared common interests. We even flew to San Francisco to see real cohousing communities in action. Our idea was to find folks who were aging and had similar interests and bring the idea to them.

To say we hit our presentation out of the park turned out to be an understatement, though at the time we didn't think we had done that well. We kept criticizing a sentence here or there and remembering things we forgot to say. The judges were business owners in the real world. They were tough and fair, but terrifying nonetheless, especially to us in our early twenties.

The results of this competition were announced right before graduation. When they called our names, Aaron and I were in shock. We couldn't believe we'd won. Not only did we receive the honor of winning the Rothschild Entrepreneurship Competition prize but we also won a fair amount of money too. We were even approached by some of the judges who wanted to invest in our idea, but Aaron and I concluded that we were too young and inexperienced to accept millions of dollars for a real estate development idea we had no experience in carrying out. I'll just say this. Thank God! Shortly thereafter, the Great Recession financial crisis hit the real estate development world particularly hard.

CHAPTER 7

What Goes Up, Must Come Down

As graduation approached, I came down off the high of winning the business plan competition. I truly believed one of those judges would offer me my first job. I was an over-confident 23-year-old who believed the world was her oyster.

However, when you don't put much effort toward something, you are not likely to reap very desirable results. While I was living on the high of feeling accomplished and too clever for my own good, I was simultaneously living that double life in South Beach with Jared in his world. I could barely keep up with him. He had this incredible ability to take drugs semi-responsibly, if there's such a thing, and keep his life together. Instead of starting the day with a cup of coffee, he would have a line of cocaine in the morning and then one in the afternoon. Our drug use naturally went up on the weekends. I couldn't keep up with his fast-paced South Beach high lifestyle. I was losing ground again.

Things became so intense that I found myself skipping

the last few days of classes and going out into areas of the city I had no business frequenting. I was hanging out with drug dealers, lesbian drug gangs, and folks who were living in tents in South Beach. I couldn't see what was right in front of me. I was destroying my life in real time—again!

I went so far as to tell my family not to come to graduation. My mother, of course, came, but I didn't want to see anyone. Jared also attended, but we ended up spending that night at a strip club until dawn. There's no feeling quite like walking out of a strip club at ten a.m., drunk, sunglasses on, high on drugs, and just questioning your life in its entirety at that moment. It was that morning that Jared told me we needed to reduce our drug habit. I knew he could do it, but I couldn't. I was so in love, and I wanted to be with him forever, so I did the only thing I knew how to do. I left town.

I needed, once again, to convene with nature to get myself straightened out and start my life over again. The money I still had from the business plan competition combined with my parents' graduation present was enough money to pay for another wilderness survival program. I researched and found the toughest program of them all, National Outdoor Leadership School (NOLS).

National Outdoor Leadership School in Australia

THE PROGRAM I SELECTED was in Australia. I told my parents I needed this and informed Jared this was how we could stay together. I think back and understand that I was probably going for the wrong reasons, but it was a trip that changed me forever.

When I embarked to Australia, I chose a very remote arrival location called Boone. It's on the west coast of Australia with gorgeous ten-mile long white sand beaches and hundreds of miles of outback to the east. It's one of the most remote places in Australia, and I would be spending several months there. Again, I quit drugs cold turkey. I had renewed hope, faith that this program would kick my butt back into shape, that I would come back and my life would continue on track as I had envisioned it. I imagined that this trip would be life-changing, but I had a long road ahead first.

Maybe I really am genetically wired this way, but I do always seem to find optimism and opportunities in the darkest of times. I won't say I am consistently positive, but usually I can see the flipside of a bad situation. This ability had served me well in surviving over my years, and I called on it for this adventure.

We had one senior leader instructor in the NOLS program, and, as I recall, six of us flew from around the world to participate. This was not like an Outward Bound trip because everyone in NOLS voluntarily hiked into the outback for weeks and months. This would be my toughest trip yet.

We each carried about an eighty-pound backpack with enough food for a week at a time, a topographical map, a compass, and our intuition. There were food drops scheduled after the first week. I was pumped. I couldn't wait to feel the sweat roll off my back and hike in 100-degree heat, in essence, to melt away my sins. It almost seems masochistic, but something about pushing your physical limits really does unlock your capabilities.

I know it may sound silly, but I felt like I was on my own personal walkabout. On the first day of the hike, I was thinking about how on earth I had gotten myself into this life mess again, but like always, I was going to get out of it on my own.

This was no ordinary hiking trip. Each day one of us would take the topographical map and a compass and be the leader for the day. The objective was to hike to a water source each night as we could carry only so much water. The water source? Waterfalls. There were days with 100-degree heat, carrying our eighty-pound backpacks, that it felt like our feet were encased in cement. We hiked very early in the morning, took a siesta during lunchtime to avoid getting heatstroke, and then carried on the latter half of the day.

There is this special feeling when you've been hiking for eight hours, and you turn the corner to finally find lush bush with a waterfall that is so unspoiled and pristine. We stripped down to our underwear and dove in headfirst, not knowing what might be in the water. We hiked up the waterfalls and bathed in the warm pools at the top before setting up our tents for the night.

This was the kind of trip where you were not allowed to bring toilet paper, deodorant, or anything else that was not biodegradable into the wilderness. When you went to the bathroom, you dug a hole, found a leaf that hopefully was not poisonous or scratchy, popped a squat, and hoped some little creature didn't come out of the woodwork while you were doing your business.

We sat around the fire at night and talked about what we learned that day and what we could improve upon as leaders. Frankly, it was really a session where we bitched about another person's ability to get us lost that day. It was quite brutal. We sat in a circle with the leader of the day sitting in the center. I was transported back to middle school once again with kids throwing things at my head. I didn't realize that experience was teaching me lessons in leadership that stuck with me. I learned that you are only as strong as your weakest link, not to let the softest voice get drowned out among the louder ones, and to take constructive criticism and use it. I appreciate all that now, but it completely sucked in that moment. I felt like a failure.

On a day when I was leader, I got us lost. We hiked down the wrong ravine. There was mud everywhere, and we were covered in it from head to toe. It was the middle of the day. I insisted everyone push on (bad idea). It was too hot to breathe, and we had mosquito bites on every inch of our bodies. You could pretty much sum it up that I was a terrible leader that day. We were also going in the wrong direction, and this is quite dangerous because you were supposed to meet your group at a designated location. It's really life or death out there. Truly. You could turn the corner and there could be a king brown snake. If it bites you, you're dead in minutes.

When we were turning the corner, I was thinking everyone was going to leave me for outback roadkill. Then a waterfall that was not on the map just appeared. It was like an oasis in the desert with beautiful striated red rocks, many tumbling waterfalls, and an inviting pool right in the center. We were stunned. No one spoke for a moment. Then, clothes came off (except shoes of course—keeping pristine feet is always of the highest priority as I will soon share), and everyone jumped in. This was a stupid thing to do because we didn't know how deep the water was. I guess you could say we took a leap of faith. We were splashing, singing, and laughing. It was as if my leadership indiscretions were wiped clean while the water washed away the dirt covering our bodies. Wiped clean that is until that night around the fire when my comrades took the time to tell me what a terrible job I had done.

We even hiked into caves, and once we discovered aboriginal art that had to be several thousand years old. Later we learned that the cave art had not been documented previously, so we were able to name the find and be noted as the discoverers. This is my only claim to being an archaeological celebrity.

One of the most painful things that I had to deal with on this venture was my feet. Feet are funny things. They are so resilient and can take you around the world, but they can ruin your immediate existence very quickly and immobilize you in an instant. I made a very foolish rookie mistake. I purchased a gorgeous pair of North Face boots for the wilderness, but I did not break them in before my trip. A rookie mistake if there ever was one, or, rather, I think I may have been too wrapped up in my drug-filled lifestyle at that moment. I knew better, for sure, but it was too late now.

In any event, after about seven days, I developed bleeding quarter-size holes a few millimeters deep on the back of my heels due to my unbroken-in boots. I was the weakest link in the group at that point, and we did have to slow down a bit. What are you going to do about a situation like this when you're in the wilderness hundreds of kilometers in the middle of nowhere with a group of folks hiking? Cry about it? Complain? Sure, you could, but that would not get you anywhere. No one could carry me. I had to hike.

And so, I hiked with tears running down my face each and every day with my fellow hikers giving me looks of empathy, knowing they could not help me in any way. There were days when I was trying to get up the mountain we had to climb, and I didn't think I could take one more step. Really. I wanted to lie down and die right there. That's how intense the pain was. I honestly can't tell you how I was able to keep going. I think my brain blocked out the pain at that point. Thank you, neuroscience and brain. I would try to dress my feet with bandages at night, but we didn't have the right medical supplies for this.

Then the most interesting thing happened to me. We were hiking through this palm-forest-like area and it was really muddy. I stepped in the wrong spot, and I sank. I mean I really sank. I sank all the way up to my waist. It was like quicksand, but there was a bottom, so I knew I wasn't going down much further. I couldn't move. I just started laughing and that made everyone else laugh. The damnedest thing was, I couldn't feel the pain in my feet.

After about an hour, my fellow hikers finally got me out of the mud pit. I had to trek on the rest of the day wet and covered in cakey drying mud. My feet felt about 60 percent better even though I knew they were not. Each morning from then on until the wounds healed, I purposely got my feet soaking wet with socks, which is generally a big no-no out in the wilderness, and I was proudly able to put one foot in front of the other. It took about a week for my feet to heal. If I could've called an ambulance over the course of that week to get out of the damn outback, I would have, but at the same time, I'm glad that I stuck it out. I was proud of myself for being on this trip. There certainly wasn't much left for me to be proud of back home.

There were days that were more challenging than others on our trek. One surprise was realizing at the end of that day's trek that the expected water source marked on the topographical map had dried up for the season. What do you do when you don't have water? You cannot hike the next day because you'll likely die of heat stroke. It's not an exaggeration to say situations like a dried-up water source become a life or death matter. While the waterfall dried up on the surface, the water was still running strong underground. We dug and we dug, and we hit gold. Gold in this instance was lifesaving, beautiful, sweet, nourishing water. Almost anyway. It was brown, muddy water, but it was water.

We had these special kits to clean the water to make it drinkable. Those nights were pretty god-awful though, because we were sticky, hot, muddy, and we had to sleep in our little mosquito net tents that barely provided any meaningful cover from the giant mosquitoes that could still fly in.

Every challenging obstacle we came across brought us much closer together. It's amazing how spending every hour of the day and night with another human being puts relationship building into hyperdrive. You have to rely on each other for your lives, literally, and this requires trust. Sure, we wanted to kill each other every day at certain moments, but we always banded together in the end.

As we neared completion of our trip after months of exploring the unknown, learning to kill lizards for extra protein, singing around campfires, jumping off waterfalls, not showering for a week at a time, and being hairy because you're not allowed a razor, the last part of the trip was a doozy.

Just as we did with Outward Bound and all the other wilderness survival trips I had been on over the years, we had a "solo" portion of this adventure. This one was different for me though. I felt prepared this time. I was not seventeen years old anymore and unable to sit with my own thoughts. I had a lot to think about, a lot to answer for when I got home, and choices to make.

I was assigned this pristine area with a beautiful rock to sunbathe on, a stream right next to me, and a little green fuzzy grass area nestled in between these trees called upside down trees. Whenever I meditate with guided visualizations, I still go back to this location. It was five-star outback living to me for the next handful of days. We didn't get any extra food, but I didn't need it.

The first two days were glorious. I was naked. I sat in the stream and washed myself every day. I laid on the hot rocks, burning my butt cheeks while simultaneously getting a suntan. I journaled how wonderful I felt. And I listened to nature. On the third day, however, things started to change mentally for me. I had completely and intentionally blocked out my life back in Miami. I had left it in shambles. I'm pretty sure not even my mother had a clue what was going on in my life at that point.

How was I going to salvage life when I got back? I didn't want to get back on drugs. I wanted a great job just like anyone else graduating high school or college. What about Jared? Would he still want to be with me? Was he cheating on me with some hot blonde Russian in South Beach? (The answer to that question, I later learned, was unequivocally, yes, he was.) There were so many voices going through my head, and I couldn't quiet them. I started sobbing. I couldn't stop.

When my tears dried up and I had no more left to give other than dry heaving, the gravity of my life situation really started to sink in. I had a lot of work to do to pick up the pieces when I got back. I had always been able to do this in the past, and I knew I had family support if I needed it, even though I was too proud to ask for it most times. I wanted to do this on my own and wanted to restart my life in the right way

When you cry, you release so many feelings, emotions, hormones, and chemicals, which do make you feel better. I started to journal feverishly on next steps to take when I got back. I wasn't going to screw up life again! At the end of my solo trip, I felt a renewed energy. I felt awesome. I really did.

When we arrived back at our center base in Boone, I took a few days to myself to enjoy the beach and hang out with some of my friends.

CHAPTER 8

First Job, First Failure

WHEN I TOUCHED DOWN back in the United States, Jared was right there waiting for me with open arms at the airport. My heart melted. I was so in love and determined to be a better version of myself. It worked, for a while anyway.

I quickly realized that there was no job waiting for me when I got home, and I started to apply for jobs. I thought with my business and entrepreneurship background that consulting would be perfect for me. I applied to dozens of the top consulting firms. Rejection. Rejection. Rejection. It turns out that they wouldn't even look at me without an MBA, and I had no desire to continue my schooling. I was not accustomed to rejection because even when I was somehow turning my life upside down, everything generally had a way of working out for me. It didn't happen with this job thing. I wish I had been given a life lesson in college about the real world. I was on top of the world, king of the mountain in college, and then knocked off the mountain in life.

I hadn't developed the mental fortitude to deal well with consistent rejections. I applied for some really odd jobs. Finally, someone called me back. It was a company that sold office supplies in Miami. It was not really what I wanted to do, but I accepted the job.

On my first day I was dressed in a knee length skirt, blazer, and blue shirt from Banana Republic. I looked professional. This woman in her late twenties took me around in her Mercedes sedan to the office districts in Hialeah, a largely Latino area in Miami. I was a little puzzled because I could not understand how this girl was driving such a beautiful car, and we were literally going to random businesses and knocking on their door, just like a cold call. Apparently, she had built up rapport with some of these places, because they welcomed her in, and we signed contracts for office supplies from paper to copiers to fax machines. Think of an Office Depot magazine. I only had one day of training, then I was out on my own.

I believe I went to sixteen different businesses that day and did not sell anything. Consistent rejection. Of course, this is normal in sales, especially in this type of industry, but I was still psychologically delicate. I was determined to succeed at something. I should've been proud of myself for what I endured in Australia, but selling office supplies seemed way harder.

I called my friend that night to tell him what I was doing, and he just flat out laughed at me. It was one of those laughs. You know—from the bottom of the belly, you're an idiot, I can't believe you're doing this. I was so confused because I had a job. What was I doing wrong?

Turns out this company was a pyramid scheme of sorts or rather, in legal terms, a multi-level marketing business. A very small percentage of people in these companies actually make any money. The senior manager who took me around, I later learned, received commissions for every new hire and pocketed a percentage of their sales. She just happened to be very good at what she did. She made it. I didn't.

Honestly, I was embarrassed that with all of my travel adventures and educational background, I couldn't even sell office supplies. I might not have failed had I stuck with it, but I quit after the first day. That is the story of my first job after college.

The Little Engine That Couldn't

I WAS TOO EMBARRASSED to tell anyone about that job, so I didn't. Instead, I pretended I still had the job for a few weeks. I had to fill my days somehow because people thought I was going to work. All I could think about was making my relationship work. As I look back now, it was probably more that I was trying to avoid thinking about life, so I focused on a boy. I didn't have a lot of money left, but I had some.

I was at a bar alone one night because Jared had to work. I met a girl in the bathroom who offered me a line of, you guessed it, that seductive white powder. And I recall vividly not hesitating for a moment. I didn't even think about it. And there I was, back on cocaine every day. I don't need to recount the stories again. Within three months I was back down to rock bottom.

This was a rock bottom that I can honestly admit was the worst in my entire life, and I knew it.

Fast forward to the end of those three months. Jared was clearly no longer interested in me. I was running out of money. I was a wreck. I looked and felt terrible. I gained weight. The list goes on.

I was alone and scared. I didn't call my best friend or my sister or my mother. I just kept to myself. When I woke up one morning, I had run out of drugs. I had barely any money and didn't have a boyfriend anymore. I sat on the back steps of my lousy South Beach apartment and did the unthinkable.

I told my mom and dad I was in trouble. Truthfully, I didn't have the psychological strength to tell the kindest and smartest man I know, my dad, so I called my mom. I told her everything down to the most minute detail. She was on Cat Island at the time, and she called my dad, who was in Miami.

I was asleep on the couch when my dad came over. I hid my face and would not take the covers off my head. I was so ashamed. He was so graceful. He just sat in my other room at the desk and worked quietly. He gave me water, food, and didn't talk. Two or three days later he asked me to go out to lunch at a German restaurant. I felt like I hadn't eaten in months even though I had been eating junk food. I ordered the Wiener Schnitzel with dumplings and gravy. I can still remember what it tasted like. It was delicious. After I made my way through a few delectable bites, my dad said to me, "Kid, we have a problem."

He was so calm, relaxed, and not even a little bit judgmental. Now, I can't speak to his inner dialogue of course, but he approached me with such grace and love. He didn't yell. We talked for hours, and I tried to explain why I did what I did, what happened, and how I wanted to proceed going forward. I have always been a solution-oriented person, and I very likely get that from my dad. We agreed to therapy for a few weeks and then rehab. However, I didn't want to go to a group rehab because I'm better one-on-one. I'm not sure if this was the right thing to do or not, but my family clan surrounded me.

So the plan was for me to do my own personal rehab in Atlanta, Georgia, where my brothers reside and have a business. I would volunteer at a nonprofit, clean their houses, cook for them, and try to find a job. I didn't know if I would ever come back to Miami. I packed up my things, and a week later I was off to my own self-imposed rehab.

CHAPTER 9

A Different Kind of Rehab

I spent five months in Atlanta. Life was pretty boring and probably exactly what I needed. I found myself enjoying volunteering at a nonprofit and learning to cook gourmet meals like a rock star out of *The South Beach Diet Cookbook*. I had such quality family time with my brothers. Like the old days, I still loved getting down to my underwear, getting the vacuum cleaner out, and rocking out to 1950's oldies music, so I did this when no one was home. It was very cathartic for me.

No one judged me. There were really kind and authentic conversations, and they were just so gentle. I was my own worst enemy, beating myself up. Eventually, I started to call people I knew in Miami. I had built up an interesting network. One of my best friends, who was working in politics at the time, said she had contact with a fellow about what sounded like an interesting non-profit job. I really didn't know what she meant, but I sent her my resume anyway.

I received an email from Justin Rockefeller and Adrian

Talbot. Yes, son of those Rockefellers, and son of Strob Talbott of the Brookings Institute. They were starting up a nonpartisan, civic engagement nonprofit with multiple locations around the country, and they wanted me to launch the Miami office. The mission was to get young people in the Miami community college system engaged in advocacy, politics, and change. What a perfect job! I'm not sure how I got the job because they called me for an interview when I was in the middle of downtown Atlanta traffic, trying to get home, and I didn't have my notes in front of me. I suppose my presentation techniques kicked in from my college presentations because they said I nailed it. Sure, I'm going to go with that.

I felt much more confident now, recovered and well-cared for by my family, and I was positive I could move back to Miami and stay on track this time. I don't know why, but I just knew I could do it. It's amazing what we can overcome and get through with family support.

Yet again one chapter was ending and another was beginning. This had become a pattern in my life, and still is today. I will always be eternally grateful to my brothers and parents for helping me get through one of the toughest times of my life.

CHAPTER 10

Political Life

I HAD SUBLET MY apartment in Miami, so I was fortunate enough to be able to fit right back in. There are some who argue you need to change your friends and environment in order to make a clean start, but none of my friends from my "other" life were involved in drugs. My friends forgave me and were supportive. Most of them had moved on with their jobs after graduation. So, I made new friends.

I had no idea how to open a nonprofit enterprise. Justin and Adrian were fantastic, and the other virtual colleagues on our team calls each week were amazing. Everyone was working toward the same common goal—to help people become engaged to improve their community.

I turned out to be quite good at this and attribute that to the way I grew up around the world, always having to adapt to my environment and circumstances. I was introduced to donors and senior leaders at different universities. I went to countless events to build political capital, and I got on well with a wide range of people. Not having a clear plan at the outset turned out to be the best thing for me.

It's counterintuitive, but while I do love organization and process, I have an ability to take things from here and there and make them into something. I was finally putting my entrepreneurship major to use a year later!

I hosted very successful, non-partisan events as well as political debates, and one time I even hosted colleagues from around the country for a major political debate I arranged during the 2004 presidential elections. I was making friends with the right kind of people and doing a good job.

Sometimes I attended local events, after which some of the folks would go clubbing later. I was only in my early twenties, so that part of my life was not over yet, although I tried to party a little bit more responsibly. One night I walked into a club restroom, and there was a young woman with guess what? That's right. White, silky powder in this little contraption called a bullet. She offered me a line.

I didn't even hesitate, but in the best way this time! This encounter still makes me smile sometimes because I said to her, "No thanks, and you know that stuff will really ruin your life, right?" Yes, I gave a totally judgmental and snarky response as I judged her, knowing full well I would hate it if anyone judged me that way.

The point is, I said no. I still remember thinking that I had stuff to do, I was busy, and I didn't have time for drugs. I was offered cocaine over the next several years and always said no. I had a purpose—a sustainable purpose—in my life.

As for my personal life, I was having a ball in true Ali casual fashion. I met a bunch of guys in the political world, in the nonprofit world, and out and about in town. I was going to work every day, casually dating young men, drinking responsibly, traveling, and just enjoying life.

Not What I Expected

I STARTED TO WORK my way up the political professional ladder and networked constantly. I'm a good networker, perhaps because I really like most people, and I smile easily. Either people take this as me being genuinely authentic or they think I'm a flirt. Sometimes it's both.

I recall one night when I picked up some politicians arriving for an event we were having the next day. They didn't want to go to their hotel but instead asked me, without giving it a thought, if I would take them to a Miami strip club.

First, they tried to hit on me, and I absolutely, positively was not having it. I had really come to care about the nonprofit world and the people in it. I kept wondering why I was taking them to a strip club, but I did it anyway. These seemed like important men, so I just went with it, acting like kind of a bodyguard for them. I watched that no one was taking photos and that they didn't get too hammered. They were doing drugs off the breasts of strippers, and they were quite arrogant. I felt like a grown-up on that occasion. Yes, I appreciate the irony!

This happened more than once. I would bring such men back to their hotel room, and then they would get up the next morning and give their speech. These people were speaking publicly about progressive change, while less than twelve hours earlier they were engaged in illegal drug activities. To say I started to become jaded might have been an understatement. Nonetheless, I carried on and ensured our non-profit organization was successful.

Eventually, our Miami non-profit was merged into a similar organization in Washington, and I recognized that I was again at a crossroad. What happened surprised even me.

I found myself talking to my dad one night and said I didn't feel like I was on the right life path. I was wondering how I could be more effective in the non-profit world. Something felt off to me, that I wasn't doing what I supposed would be of great value to others. I wanted to help people with real problems but didn't really understand the non-profit world.

Dad shared an observation that really resonated with me. He said the best way to help people in a non-profit organizational structure is to be a donor if you can, and the best way to do that is to make money first. Non-profit donors have historically either made money in different business activities or inherited money and then used their capital to help others in society.

I instantly said, "Great, sign me up. How, Dad?"

He responded that he'd been asked that question (that is, how to make a lot of money) by lots of young people over decades and noted that his answers had varied, running the gamut from manufacturing to services to trading financial assets. He also observed that presently the largest sums being made by young people in the shortest period of time appeared to involve working with financial assets. At that time there were people in their mid-twenties in New York making tens of millions a year just working for banks without being officers or directors.

So, I asked how one could learn about trading financial assets. And he suggested I first study the history of financial assets, notably from the end of the 19th century when Charles Dow founded the Wall Street Journal and Dow Theory, which laid the groundwork for what came to be known as technical analysis.

This sounded interesting, even though I had really little understanding of what this entailed. As my dad advised, I took a couple of weeks to read up on this history and then, just like that, I gave notice to my organization and resigned. My decision was made easier with the merger of my non-profit with one in Washington. I wasn't keen to move to Washington.

My new plan was to move back to Cat Island. I made preparations for the move, including selling my car. It's incredible today to reflect that at twenty-six the sum total of my savings was about $5,000. That's all I had to show after all that cocaine, but it would be just enough to open a trading account.

I seemed to be pretty much re-inventing myself every several years, and it was time to do it again. This pattern would become critical, as I was soon to learn.

CHAPTER 11

Home Is Where the Heart Is

So NOW I AM twenty-six years old and moving back home. The agreement my parents and I had was that I would move back home to Cat Island, take care of the property in exchange for room and board, study technical analysis like my life depended on it, and help out whenever they needed.

I was elated to live back on Cat Island full time. My parents had been living there for years, but I'd only spent periods of time there throughout life in between schools. I said my goodbyes to Miami friends and invited them to hop on a quick flight to visit me on the weekends, which they did.

Trading Financial Assets

LET'S TALK A MINUTE about trading. There are so many misconceptions about trading. Sure, trading can be fast-paced and really stressful if you let it, but misconceptions run rampant. Trading can be very relaxed and learning to trade any asset is usually about 90 percent psychology with 10 percent technical methodology.

First you have to figure out what kind of person you are, what your temperament is, if you're anxious or not, and if you're high-strung or low-key. The type of trading you do really depends, importantly, on the kind of personality you have.

There's pretty much zero barrier to entry for anyone who wants to trade financial assets. You can open up a brokerage account if you're a student or doctor or a small business owner or retired. This is what makes it so dangerous, because people think they can just read a few books, and off to the races they go.

If you want to be a doctor, you have to spend years training for it. To be a proficient trader is no different. It takes a tremendous amount of sweat equity, time, practice, failing, getting back up again, money management skills, and more to become a successful trader. There is no right or wrong way to trade, you just have to find out what works for you through trial and error.

I embarked on the mission of becoming a competent trader using a technical methodology called Drummond Geometry, a methodology my dad was interested in at the time. This entailed studying a 12,000 page course (several times) that I kept plugging away at each day. I would read, play around on the computer to see how a certain indicator would work on a chart, take notes, highlight the notes, memorize the notes, and then at night I would review my notes before going to bed. I was meticulous, as I was on a laser-focused mission for a straight year with the goal of trading live money (real money, not just pretend money in a practice account) by August 2010. I was not going to let anything derail me.

Dad advised me to steer clear of the New York stock markets and instead focus on the Chicago markets, where U.S. Treasury futures are traded. This was partly because trading volumes for U.S. Treasury securities are much higher than for individual stocks while also being generally much less volatile. So, I focused on the 10-Year U.S. Treasury Note and the 30-Year U.S. Treasury Bond.

Island Lifestyle

THE WAY OUR PROPERTY on Cat Island came to be built over the decades is with one larger main house in the middle and then two smaller houses north and south connected by sand pathways with conch shells lining them. It's beautiful unless you're trying to run from one house to the other and stub your toe on a root. I still have scars on my feet from ripping open the skin on my toes. Builds grit I say.

During the day, my dad engaged with his interests in an office in one house on the south side, while my mom was usually in the central main house. On the north side, my sister and I had our own house, named Bamboo, where I would be studying solo most of the day. These houses were separated from one another by less than 100 yards. We could literally yell a couple hundred feet away to get one another's attention. This was handy because local island phone lines were often out and there was no cell service.

My mom took care of the property and ran a beautiful nonprofit, taking care of many of the older folks up and down the island after the 1999 Category 5 Hurricane Floyd did a great deal of damage to island communities.

She has always been the heartbeat of the island in the way that she is involved with the community and how people respond to her.

It was really tricky in those days living on an out island because you had to think way in advance about food and supplies, knowing that the large mail boat from Nassau, 150 miles away, only came in once a week with the supplies you needed. Plus lots of things break on an out island. Living about 100 feet off the beach, the salt air corrodes anything you touch. Cars generally last only a few years before they bottom-rust out. We've had plenty of cars where you had to watch where you stepped when you got in so your foot didn't hit the sand beneath you.

For my work, I gave myself a pretty strict schedule. I would wake up at six thirty six days a week and start my morning by working out for ninety minutes with weights, sit ups, crunches, and more. Then I would walk over to the central house for breakfast.

Once I ate breakfast, I would get back to work for hours, reading and studying. I took a brief break in the middle of the day to have half a sandwich for lunch and then went back to studying. Laser focus, I tell you. Around four o'clock, I would heat up my enclosed bathroom and work out again. I was really into Bikram yoga, also called hot yoga, because it simply transformed my body and helped me be in my best shape. Following the yoga, I went for a half mile run, then stripped down to my bikini for a twenty-minute swim. There are days I still can't believe that was my life.

Each evening, I would shower and go to the main

house for dinner. Mom cooked gourmet meals for Dad and me, like local lobster or grouper fish, sugar snaps, and the most exotic salads. She baked her own bread, grew her own vegetables, and she always decorated the table as if a dinner party was about to commence. She would put bougainvillea flowers with sea grape leaves around our dinner plates. My dad and I were served these beautiful meals every single night. Yes, every single night we had a sit-down dinner together, and we talked. No phone. No TV. Just conversation.

While Mom was preparing dinner, Dad and I might break out the tunes on a CD player and Mom would join in on a dance party. Oh, so many great dance parties. My parents were and are my best friends. They support me when I am at my worst, push me when I need my butt kicked, and lift me up whenever I need that. I know I am the luckiest girl in the world to have them as parents, and every single day I let them know how much I love them and thank them for everything they have offered me in life. I do whatever I can to help them whenever they need it.

At the end of each dinner, my dad and I would have espresso and sometimes a cigar. Dad had me print out online stories from Reuters, Bloomberg, or *Financial Times* and asked me to read them before coming to dinner, highlighting sections I didn't quite understand. We then spent our time after dinner talking about macroeconomics as well and trading stories of interest. Sometimes, during long summer daylight, we would take these conversations outside to a little beachside cabana and watch the sunset. My dad is annoyingly smart in the best way possible.

He's also a brilliant teacher. If you don't understand a concept, he never makes you feel stupid when he explains it. He has beautiful metaphors to explain everything. I'm not saying this because he is my dad, but he is one of the smartest people I know.

On the weekends, my dad and I would take our masks and snorkels and go repair a boat mooring, clean our sailboat, or take picnics to smaller nearby beaches. I would also help my mom in her nonprofit work with some of the folks on the island.

Of course, whenever possible I also carved out a few hours each weekend for sunbathing on the most pristine, beautiful white sand beach with water so clear you can see down a hundred feet. I'm not ashamed to admit that I'm absolutely spoiled when it comes to beaches. How could I not be? Our houses are on Fernandez Bay, which is shaped like a crescent moon sprinkled with some private residences plus a rustic island resort. If you see five people a day on the beach, that would be crowded. I naturally didn't wear any top as I was raised by my European mom. I wish someone would've given me a different memo my freshman year in college, when I was berated by my girlfriends who asked me to please put on a bikini top!

I had friends who came over from Miami for the weekend never want to leave this magical place. I might head back to Miami for a supply run for my mom every few months, but I really didn't want to go back. I was an island girl again. I knew everyone on the island. Friends would get together at a local restaurant or bar every Saturday night, which was my "fun" night.

Fun in the Sun

YOU DIDN'T THINK I wasn't going to have at least a little fun while living in The Bahamas, did you? There was a handful of people around my age whose parents had homes elsewhere on the island. I also had grown up pretty much knowing most of the local young folks living on the island and attended the local high school, where Dad gave the commencement address one year.

We had a very old-school text group, and we would all agree where on the island we would meet that Friday night or Saturday night to party. We would carpool with each other down the 50-mile-long island to a tiki bar on the water. It was more of a shack really, decorated with great fishing nets and things that washed up on shore. It had charm, pizzazz, and would've looked like an abandoned house if you drove past it.

We brought drinks, music, and dancing along with the rock-it-out attitude. It was good old-fashioned fun that anyone in their mid-twenties would enjoy. Oh, and moderation too, of course, so we could get back home safely. We would get hot and sweaty dancing to reggae music and enjoy cold Bahamian Kalik beer together.

I'm pretty sure there was one thing that really did not amuse my mother. When I came back with friends late at night, we would be hungry, even ravenous, as we had been dancing for hours. We would raid my mother's beautifully organized fridge, sometimes for her famous sixteen-layer, homemade frosted chocolate, vanilla, and coffee icing cake. This was a masterful piece of art that she made for special occasions, like birthdays. My dad and I also loved to nibble on it while smoking cigars and diving into lengthy conversations.

On one such night, it got worse, as we didn't just eat her special cake, we had a cake food fight with some of it and rubbed it in each other's face. Of course, my mother woke up and shot us that don't-ever-do-this-again glare, but she could not help but laugh because we looked absolutely ridiculous.

Karma did get us that night though. What goes around comes around. We headed back out onto the beach, and, for some reason, we fell asleep on the sand, waking up covered from head to toe in welts. We had been attacked by the infamous sand flies while we were sleeping, but we were too tipsy to notice and wake up. Like I said, karma is a bitch. My mother did catch us on camera with a classic photograph.

Suspicious Characters

SUSPICIOUS CHARACTERS USED TO turn up with some frequency on this kind of remote Bahamian island, albeit not so much anymore. I know about this history, much of which predates my 1983 birth, because I have met a few of them over the years. Indeed, in the late 1970s, my parents indirectly acquired one of our houses from two "nameless" drug dealers who got arrested elsewhere and never returned.

This was before my time, but I'm told the house was packed floor-to-ceiling with marijuana. That house is named "Boys House." I used to think this structure was named after my two brothers. But, no, it was just always known as the "Boys House," and my parents kept the name it had when they purchased it. I used to walk into the house and try to envision it literally filled to the ceiling with drugs. That was back in tamer days, for sure, before the much more profitable cocaine trade pushed out marijuana. Drugs used to come by small planes directly to The Bahamas from South America before the DEA pushed them out to Mexico.

Mr. X—A Brief Romantic Dalliance

ON THE SUBJECT OF suspicious characters, I will share one particular romantic dalliance I partook in for a short time. I bring up this story because this was the last person I slept with before my accident, and it actually involved a funny twist with my parents.

My parents invited a couple to dinner one night. We often had dinner parties for different folks around the island. When this husband and wife walked in, I was completely smitten with him. Let's call him Mr. X because he really was that ominous. They had just purchased a home down south, and I learned very quickly that things were not brilliant in their marriage. In fact, they had an open marriage.

He was tall, ruggedly handsome, had salt and pepper hair, and was twice my age (maybe three times, unclear on that one). I didn't make much of the dinner other than thinking he was very attractive. His strong accent intrigued me. I wondered what his profession was, but I didn't dare ask. I thought maybe he was hiding out on this remote outlying island for some reason.

After dinner my dad casually said Mr. X was a legal arms dealer. I wasn't sure I understood what that meant, but okay. Of course, me being me, he became even sexier. I thought about him that night, but then he fell into the "out of sight, out of mind" category.

A few weeks later I was headed down south to one of the largest fishing tournaments on the island and quite an international one because Cat Island is located right next to the Atlantic shelf. Great for marlin, tuna, and everything in between. The tournaments were always fun because a bunch of guys from Florida would come over, and it would be good old-fashioned debauchery for days. I ran into Mr. X. To be fair, he lived down that way, so I'm not sure if I ran into him or was purposely watching for him.

He was a smooth talker. He made me feel like a teenager all over again, but in a very adult way. One thing led to another, and we quickly embarked on a torrid love affair. It gave me something to do on the weekends. He even flew his own plane. He would take his plane down south to fly up to the airport in the middle of the island to pick me up. He would whisk me off to five-star resorts all around the Bahamas.

We were treated like royalty. We had the best of the best—dancing all night, drinking, passionate lovemaking, and genuinely rolling around laughing in the sand during the day. It was invigorating, it was forbidden, and boy did I pay for it!

A month after my affair with him started, my mother asked me to come to dinner early. She printed out an email. I laughed out loud when I read it. My mother did too. Mr. X's wife wrote a variety of really inappropriate words about me and said that I needed to leave her husband alone. She then proceeded to ask my mother if she knew what kind of girl she raised and that I should be ashamed of myself. Their open marriage arrangement was none of my business. It was actually a little comical. Mom asked me if I was in fact having an affair with the man, and I told her yes. She rolled her eyes at me with the internal dialogue probably going something like, "Oh, Ali. Really?"

My family is very open, so we showed the email to my dad. He asked me if this was true. I told him yes. He looked me in the eyes and said "right." This is pretty much my dad's translation as "Girls will be girls. Boys will be boys. Moving on."

And that was it. We had a giggle. They just told me to be careful because of gossip on the island. Oh, the gossip. I got the side-eye from a handful of folks.

One day Mr. X and his wife with their open relationship were at the resort on the bay I live on having lunch. Dammit, they were supposed to stay on their side of the island! I walked right into an ambush. Mr. X didn't want any part of it and left me alone with his wife. I should add that she had an American lover she'd brought down to the island.

Mr. X was a nice enough guy to me, and I had a great time, but, as usual, I was in for a fun time, not a long time. This was seeming to become a life motto for me. After that day, I decided to call it quits with him. I didn't want to disappear on an out island never to be found again.

PART 2

CHAPTER 12

In the Blink of an Eye

AUGUST 1, 2010, WAS a memorable day for me. I had completed my technical analysis trading studies, and I started to trade U.S. Treasury futures with real money from my bank account. Admittedly, I had a few small missteps, but that's part of the learning process. Every time I tripped, I just looked at it as a learning experience. I looked at failure as the acronym F.A.I.L. for "First Attempt In Learning."

Life couldn't have been more perfect. I wanted for nothing, I believed I had everything I needed, and I didn't plan to ever leave the island except to travel. I just wanted to trade and take care of the property as I got older. That was pretty much my life plan at that point.

Then came August 21, 2010. I was 27 years old. It was a typical hot summer Saturday where a bunch of us decided to meet at a new shoreline tiki bar owned by some local boys I'd grown up with. This was about four miles south of Fernandez Bay. I awoke that morning without so much as a hint it might be the last morning that I would ever be able to get out of bed independently.

Sometimes I imagine what I might have done with such a hint. I probably would've savored stepping into my string bikini and tying the little knots on the sides, taken in what it felt like for my fingers to grip my hairbrush as I pulled my hair up in a haphazard ponytail, and marveled at that feeling of squeezing a suntan lotion bottle with my hand and rubbing lotion over my flat belly.

I have often thought about that day, not so much in a melancholy way, but rather in amazement of how many body processes must work together to simply bend a finger or do one ordinary little thing. But, of course, I didn't know, so I rushed through it unaware, like every other day.

I arrived at the tiki hut about noon. My mother and a family friend from Germany decided to join us that day for our daytime dance party. The tiki bar couldn't have been more than 30 feet in diameter with a little thatch roof, a wooden bar, and then steps leading down into the water. Based on the tide, the water ranged from three feet to six feet deep. We would splash around in the water, walk up those little steps to have a dance party, and then go back into the water again. This continued for hours. I have so many photographs of that day, laughing, dancing, and being in the water.

I think it was probably about five o'clock. The sun was getting lower and the water depth harder to read. While I was being photographed, I stood up for the last time in my life. I can't remember whose idea it was—maybe it was mine—but I decided to dive into the water headfirst. I was admittedly quite cocky growing up as an island girl.

Truthfully, I did think the water was deeper than it

was, but I could see there was just sand underneath and maybe I would get scraped a little.

Don't underestimate how non-compressible sand is, especially depending on the speed at which you hit it! Feet first please. Gravity is the ultimate undefeated champion. Unfortunate life lesson learned right there. As I lifted my arms and tilted my head to lean forward for what I hoped would be a graceful dive, I remember calculating the angle I needed to enter the water.

3 . . . 2 . . . 1—BAM. I opened my eyes to pop back up to take a breath, but I couldn't move. I could wiggle my shoulders but nothing else moved on my body. I panicked. I screamed underwater, but no one could hear me.

Oh my God. I can't move my body. I can't feel my body. Crap. I can't lift my head. I think I'm in water. Yes, yes, I'm in water. Why can't I move? Why does no one see that I can't move? I must look like a drowning mermaid right now. I'm running out of breath. I'm not Aquaman. I can't breathe underwater. Is this it?

My thoughts tumbled as I continued to hold my breath, knowing that I was running out of time. I started to inhale some water, but I still held on. I knew if I didn't, I would drown. A lot flashes through your mind when you are about to drown, about to die. I suspect this is not how most of us imagine our end credits rolling. I certainly didn't.

Mom was standing near where I'd dived, and she had a sense I wasn't clowning around. Mom jumped in feet first and flipped me over. I gasped for air. I couldn't get enough air in my lungs. I could barely talk. It felt like someone had knocked the wind out of me.

By now Mom was yelling and asking me if I was

okay. A local friend jumped in and picked me up, putting me over his shoulder in a fireman's carry. I couldn't speak very loud, but I wanted to say, "Do not pick me up. Lay me completely flat, and do not move my neck." I couldn't though. I whispered in his ear, "Please, lay me flat. Please." He did not hear me. I was carried up the steps and then put flat on my back. I couldn't feel anything. I was paralyzed. By now Mom was screaming with panic. No one knew what had happened or what to do. I whispered to Mom, "Go get Dad. Dad. Go get Dad now."

My dad is one of those men you want by your side when you are in a war zone. Maybe this comes from his aviation experience or perhaps it's just his nature. Under pressure, even extreme pressure, he is levelheaded, calm, strategic thinking, and can make quick adjustments in an instant. Dad didn't pick up the phone, and I believe Mom sent her visiting German friend to race about four miles in our pickup to get him.

I was lying there, flat on a piece of plywood and terrified. A friend was with me. She kept telling me I was going to be okay, but I didn't believe her. I knew that we subscribed to an emergency medical evacuation jet service, so I figured they were the ones who would come get me. There were no doctors on the island at that time, just a nurse at the local clinic.

I tried with the little breath I had to direct my own medical care. I was well versed in medic first aid training, so I was familiar with spinal cord injury. I knew I shouldn't be moved. They made a makeshift neck brace after I was gently placed on a sheet of plywood.

I was not privy to all the conversations my dad was

having at the time about getting the medical evacuation plane, but I overheard that they could not get hold of anyone on the island who could help. Nor could Dad reach either of my brothers or my sister by phone. He was on his own—we were on our own. We were now stranded on our beautiful island that had become a prison for me.

Gossip on Cat Island spreads like wildfire. My dad was now back with our pickup truck. The plywood I was on was lifted onto the back of a pickup truck to go to the nurse's little clinic to figure out what to do next. When I arrived at the clinic, I could lift my head. I saw dozens of people crowd around me.

Luckily, the local nurse had the forethought to put in a catheter. Thank God!

When you sustain a spinal cord injury you will no longer have full control of your bowel or bladder. If your bladder overfills with urine and you can't release it, then your bladder will explode. The chance of sepsis setting in is high, and you will die. Though I didn't realize it at the time, this was quite an important and life-saving action. I didn't yet know my catheter would become one of my best inanimate object friends. I cannot live without it today.

I was frightened even though I knew what was going on. Who wouldn't be? I was talking to those crowding around, trying to calm them and myself, but I knew this was serious. When I did see my dad, he was telling me that everything was going to be okay because possibly I was just experiencing spinal shock, which the nurse had told him.

Did you know that if you injure your spinal cord, whether it results in permanent or temporary damage, your body will go into safe mode just like when your computer detects a corruption it will restart in safe mode?[i]

It's the same concept with a spinal cord. Your body puts itself into paralysis for twelve to twenty-four hours as a way of trying to protect itself. If you're lucky, about twenty-four hours later, you will be back to your old self. I somehow knew I was not going to be so lucky, but I really believed my dad for a few hours. I needed to believe my dad. I needed what was happening to be just a nightmare. I think, however, I sensed the reality.

The Florida-based air ambulance medical rescue service to which we had subscribed for years did not have a plane available and defaulted. Somehow, someway, my dad found an emergency plane in Nassau to come get us about an hour before sunset. It was a small King Air turboprop and not really fitted out or staffed for medical rescue.

With me on a stretcher, only two of us could go. Mom grabbed our passports, and Dad became my traveling companion. When we arrived at the airport, there were now hundreds of people there. I could see them in my peripheral vision. Everyone was praying for me, screaming, and terrified about what happened.

I learned later that the beautiful tiki bar where we had had such a wonderful afternoon would never be used again. Everyone believed bad spirits had cursed it because I had broken my neck there. Our fun that day was the last happy memory in that place.

The plane's pilots were not medically experienced. Dad was directing my care as they tried to squeeze me into the airplane. They kept bumping my head in the process. They tried improvising a neck brace, but it was too big for me. And there was a giant shard of something cutting into my head. I had full sensation of it and the blood that was dripping down my neck.

After we took off, Dad followed the nurse's suggestion and worked to keep me conscious and hydrated by feeding me ice chips. Meanwhile, things went from nightmare to catastrophe. Approaching Florida, we encountered a wall of huge thunderstorms, not uncommon for the season. The pilots decided to turn back east to Nassau.

To this day, Dad remains distraught about these pilots' decision, as it turned out time was critical for getting me into surgery. He knew very well how to fly a King Air and would have opted to drop down 100 feet above sea level to run around and under the storms to get me to the University of Miami's Ryder Trauma Center. But in the circumstances, he had to choose between keeping me conscious with ice chips or engaging in a heated argument with the less experienced pilots. Dad opted to stay with me, as it still wasn't at all clear to him exactly what was wrong or how serious it would turn out to be.

We ended up landing in Nassau, the capital of The Bahamas and the largest city. When we landed, there was an ambulance standing by to pick us up.

I remember transferring from the King Air to the ambulance and riding to the hospital about thirty minutes away. The roads were full of potholes, so we were bouncing around.

Tears were rolling down my face. I was not scared of spinal cord injury in that moment. I needed my head to stop bleeding. I didn't know until a week later that the dive had also cracked my head open. I can only surmise the medical team decided that injury wasn't serious enough to treat as paralysis seemed to be the primary concern.

When we arrived at the hospital in Nassau, I was assessed by the doctors and told that the hospital had no MRI available that night. An MRI was needed to confirm how much damage had been done to my spinal cord. All the hospital had that night was a CT scanner. I went in with some of the worst bedside mannered medical staff I have ever encountered. They didn't have any private rooms. They put my gurney in an open area and then just divided the sections with a curtain between patients.

One doctor told my dad, with me right next to him, that it appeared I had broken my neck at C6 and that I likely would never walk again. There was no compassion. He did say that the best course of action would be to get me to Miami as soon as possible, as this hospital was not equipped to deal with spinal cord injury. I could not believe the words coming out of his mouth.

Dad quietly assured me that the doctor had acknowledged his limited experience with the injury confirmed by the CT scan and that I should still have hope because spinal shock was still an open issue. In that moment, neither Dad nor I was able to assess exactly what my recovery prospects might be. But we did grasp the need for speed to get to the Ryder Trauma Center in Miami.

The pressing problem of the moment shifted. It was not because of spinal surgery, but because of a hormone. Dopamine is a complex hormone necessary to your system for many reasons, including maintaining your blood pressure. If you don't have enough dopamine, your blood pressure will slowly tank until you black out and die.

When you break your neck or suffer any traumatic injury, your body stops producing dopamine and starts releasing adrenaline instead. You have roughly twenty-four hours of adrenaline in your body and then you need dopamine.

The hospital in Nassau didn't have any dopamine, and my shattered body was no longer making any. I was on the ultimate time clock. Dad left my side. I don't know for how long as I was in psychological shock. When Dad came back, he told me that we were going to Miami. He had found new pilots and hired another aircraft. I don't know how, but he did it. And fast.

I distinctly remember getting very tired. I was so sleepy. I just wanted to go to sleep. Dad kept telling me to stay awake and kept talking with me. I didn't know why it was so important. Why couldn't I just take a nap? I didn't realize what was happening, but Dad did. I knew how dopamine worked, but in that moment I was not thinking clearly.

My blood pressure was dropping. I had been running on adrenaline at that point for about 18 hours, and my body was running out of it. I had hours to live, if I was lucky. Dad kept putting ice all over my head, talking to me, squeezing me, and refusing to let me fall asleep. He's my hero each and every day.

When our flight finally took off, Dad was so kind. I asked him to please take the ice cubes and hold them on the back of my neck to numb my skull. He didn't leave my side for a second. When we landed at Miami International, we had an entire medical team waiting to bring us to Jackson Memorial Hospital, home of the Miami Project, for emergency surgery with renowned neurosurgeon, Dr. Barth Green.

I had no way of knowing this at the time, but Mom was a registered member of a Miami concierge medical practice, and, while Dad and I were airborne, Mom reached her doctor, who was friendly with Gloria Estefan. Gloria had broken her back in a bus accident in 1990, but she had miraculously recovered and remained in contact with Dr. Green. My story was passed on to Gloria, and she called Dr. Green at home right away, and there he was by my bedside on arrival at the Ryder Trauma Center.

The last thing I remember was hearing the plane land on the runway. I don't remember getting into the ambulance or the drive to the hospital. I was later told that my blood pressure dropped to 40/20. Moments to live. I was immediately given an infusion of dopamine in the ambulance, which is what brought me back to consciousness by the time we arrived at the hospital. I woke up surrounded by residents in a room with an MRI machine.

I had many questions. Where did my dad go? Who were these people? What was happening? I immediately started to ask questions and started to move my arms around for what little movement I had at that time. One of the residents explained to me I was about to go in the MRI to understand the level of damage and then right into surgery. I kept asking questions, but everyone kept telling me to be quiet.

And then, for some reason, I decided to fight back. How did I fight back? I saw in the corner of my eye a resident pick up a pair of scissors as he was telling his fellow doctor to cut off my bikini. I thought to myself, *Are you crazy? Just pull the damn string.* What came out of my mouth was, "You don't have to cut my bikini. It just comes off. I like that one. I will need it again."

I didn't know that was the last time I would ever wear a bikini, but it was so important to me in that moment. It wasn't until years later, when I started to study neuroscience, that I understood it was my brain's way of trying to control the uncontrollable. I had control of my bikini and that was pretty much it. They also had to pull out my belly button ring because you cannot have any metal in an MRI. I did tell them to take very good care of it, because I would like it back on after surgery. That poor belly ring was never seen again!

That night the surgeons performed something called a spinal fusion between the C5 and C6 vertebrae. I had countless vertebrae shards floating around my spinal cord, and the surgeons had to carefully pick out each piece. Then they inserted two titanium rods through the anterior (front) of my neck to stabilize my spine. It's a pretty standard procedure after a spinal injury of this nature. My Miami surgeon did not even stitch me up. Instead, he superglued the front of my neck back together, because, as he later told me, he did not want me to have a scar. As if that was my immediate concern. But I do thank him now years later. You can barely tell I had that surgery. I was now a bionic woman!

CHAPTER 13

ICU Life

IF SOMEONE WOULD HAVE informed me of my future frequent-flyer ICU status over the next seven years, I probably would've opted not to wake up from surgery if given a choice. The first few days were very fuzzy. I was on a lot of narcotics.

I remember waking up and then falling right back to sleep. I did see my brothers, my sister, my best friend, my dad, and my mom when I opened my eyes. I could see people crying. When I closed my eyes, I could hear them crying, but I was still too tired to engage with them. I was also on this bed that rotated at an angle back and forth and back and forth. I was in constant motion. I was very uncomfortable and had tubes coming out of every part of my body.

I came to more fully a few days later. Dr. Green came into my room to break news that no one should ever have to hear. Truthfully, I think it was harder for my family than for me. I don't think we give enough room for our family members and their grief when something dramatic happens to their loved ones. He told me the days were early, but as of right then, I was presenting as a C6 quadriplegic. I had crushed my C5-C6 cervical vertebrae and would leave the hospital in a wheelchair.

I remember looking into Dr. Green's eyes and thinking, *You think I'm paralyzed? Really? What gave it away?* In really stressful times, I turn to dark humor, so my humor level was running pretty high at that moment. Dr. Green explained to me I would need to spend about a month in the ICU before I would go to the rehabilitation unit for occupational therapy and physical therapy, among other things. I couldn't process rehab. I was still trying to process what was happening to me.

Here's the thing, breaking vertebral bones is not actually what causes paralysis. It's the swelling and contusion (bruising) around the spinal column that deprives nerves of capillary blood flow that causes paralysis. This is the body's way to protect itself by stopping the bruise from rising up the spine to the brain, which would be fatal. It's that protection mechanism, that stopping the bruise from spreading, that causes a life-changing result. Your body saves itself from dying, but now you're stuck with nerves that have starved to death in your spinal cord, which results in paralysis.

I didn't know it at the time, but I was a lost cause even before I rolled into surgery. It took about twenty-two hours for me to get to surgery, so that swelling had already set in and spinal cord nerves were already dying off. I think when the doctors explained to me that I might regain some function over the next year, they were just trying to give me hope. Honestly, spinal cord injury is so complicated that it really is hard to tell what will or won't happen during the recovery phase, so maybe that was fair.

Within a week, I started to fully regain my conscious thoughts. There was so much going on around me. I could tell my family was trying to be brave for me. They would come in with big smiles, but I could see them fighting back the tears. My family and friends had to leave each night. It was against hospital policy for even family members to stay in the ICU. I was terrified. It felt like ages before anyone would come to me when I pressed the call button. I had some ICU nurses I will forever be grateful for and some who were plainly so jaded they just didn't give a damn.

Within the first week, one of the nurses sat with me to explain something else that was happening. She told me that I had not been turned from side to side on the medical evac board for twenty-two hours and, as a result, I had something called a Stage III pressure sore.[ii] I had no idea what she was talking about.

While she was talking, I suddenly realized I had not peed in days and inquired as to how I was able to pee. She explained that I had a catheter in my urethra, so I was good to go—literally. I asked her how long I would have this thing called a catheter. She replied, "The rest of your life, dear." What? Hell no. Not in my mind. I was going to kick spinal cord injury in the butt and recover just fine, thank you very much.

I asked the most dreaded question of all, "How am I pooping?" She explained that I would be learning about something called a "bowel program" routine to regulate how I go to the bathroom in the future, but for now I was just pooping as my body wanted to on a disposable under pad. I was so disgusted that I didn't know what to say. I didn't know what to think. I'm pooping on myself? Gross! I don't know why my bodily functions were such a priority when I should've been focusing on my spine or my pressure sore, but there you have it. This is precisely why I choose to normalize highly uncomfortable topics in my daily life and in blog posts as relates to every taboo topic I can think of. Big questions and concerns do arise on these topics and need answers.

Of course, the pressure sore had to be dealt with, and that turned out to be pretty darn serious. Here's a thing to know about pressure sores. They can be truly life-threatening. Pressure sores are my arch nemesis with respect to secondary complications I endure, even today.

If your skin is pressing on something for more than two hours, and the external pressure is higher than the internal capillary blood pressure, the skin cells start to die inside. There are four stages of pressure sores: Stage I, II, III, and IV, with IV being the most severe and often the wound is down to the bone at this point. Sometimes pressure sores require surgery, which is not always successful. When you are paralyzed, you must be extremely careful to prevent pressure sores, otherwise known as bedsores to many people.

This was my general life routine in the ICU over the next month:

- I was turned every two hours for my Stage III pressure sore.

- I was peeing in a bag.

- I pooped on an under pad.

- I was being pumped full of more drugs than I can recall.

Doctors and nurses were in and out of my room every few hours. My family would take turns sitting with me, and my mother was by my side every single day. She would bake brownies and other delicious treats, which I really didn't need to eat because I ended up gaining forty pounds over the next three months, but I loved her trying to help me cope. Everyone would giggle with me, and I think I really did have a fantastic attitude for the ICU. I was abnormally positive. I joked with the nurses, I laughed with the doctors, I put on a brave face to my family. I don't know if I believed I was going to regain function, but I sure acted the part. The darker things get in my life, the more I battle back with humor, then and now.

Generally, I find that people like to help you more if you're friendly and smiley. Who wants to be around a grumpy person every day? It can really wear on your own spirits, so I decided to keep my own internal trials and tribulations to myself.

I do recall overhearing my brother talking to my sister one day. He didn't know what was going to come next for me in life. How would I ever get married? How was I going to live this life? I had already pondered these questions myself for years. They were legitimate questions.

Family and friends came to visit me, paint my nails, and do my makeup. I have very blonde eyelashes that I'm very self-conscious about, so I always wore makeup when I went out. My sister and Mom would put eyeliner and mascara on me before the day would get started. It was very important to me to look presentable. I suppose I could probably chalk it up to "if I can't control how my body is functioning right now, I can certainly look good." I thought I looked adorable. I might've been the happiest new spinal cord injury patient on the planet, or at least in this hospital.

Do you know what likely did save my life in the ICU? My dad. One day he said to me, "Ali, you broke your body, not your brain. Get back to work trading." What he meant was that my mind was intact even if I didn't have control over my physical body, and I could still live a full life. This insight turned out to be hugely important for me at that time and ever since.

Dad created a whole technology set up on top of my bed for me to continue trading. I would look at the screens, and he would be my hands. I would tell him what to buy or sell at a certain price. We had a schedule. I would wake up, do all the medical stuff I needed to do, have a few visitors, spend a few hours trading, sleep, rinse, rest, and repeat. I was a busy girl in the ICU. I didn't have time to think about what was happening to me, because Dad kept me on task. One day he even told me that we needed to focus when someone wanted to come visit me.

I recall having had a live Treasury Bond trade, an actual at-risk open position, over the weekend I was injured, and when I woke up from a surgery on Monday, I told my dad my password and urgently asked him to please close my position. He did, and the position was slightly in profit.

Again, I don't know why this was so important at the time, but it was. Thank you, Dad! Staying on task with self-discipline saved me in the ICU as it has in my ongoing life.

Time passed. I was ready and packed to go down to the rehab unit when disaster struck again. No kidding!

One afternoon I couldn't breathe. I was gasping for air. Turns out I had developed a life-threatening pulmonary embolism. A blood clot in my leg broke off and traveled up to my lung. If these are not caught in time, they have a very high mortality rate.

I was immediately put on an intravenous blood thinner and held back for a few more weeks in the ICU. This delay was actually very dangerous. It's so important to start moving the muscles that are functional so that they don't completely atrophy and present as "more" paralyzed. By now I could barely lift my arms at all. One would've thought I was paralyzed from the neck down.

Then came the next crisis. I was chatting with my mom and sister one afternoon and said, "I feel funny." And, just like that, I was dead. I can't tell you what happened during that period because I was not conscious, but I woke up to paddles and really bright lights. I had been revived. But, oh my goodness, I think I had what's called an out of body experience. I'm more of a science girl, so I think what happened is that I died but the neurons were still firing in my brain, but most people call this an out of body experience.

I remember I was running down a very dark hallway,

an abyss. There was nothing. I was all tangled up in these rubber bands, and I saw some kind of bright light ahead of me. I was running with all my might with all of this elasticity pulling against me. I knew if I made it to that light, I would be okay. I grabbed onto the brightness and started to rip open a hole in space to pull myself out. Then, the next thing I knew, I was looking at hospital lights above my head.

I tried to tell the nurses what had happened to me, but someone told me to stop talking. I really wanted to tell someone, but they seemed more interested in keeping me alive, probably a good idea.

I don't know exactly what happened to me, but that night, when my family departed, I asked if the nurses could please keep me alive. I was scared of death at that point in my life. I didn't want to die just yet. It wasn't until many years later I came to live in peace with the concept of death. That night, I called my sister. She snuck back in the room to give me a hug. With tears streaming down my face, I begged her to ask the nurses not to let me die again.

I don't know what happened next, but my sister was sleeping at the foot of my bed for the rest of the night. This started the trend. My family would take turns for a week at a time to sleep over with me. No one was going to let anything happen to me. I can't even imagine trying to recover from a spinal cord injury with no family or friends to support you.

I have deep empathy for those who go through this alone. This is why each and every day now I work toward helping injured and disabled people, because no one should be alone through such horrible times. Empathy, compassion, love, and understanding need to be there for everyone—even total strangers.

CHAPTER 14

Rehabilitation

FINALLY, THE DAY ARRIVED when I was on the rehabilitation floor, ready to start trying to regain function and get back to my life. It was eight weeks of hell. Honestly. I was so weak I could barely sit up. I was now an adult pooping on myself. I had an intermittent catheter, meaning I had to get in bed every few hours so someone could insert a catheter into my urethra, allowing me to pee into a bag, and I was waking up every two hours at night to be turned for my pressure sore. I was one of twelve patients per caregiver on the floor. This is not the space to speak about the structural failures of our healthcare system, but let it be said they exist.

Do you know what sleep deprivation feels like? Waking up every two hours for almost a full year? For one thing, you start to hallucinate. It's challenging to form a sentence, and it's one of the worst forms of torture. I would be remiss not to point out that lack of sleep also leads to lack of regeneration in the body, thus making healing immensely less efficient.

Despite all of these challenges, my sister taught my brothers how to French braid my hair and insert my contacts (not an easy task). I wore bright green scrubs. I looked freaking adorable. I was bubbly and energetic even though I couldn't drive this thing called a power wheelchair for the life of me. I couldn't figure out how I was going to be a successful person living with paralysis if I couldn't even drive my wheelchair. I kept running over the nurses' toes. Sometimes my blood pressure would get so low I would pass out and run into the wall. I learned this is commonplace for newly injured folks who are trying to regain control of basic bodily functions.

I developed strong friendships with my physical therapists and am still friends with two of them today. I slowly got stronger, was fitted for a wheelchair customized for my body, and figured out how to manipulate and twist my wrists even though my fingers were paralyzed (called tenodesis in medical terms). By the time my customized wheelchair arrived, I had gained serious weight and had to start all over again. A very common problem by the way.

Every day I would bite my right pinky because I started to have little sensations return in just a few fingers. A month previously there had been no sensation. I told everyone around me how excited I was, but you could see they were just trying to stay positive for me. I did eventually get to a point where when I bite down on my right pinky, I know I'm doing it though I would not feel any physical pain if it was stuck with a needle or touched by something hot. That one sensation when I bite on my pinky is pretty much the only sensory function I recovered.

There was this one patient, also a cervical level

injury, like me. Over the months I watched them regain physical function. I was envious. I'm not going to lie. I couldn't believe they were starting to walk and I wasn't. They were even quite grumpy, and I thought how is this cosmically fair that I can barely feel a pinky after I chomp down on it, but they could walk again? In any event, years later, I truly am glad that this patient was able to walk again.

There were quite a few atrocious medical situations we had to endure, but I think most of the time we handled them pretty gracefully. We definitely started regaining the ability as a family to engage in dark humor. On one such occasion I saw a water drip in my room. I kept watching the water line creep toward me on the ceiling. I told my best friend and my sister-in-law what was happening. They went to get help. It was too late. By the time they returned to my room, the ceiling had fallen directly on top of me. A water leak. The ceiling could've fallen anywhere else in the room, but it had collapsed on me.

In the department of dark humor, my brothers joked around that since I had already broken my neck, a ceiling collapse was no problem. They told me it would just add to character building. They were right.

On another occasion, a nurse came in to put a catheter tube up my urethra to drain my bladder into a bag. She kept missing the urethra opening. I had had too much water to drink so my bladder was overfilled, and my body went into what called dysreflexia shock.[iii]

When you sustain any damage to your nervous system after a spinal cord injury, a lot of really gnarly stuff can happen to you, and what's known as "autonomic dysreflexia" is one of them. For example, I can't feel my leg, but if you stab me in the leg, I will know it, just not from a sensory perspective. My body will tell me something is wrong—like getting stabbed in the leg or having an overfilled bladder—first by raising my blood pressure. Then I will start sweating above the level of injury (my breasts up), chronic nerve pain will increase, I will get goosebumps, and then I can have a stroke. This is dysreflexia. It's life-threatening if you can't figure out what is causing it to happen and do something to alleviate it.

So, my body was sounding an alarm by skyrocketing my blood pressure, and I was profusely sweating from my shoulders up. Half my face was beet red like Two-Face, the DC comic supervillain. I couldn't breathe and felt like I was dying. When the nurse finally released the urine from the bladder, all we could see was blood. You're supposed to slowly release the urine. Think of a balloon that you deflate. It just squishes together once the air escapes. This was what happened to my bladder with the fast release of the urine. I remember saying, "Well, at least I'm alive." What's the alternative? Cry about it? Sure. I did that sometimes, but that wasn't going to reverse the universe's twisted sense of humor with my paralysis. It is better to try to make the best of things and move on, but there are times . . .

Chronic Pain Activates

ONE NIGHT IN REHAB I started screaming. It felt like my entire body was on fire. Every cell was burning like hot pins and needles were being shoved into my body. My whole body felt like it was on hot coals. The doctors immediately thought a titanium rod holding my spine together might have come loose. Off I went into the MRI. Nope. Clear. Nothing wrong with the hardware in my neck. They doped me up on so much morphine for two weeks that I could barely open my eyes.

When they weaned me off morphine, I told the doctor the pain was still there and while I can't feel my legs per se, I can spatially understand where my toes are in relation to my body because of the burning pins and needles. Think of it like this, your arm falls asleep and you shake it to wake it up. When it's waking up you start to feel those little burning pins and needles. Yes, like that. That is the pain I was feeling and currently still feel every day raised to the power of ten.

A nurse came into my room and told me she thought she understood what was happening to me. She thought I was experiencing something called neuropathic pain, essentially chronic nerve pain. She said this is very common in spinal cord injury and added I would likely have to live with it the rest of my life. I didn't believe her at first. I couldn't live in constant chronic pain like this every day of my life. Could I? People kill themselves over chronic pain.

That was my introduction to neuropathic pain. I would have preferred we not meet, but we're in this together now. The nurse said there were a few options such as narcotics or specific medications that help with how loud the pain essentially screams in your body. She said I was going to have to adjust. The next morning when I awoke, my brain somehow comprehended that I was going to have to find a way to live with this pain.

Once our brain has time to catch up to the reality

of a situation, we have this incredible ability as human beings to find ways to cope with it. Yes, there's a bunch of neuroscience behind that. The pain volume turned down just a little bit because my brain had time to catch up to the reality of what was happening.

At this time in my spinal cord injury life, the constant neuropathic pain was about a five out of ten every day and night. It was horrible, but I could find a way to live with it. Over the years I tried a few of those meds the nurse talked about, but to no avail. At least I wasn't going to get addicted to narcotics, because they don't act on the pain receptors that nerve pain does.

About two years later, my pain scale jumped up permanently after a disastrous experience in the hospital. This constant, chronic pain was my most debilitating disability, and it has remained so. I just don't give it the power today that I did back then. Being paralyzed is quite easy. I just sit there, drive a chair, and people help me live my life. Constant severe pain, on the other hand, has the potential to drive a person to become suicidal. It took me many years of hypnosis to basically detach my mind from the pain in my body.

I am a huge believer in mind over matter and putting consistent effort toward how I shape my internal thoughts, basically, using applied neuroscience to re-wire my brain. This involves a concept called neuroplasticity: neurons that wire together fire together. Think of your brain as a hiking trail. The more you walk the same path, the more worn and easy to follow the path becomes. But if you stop using the path, nature takes over, and the trail disappears. The good news? You can carve out new trails anytime. The more you practice a new way of thinking or responding, the stronger that path becomes until it's the path your brain naturally takes without coaxing.

Goodbye to Rehab

THE TIME WAS NEARING for me to head home. My dad rented an apartment in Miami, we adapted it for my needs, and we started the hunt for caregivers. I am so grateful that I had an exceptional network to help me. So many others do not have the family network I have been afforded in life. I went through an agency at first to find caregivers. I didn't want to rely on my mom, who was sixty-five at the time, to be my primary caregiver.

When I rolled out of the hospital, a burnt orange adapted van was waiting for me. I cried at first, because I could not believe I was going to be driving an ugly orange van the rest of my life. One of my siblings told me it was my pumpkin, and I was Cinderella. I still cried, but Pumpkin has been part of the family ever since. I know that I am fortunate to own my own adaptive vehicle, whatever color it is.

As a delightful parting gift prior to being discharged from the hospital, a woman from the billing department came to pay me a visit. She proceeded to try to get me to pay a bogus seventy-thousand-dollar invoice for the medical evacuation jet that supposedly rushed me to surgery. Nice try. I was not so naïve as to take ownership or give her a credit card for that invoice. This actually started our first of numerous battles with health insurance, but it was a dear family friend who navigated health insurance for me for the first several years. I was just trying to survive from day to day. This was my first experience with health insurance that shaped my purpose-driven life to fight for health equity for others many years later.

CHAPTER 15

Back into the World

I HAVE SPOKEN WITH dozens of friends and colleagues about their experience of getting back to life right after rehab. Most folks seem to adapt quite quickly, but I was in for a much longer road. Seven years to be precise.

I was regularly in and out of the hospital for infections, pressure sores, autoimmune diseases, cervical cancer, spinal cysts, pulmonary embolisms, and countless other secondary complications. I went back and forth between home and the hospital often. The hospital became my second home. When I was first discharged, I was trying to find some kind of normality in my life. It was challenging because I had to wake up at four o'clock, exercise in my carefully designed adapted home gym, go to daily physical therapy appointments, participate in spinal cord research at the Miami Project, come home, trade when I could, shower, teach new caregivers, and then do it all over again the next day.

Life was pretty monotonous and soul sucking, the first

two years in particular. I didn't really have a life. I would arrange outings with my friends on Sundays, but I could never venture far from home because I still didn't have a permanent (Foley) catheter yet, I was having bowel accidents while living in disposable adult underwear for years. I couldn't even look in the mirror. I gained so much weight I could barely fit into any of my clothes. I had to get rid of my entire wardrobe from before the accident. That was painful. I basically lived in scrubs for the first six months after rehab. I was disgusted with my body and couldn't even fathom finding a partner.

The concept of a relationship and love was a distant memory for the next five years. You could say I became asexual. I didn't think about lovers or sex or anything in the realm of affection. I was living in beautiful, tropical Miami, but I wasn't even getting outside. I couldn't control how I went to the bathroom, let alone how I looked. My face broke out with acne from all the countless medications I was taking. I developed hypothyroidism, an autoimmune disease, causing my weight gain, which was exacerbated by contraindicated medications prescribed in error.

I went to a holistic doctor for nearly a year to help me get my period back, help me lose weight, and get me off twenty-two medications. I kept getting over prescribed. It seemed like when a doctor didn't know what to do with me, I was prescribed more medication. No one seemed to look at the drug side effects or how one drug interacted with another drug. It was a nightmare. I was even eating based on a physical Excel spreadsheet at about six hundred calories a day to lose weight, and I wasn't losing weight.

I was gaining weight. My hormonal system was completely out of alignment.

Then there was the pressure sore. For eight straight months, I had a Stage III pressure sore I was trying to heal. We brought in this amazing nurse from the Veterans Hospital to help. I was turning every two hours at night. I was still sleep deprived and surprised I could even make a sentence. I muscled through though. I think my brain has overwritten specific periods during that time to protect my sanity. I often look back and don't know how I did get through it, but I did. I was no stranger to getting my butt kicked in life. Murphy and his crazy law were kicking my butt eighteen ways to Monday.

My dad would offer me a reprieve each Sunday. We would go to Little Havana, smoke a couple cigars, and talk about news and geopolitical events. He helped me escape from my mental prison.

On one such day, I recall Dad presenting me with five different qualities of cigars along with a small Cuban coffee called a Cortadito. This was a fun cigar evaluation test. My family had become very loyal to one particular Miami family who produced (in Nicaragua) what we think are the world's very best cigars.

My dad's life lesson here with the cigars was to teach me about the challenge of understanding perfection before one understands imperfection. A life lesson through cigars and a great diversion from my daily miseries. Same goes for wine, chocolate, coffee, and many other of life's little treats. Welcome to my family. And so each Sunday, Dad and I would escape the walls of our apartment into a fantasy land where I didn't have to think about my paralysis.

ALI INGERSOLL

Caregiver Life

I THINK ONE OF the hardest things about losing your independence is that you have to rely on another person all the time to physically take care of you. My mom has always been front and center for me. She would, and still does, teach my caregivers how to put their fingers up my bum with suppositories to help me poop, teaches them how to dress me, administer my meds, and give me a shower. I didn't have it quite figured out in the beginning.

Mom's coping mechanism is to be a little bit overbearing—not blaming her—because she was in a sense also dealing with the loss of her child. After all, from the moment she flipped me over face up in the water, life changed forever for her too. She has been by my side in every imaginable way and then some in the fifteen years since my accident.

A piece of me died the day I broke my neck and my independence was taken away in the blink of an eye. It took years, and even becoming suicidal, for me to authentically process what really happened to me. I was grieving the loss of the old, carefree Ali. She was gone, or so I thought back then. I acted bubbly, but I don't remember feeling remotely like myself for years.

I have trained many, many caregivers on how to take care of me. At first, I hired people based on their credentials, which was a huge mistake for me personally, because if you are around someone all day and night, you want to make sure you like them as a person. I carried quite a lot of trauma surrounding the early days as it relates to caregiving. I had caregivers leave me alone in the middle of the night, try to jerk out my catheter, come to work on drugs, steal my money, take my medication, lie to me, and even hit me. I was used to being a very independent woman, but now my life was physically in someone else's hands. When they abused me in these ways, it was as if all my strength would disappear.

It wasn't until 2021 that I finally learned to let the trauma go through a great deal of therapy, personal mental work, and other strategies I learned.

I sat with this and struggled with how much to write about caregivers in my life. On one hand I've had fantastic caregivers stay with me for years and others who have just been downright abusive and probably should've gone to jail. When you find an amazing caregiver, oh my God, life just seems so seamless and everything seems possible. When you have one who is highly abusive, you feel like an emotional hostage in your own life. If I were able-bodied, I never would've put up with what they did to me, but when I was dependent on another person and my mom wasn't around, then it was a tricky balance. I had to consider their feelings and thoughts as human beings while simultaneously trying to create a boundary to live my best life and not get taken advantage of.

Let's just say I didn't really get it right or know what I was seeking for a very long time. I truly believe in growing through even the most challenging of times, and I know I have. I still struggle at times, but I generally keep moving forward regardless. In my life today, I do try to surround myself with really great human beings. Sometimes it works out, sometimes it doesn't, but I have learned never to carry the baggage from one caregiver to a new one. Now, that took quite a lot of therapy!

Everyone has a clean slate when they walk into my home, and they have my full trust. If they break that trust, that is a different story, but I choose to live my life believing the best in people because if I didn't, well, I probably wouldn't survive. I will just say my first few years out of rehab, we went through a lot of folks, but, through it all, I'm still here today to share the stories and lessons learned.

Cervical Cancer Carnival

A YEAR AFTER MY accident, I still had regained no meaningful function. Okay, I accepted I was going to have to live as a complete quadriplegic. I'm a realist. I'm not much of a hope spree person. This didn't stop my dad though. Science is his forte, and I think it is his personal coping mechanism as well. You'd have to ask him about that. He traveled around the world for me for years to meet with top scientists interested in spinal cord injury. Really. He interviewed the best of the best.

He would come back full of hope about new discoveries, but nothing really materialized over the years. I joke with my fellow quadriplegic friends about "new advancements" because all of us had heard so many times that a cure is just a few years out. A person I spoke to recently about this is sixty-five years old now. He was told the same thing when he was injured in the late 1980s—just another five years before a breakthrough emerges.

I could tell my dad was full of hope based on what he learned in the field, so I played the proverbial part. I think it made him feel better. I was, however, planning to live my life as is and figure out how to make it the best life I could.

Most days felt like I was just living the movie *Groundhog Day*. I didn't find much joy in anything anymore, but I was still wildly bubbly. I smiled, I laughed, and I figured that if I could just fake it, I would eventually make it, as that tired old saying goes. I have since turned this into "face it until you ace it."

About this time, I realized I had not gone to the gynecologist in ages to get a Pap smear. I had been diagnosed years earlier with some strain of common HPV. I was also tested for the genetic markers, and it turns out I have the cervical cancer genes. HPV can express itself in dozens of different ways from genital warts to cervical cancer. Back then, in my teens, I was happy I had the cancer genes, because I certainly didn't want to have genital warts. Typical Ali thinking, I guess.

It was quite an undertaking to get up onto an exam table at the gynecologist's office. It was quite comical figuring how to roll a quadriplegic on the table and have my caregiver and my mom hold my legs open. If that wasn't challenging enough, my bowels were still not quite trained. My body just did what it wanted to do although I was teaching my body with suppositories to poop once a day. Well, on that day, my body decided to poop all over the gynecologist. She was tremendously open-minded and just cleaned me up like nothing had happened.

I went on my merry way, thinking nothing of the exam. A week later I received an urgent call from the GYN's office telling me to come in immediately. She told me that my Pap smear was abnormal, and they wanted to do more testing that involved scraping cells off my cervix. I went back to the office a week after that testing and was told I had cervical cancer. Stage I, thank goodness, but they wanted to operate immediately before it spread. I didn't have much time to process. I had to tell my dad, who then asked the doctors a thousand questions. We made quick work of getting me into the OR.

They didn't anesthetize me because I have no feeling below the chest, so they gave me an epidural. I don't think they gave the OR folks the proverbial memo, because the OR staff started talking and didn't realize that the patient was awake. I heard the funniest conversations, just like in *Grey's Anatomy*. I was in and out of the hospital pretty quickly. I thought that was it. Great.

A day later I started to get a splitting headache. I'd never had a headache like that before. In the spirit of saying more with less, it turned out I had a cerebral spinal fluid leak. Basically, the gauge of the needle used to give me the epidural was too large, allowing spinal fluid to leak out of my spine. That's not as scary as it sounds. It was fixable. I needed to return to the hospital where they would take blood from my arm and inject it back into the spine where the leak was located—usually a quite simple procedure. I scheduled it for the next morning.

In the middle of the night, I started to suffocate. It felt as though my lungs were collapsing. They attributed this to the cerebral spinal fluid leak. I arrived at the hospital in the morning as scheduled and told the doctors I couldn't breathe. They assured me that the blood patch would do the job. We rolled into the OR, and they told me I needed to sit up perfectly straight for the blood patch. I couldn't do this. They didn't have a way to keep me straight, so they sat me up against a structural pole in the room and tied me to it. It was absurd, but I went with the flow. They completed the blood patch and then left me alone in the OR for a good ten minutes. I didn't know what to do, because I couldn't call for help.

They rolled me to the recovery room. I told them my lungs still felt like they were collapsing, and it was getting harder and harder to breathe. They were very puzzled because a blood patch was supposed to fix the cerebral spinal fluid leak immediately. They did some quick testing and found I had developed a massive pulmonary embolism. By now these doctors were not even trying to hide their conversations. They could not figure out how I was still alive after forty hours with a massive blood clot in my lung.

My medical team immediately administered a blood thinner. A few days later I was sent home with a machine to test the thickness of my blood. I adjusted medication accordingly, and that was that. I should have known that the story would continue, but I was just happy to leave yet another hospital.

Over the next few days, life went from challenging to a nightmare once again. One night I started to go into dysreflexia shock. My blood pressure was skyrocketing, I was sweating profusely, and I felt like I couldn't breathe. I was on the verge of a stroke. I was immediately rushed to the ICU.

They couldn't figure out what was wrong with me. Honestly, they were puzzled. Too many cooks in the kitchen from pulmonologist to cardiologist to neurologist to primary care physicians. They just kept talking over one another. So, what do medical professionals do in general when in doubt? Enter morphine, again!

I kept getting dysreflexic, and they kept combating this by giving me different drugs to bring my blood pressure down. After two straight weeks of this, I woke up one morning and felt fine. The nurse came in my room, pulled the covers off my body to wash me, and looked horrified. She rushed out of the room and came back with the doctor. Mom was right behind them. A football-sized blood clot had passed through my vagina in the middle of the night. What really happened? Here's the gist of it.

After my cervical surgery I was lying in bed because I'm paralyzed. I was not draining the blood downhill as most women would because they can walk. The blood was pooling back inside my abdomen. It caused complete toxic shock in my body. Essentially, I had been hemorrhaging slowly for two weeks, and no one caught it. A simple CT scan of the abdomen would've shown this immediately, but no one thought to give me one. I don't know what to think about that. Shock? Disbelief? Standard-of-care?

The reason I bring this up is those two weeks changed my life forever. There is an unfortunate complication that can arise with long-term morphine use. Increased chronic pain. Permanently. My daily twenty-four seven chronic burning pins and needles pain throughout my body went from being a five out of ten to waking up with a seven out of ten in the morning and going to a nine out of ten at night. Once again, I had to learn to cope with a new reality, seemingly a daily occurrence at this point in my life.

The Paralyzed Mermaid

AFTER THIS VERY DIFFICULT first year with its many medical

debacles, I was craving the ocean. I was living right on the ocean in Coconut Grove, Miami, but I longed to get back in the water. My dad could tell. Everyone could tell. If there were such a thing as a past life, I would have been a mermaid. Most quadriplegics I know who injure themselves from shallow water diving have quite a fear of water. Not me!

I'm not sure where my dad found this wonderful Venezuelan swim instructor, but she changed my life.

My pressure sore had healed enough that I was allowed to start swimming. I didn't know how I was going to swim as a quadriplegic paralyzed from the chest down with paralyzed triceps and paralyzed hands that I call my "paws." When we first entered the pool, I was in heaven. I couldn't feel the water until it hit my nipple line, but I felt free. I was floating. I was on top of the world. I felt like Superwoman. Nothing could stop me.

Then . . .

Face plant in the water. I couldn't move. I was flailing my arms. It felt like I was drowning all over again. I was having a flashback to the day of my accident, and I'm pretty sure my very experienced swim instructor let me flounder around in the water to teach me a lesson. The lesson? Slow down. You're not ready, little one.

Three times a week for several hours at a time I would meet her at our pool at the apartment complex. It was a gorgeous infinity pool overlooking the ocean. I learned different adaptive strokes. She refused to let me use any type of flotation device. She wanted me to learn to swim independently as a C6 quadriplegic. I have since spoken with dozens of other quadriplegics, and none of them succeeded at this. I still have not found anyone who swims like me. I even applied to the 2012 Paralympics. Unfortunately, my swimming level and style was such that no other swimmer on the Paralympic team could swim like me. They would swim on their backs into a backstroke. I could flip over, roll over, swim the butterfly, and do a backstroke. I was flattered and slightly disappointed at the same time. Of course, I had much to learn before I achieved this.

My instructor was relentless. I swallowed mouthfuls of water, choked, wiggled around like a worm on a hot pavement, and I just couldn't get it. I was getting frustrated with month after month of unsuccessful efforts. She was trying to teach me a log roll where I would float on my belly and then figure out how to twist my belly so I could roll on my back for safety. This was such a key maneuver as I could swim strokes, but I could not raise my head out of the water to get a breath of air.

Then, one day the "aaahh haaa" moment hit when I was squirming around and, suddenly, I flipped over onto my back. I screamed in elation, but I was still stuck. It took some time for us to figure out how to move my body vertical so I could swim upright, my special way of swimming, but I eventually triumphed. Swimming was the only thing I looked forward to each week. Okay, not the only thing. I did look forward to Mom's cooking and cigar time with Dad, but swimming was mine. It was a step of independence.

Some women want to learn how to put on their makeup after they break their neck, but I just wanted to swim. Sadly, what happened next would keep me out of the water for the next four years of my life. But don't worry, my swimming career was far from over!

On Death's Doorstep

ABOUT TWO YEARS AFTER my accident, I was still trying to settle into the normality of life in Miami when I started to develop trouble breathing. Slowly, for sure, but the new difficulty was persistent. I went through a battery of tests. Eventually, the surgeons found something called an arachnoid cyst[iv] inside my spinal cord. It's a fluid-filled cyst inside the spinal cord, and it was slowly ascending toward C5 and maybe eventually beyond. At C5 I'd lose independent breathing. I needed surgery to remove the cyst.

The progression of my breathing challenges steadily increased, but insurance would not approve my surgery until I exhibited more symptoms, such as losing more motor function. The other challenge was that the MRI showed a kind of fuzzy image of the cyst, and insurance used the excuse that they did not have full confidence there indeed was a cyst.

But there was another, more significant issue than distraction with medical insurance. And this concerned the surgical skill to remove the cyst. On this, we learned that only about 5 percent of the world's neurosurgeons have ever opened a spinal cord. No problem with operating on the brain, but going inside the spinal cord was exponentially riskier due to the risk of collateral damage to blood vessels feeding spinal cord neurons.

The original surgery after my injury served only to

rebuild vertebral stability, but no one actually touched my spinal cord.

My dad immediately sprang into action, as we were now dealing with a ticking time bomb. He departed on both national and international trips to interview top neurosurgeons and find a solution. He ran into the same problem repeatedly in the US—experienced neurosurgeons declined my case. World-class surgeons in the US rarely got to operate on spinal cords, given malpractice risk from ambulance chasing lawyers and profit-protecting insurance companies.

Exasperated, Dad finally hit upon a simple new question that went like this: "If she were your daughter and had this problem, what would you do?"

He hit pay dirt, as it were. Over and over he got the same response from experienced American neurosurgeons: "I'd take her to China."

Why? The answer turned out to be pretty straight-forward. China has a population of over 1.5 billion people, so not surprisingly they have a lot more spinal cord injuries than we do in the US. Perhaps just as importantly, in China the doctors do not have to contend with constant threats of malpractice litigation, and there are no private insurance companies to worry about. Chinese surgeons just practice medicine, and some of them have successfully opened spinal cords hundreds of times.

Dad met a neuroscience professor from Rutgers University in New Jersey who was able to introduce him to a Chinese neurosurgeon who had worked for years for the Peoples Liberation Army (the PLA) in what was the equivalent of the American VA hospital system.

After Dad showed my scans to surgeons around the world and discussed my case with them, he found another key player in perhaps an unlikely place, Norway. To make a longer story shorter, Dad needed a way to vet the surgical competence of the PLA surgeon he had identified.

As it happened, he learned that a group of Norwegian doctors was visiting the largest PLA medical center in China, in the five-million population city of Kunming, located in the far west corner of China.

The Kunming neurosurgeon Dad had identified with the help of his new friend at Rutgers University was happy enough to allow the obviously experienced chairman of the department of neurosurgery in Oslo, Norway, to observe an actual spinal cord surgery in Kunming.

The upshot of this initiative was that the top Norwegian neurosurgeon was amazed and impressed by what he observed firsthand in Kunming, noting that the Chinese neurosurgeon needed less than half the time that would have been required in Oslo to do the same thing and with the same high standard outcome.

Why was this?

The answer was pretty simple. The more often a surgeon does the same procedure, the faster he or she typically gets and with fewer mistakes. This Chinese neuro-surgeon had opened spinal cords literally hundreds of times, and his only special requirement was to prevent any involvement by any orthopedic surgeon. Indeed, he had taught himself orthopedic surgery to minimize the surgical risk of nicking even the tiniest blood vessels feeding cells inside the spinal cord.

Now we needed to move from Miami to Kunming,

and quickly rather than wait for me to lose even more pulmonary function, as 80 percent of my body was already paralyzed. Indeed, by now I could barely breathe and was frequently on oxygen. It was truly a monumental effort to move halfway around the world with a quadriplegic. I'll spare you the preparation we went through to get there, but it took my entire family to make it happen.

I had very little lead time before departing. I started practicing my medical Chinese right away, knowing that there would not be many folks who spoke English. I hired a Chinese tutor, studied ferociously to memorize at least twenty new characters a day with a specific focus on caregiving and neurosurgery. I rolled around the house talking to myself. I created dozens of pages of words and sentence structures on how to teach people to change my catheter or to understand different technical terms about the spinal cord.

We later learned I likely had about three months to live before my respiratory system would have failed. And, just like that, another chapter of my life was ending and a new one began.

In full disclosure, even though the triple laminectomy operation was successful, I'm not sure I would have gone to China if I had been given a preview of the next six months of my life after surgery. Of course, I did not know what I did not know, and at thirty years old, I had become pretty adept at starting and closing chapters. I figured I was ready to adapt to the next unknown—medical personnel from the People's Liberation Army and the Kunming Walking Program at the Tongren Hospital.

CHAPTER 16

China or Bust

My ELDEST BROTHER, WHO was strong enough to pick me up, and my mother accompanied me to China, as my father had gone on ahead to Kunming via Hong Kong.

We flew 15 hours from Atlanta, Georgia, to Seoul, Korea, and then another five hours over to Kunming, China. It was the second time I had flown since my accident. My brother had to carry me onto the plane. I could not fit in one of those little aisle chairs due to my weight gain. I was so terrified about having a bowel accident on the plane that I decided not to eat the day before. When we were in the airport in South Korea, I literally passed out in the middle of customs.

By the time my brother, Mom, and I arrived in Kunming, my sister, who had gone there ahead of us, had set up a beautiful ground floor apartment with the help of a local construction team. It was an all-hands-on-deck kind of situation. I needed oxygen immediately because I couldn't breathe. I was provided with a giant blue pillow (seriously, I have a photo) inflated with oxygen. It had a nozzle to allow me to breathe the oxygen.

It took us a few weeks to find the right set of caregivers, who turned out to be two lovely sisters-in-law who would become part of our family over the next several years. I will never forget trying to teach changing my catheter in Chinese when they had never even seen a catheter before. It was comical, terrifying, and you know what, we did it. We had much higher hurdles ahead of us.

My other brother very thoughtfully imported an accessible London taxi for us because there were no accessible vans to take us around the city.

I was within rolling distance of the hospital, so every morning I would go over to the hospital with my two caregivers, and people would stare at me. I was used to being stared at as a blonde foreigner in China, but this time I was a blonde foreigner in a power wheelchair. No one had ever seen a power wheelchair before. Every morning random Chinese folks would come up to me in the street and poke me, rub my head, compliment me on how fat I was, and be generally curious about every function on the power wheelchair. They weren't trying to be rude. They were just curious. Different cultural philosophies were in play on what was socially acceptable.

My dad meanwhile was working day and night with me and translators to find out exactly what the surgery would entail, how they would perform it, and every detail you can imagine. It was quite nerve-racking to translate to my father how the surgeon was going to cut into my spinal cord. I had a detailed preview for what they were going to do to me and exactly how they were going to do it in the operating room.

Proposed Surgical Plan

THE PROPOSED SURGERY THROUGH the Kunming Walking Program and the People's Liberation Army surgeons would address the spinal cyst and my neuropathic pain if all went according to plan. I was given the impression and pretty much certain guarantees from my surgeons that they could alleviate much of my neuropathic pain with a two-part surgery.

A Professor of Neurological Surgery at Indiana University, who was originally from China, expressed the strategic surgical concept this way: "The key goal here is restoration of spinal morphology."

Put another way, the goal was to restore my spinal cord as close as possible to its original design and orientation within the spinal canal. That means my spinal cord would no longer be compressed by the large cyst nor would it be tethered by strands of scar tissue left behind from my original spinal fusion surgery. Instead, my spinal cord would be floating free again with full cerebrospinal fluid (CSF) circulation—free once again, as Dr. Zhu Hui in Kunming expressed more poetically, to "dance with the rhythms of my heartbeat and breathing."

Both restoration of free CSF circulation (no scar tissue tethering) and decompression by draining the cyst were believed to be critical to achieve the optimal results for me and for the Kunming Walking rehab program to follow. Frankly, I would have been happy for cessation of the persistent, severe neuropathic pain that made it pretty much impossible for me to focus on anything else.

There was talk of two or perhaps three days in

intensive care to be followed by two weeks of bed rest. After about 15 days, I would be expected to join the Kunming Walking Program.

This surgery was complex, involving a major incision the length of the back of my neck to remove no less than three vertebrae. A wrong move and I would be toast.

The thing was, as a patient, I was going into this terrifying surgery knowing every single detail of what they would be doing as they poked around in my spine. Another life experience not for the faint of heart!

CHAPTER 17

Surgery

DAD AND I KNEW time was running out. By now I was gasping for air and could barely breathe. Soon I was going to lose function and then just drop dead.

We had arrived in Kunming in mid-March 2013. The surgery was scheduled on May 14, my sister's birthday. My sister still snarks that it was the worst birthday present she's ever received. I argue it was the best birthday present because she continues to have a living sister two miles down the road in Raleigh, North Carolina. We agree to disagree on that one in our verbal bantering, but I do think she agrees with me!

My mom, my dad, and one of my brothers were present in China during the surgery. Mom and Dad by now lived in China with me. My eldest brother came at least once a year and my sister more frequently during this period of my life.

The day before entering the hospital, I spent some time on my computer dictating goodbye notes to each of my family members. I knew what the spinal surgery would entail, somewhat unfortunately in great detail.

I was told it would normally take a surgeon in the United States about twelve hours to perform my proposed surgery, but my team in China was expecting to get it done in about four hours due to their experience and proficiency in the procedure. Dad, meanwhile, had independently hired the just-retired chairman of anesthesiology of the University of Kunming to join the surgical team.

The younger of my two brothers, who was now in Kunming, has always had a twisted sense of humor and asked Dr. Liu if he could please save a small piece of my vertebrae as a keepsake. Weird request, huh? Yes, that is how much I love my brother. How many sisters would offer a piece of their spinal vertebrae as a gift?

I checked in at the hospital the night before the surgery. The charming little nurses proceeded to shave the lower half of my head. I know that does not seem like a big deal with all that was facing me, but I cried. I looked ridiculous.

The surgeons offered to photograph and film my spinal surgery. I agreed. I admit at first I was hesitant to look at those photos or watch the videos after the surgery, because I thought they might make me a little queasy. However, I found the videos very informative, and, later, I even wound up sharing them with my regular readers on my China Quad Diaries blog. I mean how often do you get to see the inside of a spinal cord, right?

www.chinaquaddiaries.org

Post-Operative Spinal Surgery Nightmare

I THINK IT IS important to set the stage for what follows

by discussing the "culture of pain" in terms of East versus West thinking and norms. In developed Western countries, complaining about pain is encouraged. When people are in acute pain, as in post-surgery, there are many pharmaceutical options to alleviate the pain, at least short term, and it is pretty standard practice to work with a pain specialist before and after surgery to create a post-surgery pain plan.

In contrast with this perspective, the situation in China is quite different. In China, especially for the generation who lived through the Cultural Revolution forty years ago, acknowledging pain is considered a sign of weakness, and pain is generally not discussed with medical staff.

I have spoken directly with many Chinese about the concept of pain, and the younger generation definitely vocalizes pain issues more freely. On the other hand, the older generation, including my neurosurgeons, grew up in the era of keeping pain to yourself, and their answers to my questions reflect this stoic mindset.

I am sure there have been many thousands of Chinese SCI (Spinal Cord Injury) patients before me who underwent spinal cord surgery and experienced intense and acute pain afterward. However, out of respect for their doctors, they did not complain about their pain, and so the doctors seem not to have developed an appreciation of the issue.

In the West, it's pretty standard to question your doctor on his or her methods as well as to independently research your particular ailment. In China, by way of contrast, this is not the norm, and, as a general rule, patients blindly trust their doctors and especially their surgeons.

Our (Flawed) Pre-Surgery Due Diligence

IN ADVANCE OF MY surgery, my brother and my dad questioned my surgical team about post-surgical pain management and were assured that pain meds would be administered.

Thereafter most of the discussion focused on my neurosurgical team's pride in our having recruited the just-retired head of anesthesiology of Kunming Medical School to personally manage my surgical anesthesia. Thankfully, there were no issues with the general anesthesia.

I do take some responsibility for what I'm about to describe because I assumed by post-operative care, they intended to use something like morphine for pain management.

Oh boy, did I ever come to regret not doing a little bit more research on pain management protocols at Tongren Hospital before the surgery and, specifically, for not asking what drugs they planned to use on me post-surgery.

Bound + Gagged

AFTER A SUCCESSFUL SIX-HOUR surgery (yes, captured on video), I was wheeled into the ICU where my family was told that they would not be allowed to visit me for the next twenty-four hours because I needed to rest.

Well . . .

I woke up in the ICU to the feeling that somebody was slicing open my spinal cord as if they had not finished the surgery. It was a scene right out of a horror medical show on TV. No one had told me that when I woke up from surgery, I would still be intubated, meaning the anesthesia breathing tube had been intentionally left inserted down my throat. Needless to say, I was unable to speak, but I moaned and cried from the severity of my pain.

My hands flailed frantically in the air as I tried screaming through the intubation tube, while hitting doctors and nurses left and right to signal to them that I needed to speak. The pain was like nothing I had ever felt before.

I don't know how many minutes or even hours passed of me moaning and hitting people, but finally the staff took some sort of purple string and tied my wrists to the railings of the bed. I remember this vividly.

I was hysterical, but I must have passed out after a while from the sheer shock of the pain. The next thing I remember was the intubation tube being yanked out of my throat and the purple strings being cut as my outraged brother had forced his way into the ICU.

I felt like they were trying to hide evidence of an ICU torture chamber before my brother and mother discovered how they'd restrained me. My brother had a lot of work experience in China, much of it with manufacturing families, so he wasn't shy about being forceful.

I had been making such a scene in the ICU that they did not know what to do with me. They called my brother and my mom to see if they could calm me down. The instant after they took out the intubation tube, I was crying that the pain was mind-numbingly unbearable.

Now, mind you, I'd been living with severe neuro-pathic pain for quite some time and have a pretty high pain threshold. So, for me to complain about pain, it must have been pretty extreme.

The Situation Gets Worse . . .

My FAMILY ASKED WHAT kind of pain medication the hospital was administering to me through the IV. They were astonished to discover that I was only being offered ibuprofen. Crazy I know, after triple laminectomy spinal surgery to be given only ibuprofen!

My family, understandably, was outraged and demanded that they switch immediately to morphine to get the pain under some semblance of control. My brother insisted that I be moved out of the ICU and down to my room on the seventh-floor spinal cord injury unit so that at least one immediate family member could stay with me round-the-clock over the next few days.

I can't remember if it was a day or two or three, but the pain was definitely not abating though supposedly I was being given 8 mg of morphine per hour. To put readers in the picture here, that amount of morphine would have knocked me out or caused me to start hallucinating, so clearly, we were missing something.

It was only after my brother leaned really hard on the staff that we discovered what was going on with my medication. Chinese physicians generally have an aversion to the use of morphine, and sometimes they may also cut costs by diluting drugs. In any event, a junior nurse revealed to me in the middle of the night that, yes, the morphine being administered to me had been diluted.

All hell broke loose again. My brother was so angry he was speechless. He had opted to sleep in my room with me and had suffered a succession of sleepless nights as I moaned and screamed. Perhaps fearing my brother might assault a member of staff (I've never seen him so angry), the medical team changed course and the morphine pump was suddenly filled with the real thing.

Here's the crazy part. The 8 mg per hour pump setting had not been reset. I started hallucinating and seeing spiders crawling down my walls and the walls melting. My blood oxygen saturation collapsed suddenly to 70 percent from a reference normal of 98 percent, leaving me gasping for breath.

I do remember asking my brother to make sure I didn't get eaten by the spiders and asked him politely to stop making the walls melt. I'm fairly confident we can agree this was a morphine overdose!

After a few days of back-and-forth, we finally got the morphine dosing cut very sharply, but we overshot the mark, and then the pain returned with a vengeance.

My dad spoke urgently with a military surgeon in Australia, asking for Iraq battlefield triage advice on how to use what medications we had on hand at the apartment for painkilling purposes. They came up with a "cocktail" comprised of morphine sulfate and diazepam (Valium) that worked wonders and extended the half-life of our very limited remaining supply of morphine brought with us from the Miami pulmonary embolism episode. And that's how Dad also ended up practicing medicine in a Chinese hospital.

After about seven days, I was able to go home and rest for the next few weeks.

Truth be told, I remember the exact hours after the ICU very vividly, but much of the rest of the seven days in the hospital is a blur. I think my brain shut out that experience because the pain levels were just intolerable.

I have to give all the credit to my family, who designed our own, successful pain management cocktail and then stayed up with me day and night, making sure that I survived this ordeal.

Obviously, I already had been through several nightmare ICU experiences before this one, and I have a hunch that many SCI patients may have equally terrifying stories. We thought we were prepared for almost every scenario except, as it turned out, the one we encountered after my otherwise successful Kunming surgery.

CHAPTER 18

The Kunming Walking Program

AFTER SEVERAL WEEKS OF recovering at home, my medical team was determined that I get up and get moving. Indeed, they had even built a new rehab gym for me to accomplish this. I was evidently slated to be their international poster girl for the program.

Of course, our main reason for going to Kunming was to deal with the spinal cyst that was shutting down my breathing and about to kill me. The Kunming rehab program was envisaged by us as sort of a bonus.

When I look back at this time in my life, I remember I had developed hope again. Hope has the potential to be powerful while simultaneously being extremely destructive. I had become accustomed to grounding my life in reality and making the best of my life with the functionality I had left. My surgeons had given me hope that their surgery would reduce my chronic pain and that I might start gaining functional mobility.

In any event, I could not have anticipated what came next nor would I have wanted to know. Despite still having stitches in my neck and having to wear a neck brace for months to come, the second phase of my medical treatment plan commenced as my medical team arranged to get me vertical and moving.

The Kunming Walking Program Background

THE KUNMING WALKING PROGRAM[v] was developed over the past 30 years by Dr. Zhu Hui, who for many years headed up spinal cord injury treatment at the PLA's medical campus in Kunming, Yunnan Province. Since 1989, Dr. Zhu has treated and rehabilitated more than four thousand SCI patients. So far as we know, she has an unchallenged world record.

The Kunming Walking Program is based on what might be called a holistic philosophy of physiotherapy. The process begins with three to five staff members helping the SCI patient to his or her feet by lifting from behind into a standing position at a vertical walker device and hand-locking the knees from the front. Two members of the team are positioned alongside the patient to square the shoulders. These maneuvers ensure that full body weight is centered naturally over the feet.

This initial program step is aimed at promoting Standing Balance and can last for many days or even sometimes for weeks before any attempt is made to move forward with other program activities.

Dr. Zhu explained that compelling the body to support itself vertically, bearing 100 percent of the body weight, induces the brain to force new neural connections or wake up dormant ones to "speak" to the body's core and, eventually, also to the limbs. Even standing with my former Permobil C500 Stander wheelchair was not equivalent, because mechanical stander devices hold the patient at a slight angle, therefore effectively preventing 360 degree Standing Balance training.

Just by focusing initially on the core, program head Dr. Zhu proposed that an SCI patient's brain would actively try to awaken connections and recruit related muscles. She felt the patient would begin to re-generate function at a cellular level. In contemporary science terms, we're talking about neuroplasticity.

Think about how an 8-month-old child learns to walk. Initially, the child is very wobbly and clings to a window sill or table edge until the brain learns by repetition to recruit hundreds of small core and neck muscles that ultimately enable Standing Balance. No human has ever walked without first mastering Standing Balance.

At first, progress is almost imperceptible to SCI patients, which can be very frustrating. The therapy can be reasonably described as a tough military boot camp regimen. Hard work for six hours per day (divided into two sessions) for six days a week for at least six months. New patients can expect to feel tired, discouraged, angry, and defeated—that is, until they see some results. Once the first voluntary action, Standing Balance, or a leg swing takes place, a whole new spirit takes hold. An enormous part of the challenge turns out to be having the mental stamina to stay the course.

The results of the Kunming Walking Program naturally differ from patient to patient, but virtually all who put in the work seem to gain something quite remarkable, and even chronic quadriplegics regaining bladder and bowel function is not as rare as you might imagine.

The significance of Dr. Zhu's retirement from the PLA in 2012 was that China's private Tongren Hospital Group moved in quickly to recruit her to head up their new neuro-surgery and spinal cord rehabilitation department. Thus, the renowned and successful Chinese military program for treating SCI came to be available to international patients in mid-2012.

Up Next—Walking

THE NAME KUNMING WALKING Program is slightly misleading. I did not, in fact, walk six hours a day six days a week. There simply were not enough trained physical therapists at the gym at the time with respect to the patient-therapist ratio. I would spend most of my time engaging in activities like cardiovascular exercise, stretching, weight-bearing, and being picked up to stand in a frame. Then once a day for thirty minutes, give or take, I would be picked up and placed into this rolling standing frame where four or five physical therapists would push my legs to "walk me," trying to promote neuroplasticity.

I believe in neuroplasticity. It's this concept I've spoken of already in which "neurons that wire together, fire together." We absolutely do have the power to re-wire our brains. I have read about it. I have seen it, and I have practiced it. I put it into action in my own life with respect to the way I think.

However, spinal cord injury is a bit different in that there is a physical bruise that prevents signals from passing through that part of the spinal canal. In my case, the bruise was pretty solid 360 degrees, so the likelihood of functional recovery for me was already hard to determine. I'm what's known as an "ASIA A Complete" quadriplegic, referring to American Spinal Cord Injury (ASIA) Impairment Scale.

I played along though. After a week of making my way every day to the rehab gym with my two lovely caregivers, the day had arrived where the therapists wanted to push me in this rolling walking frame to see how far my endurance would take me.

As four small male therapists physically picked me up to stand vertical in the frame and hold my upper body, two therapists held my legs. It was almost like a game of seesaw. One therapist would push one leg forward while a second therapist would push the other leg. Several therapists held up my upper body so that I would not topple over.

This continued for about five minutes, when all of a sudden I felt a rush of blood in my head. Worse, my blood pressure started to shoot through the roof, I started sweating, my face turned bright red, and I begged them to put me down immediately.

"Stop. Stop. Put me down. Now. Please," I forcefully yelled in Chinese. I didn't know what had happened, but I knew something was terribly wrong. I was extremely dysreflexic and knew I had to return home immediately.

My caregivers rushed me home and laid me flat on my bed. I was only about two weeks out of spinal surgery and should have been lying quietly at home recovering. After lying flat throughout the night, I felt better by the next morning. I was encouraged to come back to the gym with the assurance that it was just my body acclimating to trying to walk again.

I think I was naïve and still holding on to a false hope, because I acquiesced to the request and returned to the gym. The therapists wanted to try the walking frame again. I didn't want to, but I did. The medical professionals certainly had to know best, right?

Within ten seconds of being vertical again, I was in extreme dysreflexic shock, just like the day before. I don't know if they thought I was just being overly emotional or a "wussy" foreigner, but they didn't really believe me. I insisted I wanted to go home because the pain of shooting pins and needles throughout my entire body was electrifying. I couldn't think. Tears were streaming down my face.

The next morning, I woke with the pain screaming at me. My caregiver shouted that there was something wrong with my leg. I raised the head of my bed so I could see my legs. My left leg was completely swollen and red. Once again, I was rushed to the hospital. They performed an MRI, CT scan, and x-ray. There it was. I could see it in the x-ray. The femur was broken. There were other smaller bones that were out of alignment as well.

My entire medical team tried to tell me that this was a past injury that did not heal right. I had a little swelling, but I should be fine in a week or two. They sent me home and told me to recover for a few weeks, but recovery did not come as expected. Instead, my pain situation deteriorated.

CHAPTER 19

Practically Suicidal

THINGS MOVED FROM BAD to worse to catastrophic. A few weeks for anticipated healing turned into many months. I was in a constant state of dysreflexia. My blood pressure was consistently high. I was sweating profusely as a result of high blood pressure. The chronic pain was so intense throughout every inch of my body that it felt like I was literally being burned alive. I slept maybe two hours a night. I developed Stage II pressure sores from being in bed and not turning enough, and I was trapped in a room so tiny I could not even turn my wheelchair in it. To top it off, there was no air conditioning during the summertime.

Everyone thought I sprained my knee or pulled a ligament. I didn't know what was going on. I couldn't engage in any intellectual activities such as trading or even reading a book. I couldn't concentrate. Every time I would wipe the sweat off my face and neck, new sweat would form, shivers would take over my entire body, and tears would stream down my face.

This did not happen for a week or two, but for many

months. I know this is quite a statement, but if I would've had functional hands, I would've killed myself to stop that misery. I didn't want to live that way anymore. I was a shell of myself. It felt like the ghost of Ali had taken over. My mother would comfort me the best she could as I cried. I begged her to please help me take my life. I can't imagine what this did to her. We don't actually talk about it much to this day. I think it was probably more traumatic for her than it was for me.

As it happened, my mom came into my office in Raleigh as I was writing this chapter. I told her how interesting and difficult it was for me to relive those feelings all these years later. She told me, and I never knew this before, that she had slept outside my room on the cold stone floor with a blanket because she feared for my life for nights on end when I was crying night after night.

If that's not the dedication of true love and empathy, I have no idea what is! I call her the Super Spinal Injury Mom. She is an endangered species. I can authentically say she has dedicated herself to me since my accident. I don't know how I will ever be able to repay her kindness other than by showing her my love and telling her I love her each and every day. I would say my dad did not handle mental trauma much better. His coping mechanism was to get my mind engaged. When I would tell him I wanted to kill myself, he would talk to me about the news, perhaps to try to distract me. I love him for this, but it's not what I needed at that time. I'm still incredibly grateful he tried to help me.

Then late one night I decided I wanted to tell my entire family my plan to end my life. I called each one of them and my best friend. I said I would live for one year, but if nothing improved during that time, the family needed to respect my wish to die. When people express suicidal thoughts in circumstances like this, it's natural for family members not to want to let them go. I think this is a bit selfish. I was suffering. I was miserable. I was no longer proposing to kill myself immediately, but I certainly was not going to live my life this way long term.

Some of my family members were on board, albeit sad, but others refused to accept the idea of what I wanted to do. I started to devise an action plan by reading a few books on how to take your life safely and without pain. I can't find those books anymore. Back in the day, there were only two on Amazon.

I learned that if I collected enough amitriptyline (antidepressant medication) coupled with a particular type of painkiller, I would be able to safely take a large dose of this medication, fall asleep, and die peacefully in my sleep. Through my reading, I learned that most folks who take drugs to commit suicide end up choking, vomiting, and suffering in their attempt to take their own life. I didn't want this to happen to me. I was suffering enough. I simply wanted to go to sleep and not wake up.

I appreciate it's challenging to really understand the situation I was in if you've not been in it yourself, and I hope you never are. But I will try to explain because I know there are many who do not believe in suicide or physician-assisted suicide. Personally, I believe we have a right to make decisions on how we live and how we die.

I was in constant severe pain and physically trapped in my own body. I couldn't move or get out of bed without assistance. The pain was screaming at me. I couldn't put a thought together because I was simply trying to breathe to get from moment to moment without my head feeling like it was exploding.

Imagine you hear a fire alarm going off, and it will not stop. Can you think when experiencing that penetrating sound? Then, I want you to imagine that feeling when your arm falls asleep and it starts to wake up with those pins and needles feelings and you have to shake your arm because it's terribly uncomfortable. My chronic pain is similar to that, but just add burning fire, and raise it to the power of ten.

Oh, we're not done yet. Now imagine you are in a hot sauna simultaneously, and you cannot get the sweating to stop while the fire alarm is going off and all of your limbs are being plagued by the burning pins and needles sensation, but you can't move. Nope, we're still not done yet.

We are going to add a robust dose of sleep deprivation. This is one of the premier forms of torture. I want you to imagine everything above and then think about falling asleep because you are so exhausted and need rest. Then, someone starts blaring heavy metal music every twenty minutes. After days of this, you start hallucinating and perhaps even start to teeter on the edge of a full psychotic break.

That was me. I slept an average of two hours a night because of the pain, the constant chronic sweating, the broken leg that I still didn't know about, my fused together vertebrae from my recent spinal surgery, and rolling left and right throughout the day and night because of my pressure sores. All this culminated in the desire to end it all. I think what tipped it over the edge was the prolonged sleep deprivation. I was literally hallucinating.

Fast forward a few months of living in hell and my last-ditch effort to keep going after I had promised my family I would wait one year before I chose whether to take my own life. A weird peace had come over me.

I started looking forward to death in the most beautiful of ways. I was not intentionally trying to get out of living, but death represented to me then, and still represents to me now, perfect stillness. The only reason I would wake up in the morning and attempt to live through the day is because I knew if life didn't take a turn for the better, it was in my control to die how I had planned. I held on to this feeling, because, when I would think about it and dream about it, I envisioned my old self in a bikini on Cat Island with my toes in the sand, looking out on the crystal-clear blue water with a piña colada in my hand.

Whatever your thoughts are about this, I assure you it was a beautiful feeling to me. The idea of death is what kept me going. If I'm being true to myself and to you, the reader, the idea of death still keeps me going. Even today in my current reality, there are so many struggles I endure. The worst offender is actually not paralysis, but the constant chronic pain. It has not let up. On the contrary, my pain increases just a little bit more every year.

I still get comfort knowing that if things go really sideways in my life again, it is my choice to live or not. This is precisely why I choose to live every day to its fullest, or at least the very best I can in that moment, because tomorrow is not guaranteed in so many ways.

I've had this discussion many times with folks in the

disability community and in the able-bodied community, with politicians, and others. There are many schools of thought. I'm not advocating for suicide for anyone if there is a better way forward, but I can only share my authentic experiences of what I have been through. I've talked to many who have been suicidal before, and they found a similar feeling with respect to this idea of peace behind suicide.

If you have never suffered day in and day out for months on end, hallucinating due to lack of sleep, it's hard to empathize or see a different perspective on the matter. I'm leaving religion entirely out of this for the moment because, well, I am not touching that one. I respect everyone's belief system, but I also ask for mine to be respected in return.

Lithium

SINCE FATE SEEMED TO be on a trajectory of figuring out how to torture me on the daily, why not throw in some prescribed lithium? The idea behind a lithium protocol to reduce chronic pain is complex and scientific in nature. There have been many papers written on the subject. This was the final attempt in Kunming to help me.

We spent several weeks adjusting doses of lithium with the hope that it would reduce my chronic pain. Lithium can be poisonous, especially at the doses I was prescribed each day. It created nausea, vomiting, another near-death experience, and consistent chronic infections.

It finally got to a point where I could not breathe without vomiting. I was being poisoned and didn't know it. The levels of lithium in my blood became so toxic, we had to abort "mission lithium."

This was a turning point for me. I said to everyone around me, "That's enough. No more. We are stopping everything." And, just like that, I was pretty much left alone. I needed to find a new normal in my life since I didn't even know what that looked like anymore.

Light at the End of the Tunnel

AFTER ABOUT SIX MONTHS of living in my psychological prison cell, I started to notice a very small shift in pain. It abated ever so slightly. A flicker of hope.

We had my scanned images sent to the United States to a renowned sports orthopedic surgeon in Ft. Lauderdale. He assessed that my left leg had been broken in eight different places with the two worst offenders being a cracked left femur and a tibial shaft fracture (shinbone). My leg had not been placed in a proper cast to protect the broken bones and to reduce the pain through the healing process.

This resulted in my left leg permanently hyperextending backward because none of the ligaments healed properly. In my household, we call this leg "Gumby," from the cartoon in the 1980s. She is now part of the family. We love her, and we just work around her.

The reasoning behind the Kunming medical personnel denying breaking my leg, claiming it was a result of a former injury, most likely can be attributed to a concept in the Asian culture usually called "saving face." Essentially, it is a sociological construct in East Asian cultures that involves avoiding embarrassment and maintaining one's dignity and reputation.

My Kunming surgeons were some of the most highly regarded medical professionals in the country. God forbid they should have taken responsibility for breaking their prize foreign patient's leg in time to actually do something about it during the healing process. It was the PTs who broke my leg during my so-called walking therapy, but then the surgeons were responsible for diagnosing what was wrong in my body, as the x-ray clearly showed.

I really don't blame them. I don't blame anyone for anything. That would hold a lot of anger, hurt, and resentment toward so many medical professionals throughout my life with paralysis. I want to keep moving forward, not backward. I accept that their misguided efforts were not intentional.

Having experienced so much as a result of this unintentional harm, I now teach others how to redefine the concept of happiness, re-examine the idea of success, take responsibility for their own lives and what they can control through their thoughts, actions, and emotions. Part of this teaching is to determine what to let go of. I strongly believe authenticity is a key ingredient for the success of the message deliverer. Where we came from, what we have experienced, and what we have overcome is important.

The story really does matter. I have shared mine throughout this book because why would someone choose to believe me or perhaps utilize some of the applied neuroscience techniques I teach if I have not walked the walk myself?

During the first year after moving to Kunming, it

took every ounce of willpower I had to open my eyes each morning. But I did it. I didn't do it alone. I would not be here today without the unwavering support and love bestowed on me by my mom, my dad, my brothers and sister as well as family friends during that time. I am so grateful and fortunate for the support I received and continue to receive in my journey. I try every day to pay it forward to others who do not have this critically important support to the degree I do.

Sadly, the chronic pain never abated, nor am I currently walking. I do believe my Chinese medical team was desperate to help in some way, even with their one last suggestion to use lithium to help abate the pain. Little did I know at the time how poisonous lithium can be. It almost killed me.

On the other hand, the spinal cord cyst choking the life out of me was successfully removed, and that was our initial and primary reason for going to China.

So what else can I say in summary about 2013 and 2014? Well, I can say I survived with minimal PTSD and gained a different perspective on my life. I went from arriving in China with hope I might walk again and that neuropathic pain would be attenuated. Neither happened. This is not said to deter SCI people or have them lose hope, because no two spinal cord injuries are alike. Their experience might be entirely different than mine. With my new perspective, I decided that if I was going to spend the next several years in China, I needed to occupy my time productively.

CHAPTER 20

Acclimating to Chinese Life

At some point, life in Kunming became pretty easy-going. My general day would involve waking up, going to the gym to work out, coming home, reading, studying, and day trading. It was a looks-like-Groundhog-Day all over again period, very monotonous. Nothing great happened nor did anything terribly drastic occur either. I was quite content with the newfound stability. I chose to use my time to feed my ever-present intellectual curiosities.

In 2014, I read 170 books on subjects like neuroscience, particle physics, quantum mechanics, nutrition, and trading psychology. My trading was going well. I didn't love life, but I didn't hate it either. I didn't think about the future or what was going to happen to me. I lived in the moment. I didn't have any immediate plans to leave China. I was just going through the motions of life and that seemed okay. I didn't have hopes for ever finding a meaningful relationship with a partner, but I also didn't want to kill myself anymore. I think that was progress.

My best friend, my brothers, and my sister would come visit me over the course of the next few years. We took our London taxi on semi-accessible adventures all around sprawling Kunming and in the mountains, and we made the best life we could in the moment.

Little People Kingdom

ONE OF THE MOST bizarre adventures I went on was to visit the Little People Kingdom with my brother and a Kunming native who is today one of my closest friends.

The Kingdom of Little People is a theme park that features theatrical performances by people with disabilities identifying with "dwarfism," but the more socially and politically accepted term in the United States is "little people."

Look it up online if you're interested, as there are numerous media stories on the enterprise.

This theme park offers employment to a group of underserved and marginalized individuals who would otherwise be unable to find work. It is also their home. The park is criticized by some Western media for treating dwarfism as a humorous condition. I understand that Western perspective, but I received a much different reaction from the folks living in the theme park. They adored living and working there.

Their reasoning was quite interesting. They said that they faced discrimination everywhere in the country, but in this park they were together. They earned income so they could support their families. They didn't seem to care if people were coming to see them for amusement. They simply wanted to provide for their families in a meaningful way. Don't misunderstand me, the park is bizarre. Words do not do it justice. Their homes are mushroom-shaped houses that looked like they had been transported right out of the Smurf world. I rolled into one of these little Smurf houses. It had a TV, bed, kitchen, and cozy little den. There are stages around the property where the residents sing and dance for the tourists.

I really ruffled their feathers because when I rolled up as a blonde foreigner in a wheelchair, everyone kept staring at me. Then one woman whispered in my ear that she thought she would get more money from Chinese tourists if she could sit on my lap, so I rolled her around on my lap. What was I going to do? Say no? Of course not. I accepted her request. She made three times the amount of money she ordinarily earned. I was happy to participate and gave her some myself. Cultural perspectives aside, I just listened to the Little People. They were happy being together and supporting their families. I helped them for a moment, and we had a ton of laughs along the way, including capturing some seriously funny photos.

Hypnosis

I STARTED TO EXPLORE the world of meditation and hypnotherapy as part of my efforts to make my life better. Through a family friend, I met a hypnotherapist I talked with on the phone several times a week. I used to think hypnosis was ridiculous, but I learned hypnosis is complicated. I didn't get into any kind of hypnotic trance where I drank anyone's Kool-Aid, but I learned a very important skill to help reduce my pain in moments that were overwhelming.

This Chicago hypnotherapist traveled to Kunming, and we spent several weeks together working on techniques. He created these guided visualizations for me where he would play beautiful, quiet, oceanic music and walk me through a very specific image. I created a mental representation of a red door into this beautiful world with lakes, waterfalls, and oceans. He would talk me through breathing techniques as I entered my little world. I still have those recordings. I use them when I meditate today. It's personalized for me. When my pain starts jumping over a nine out of ten, I go out into the sunshine or into my closet with heating pads in the winter to step into this world to lower the pain. It really works for me.

A Lasting Present

I'VE MENTIONED SEVERAL TIMES now the chronic pain I live with, but it is more complicated than one kind of pain. After my "delightful" medical procedures over the years, I have been permanently saddled with four distinct types of chronic pain to deal with every day. I share this experience with you because it is part of my authentic lived experience and far outweighs the challenges of living in a wheelchair. I engage in a strategy of distraction, meditation, and many positive psychological mental exercises like hypnosis each day to manage my pain and keep me moving forward.

Neuropathic pain is where the 80 percent of my body that is paralyzed feels the burning pins and needles sensation all the time. This pain stems from damage to my central nervous system.

Allodynia is a type of peripheral nerve damage pain. It exhibits its symptoms through extreme hypersensitivity where I have partial sensation in my hands and forearms. Allodynia basically feels like little glass shards are cutting me all the time. The slightest feeling of wind on my hands or forearms causes extreme discomfort. I combat this by wearing little gloves and basketball sleeves unless it is warm and sunny outside. The warmth and the sun really help reduce this pain.

My musculoskeletal pain comes from my being slightly more paralyzed on the left side of my body compared to my right side. As a result, I overcompensate by using the functional muscles on the right side more than I should. This creates a feeling in my right shoulder blade of consistently being stabbed by a sharp knife.

And then there is the persistent chronic pain at the incision site on the back of my neck. When I sit vertically in my chair for too many hours, it feels as though I can't hold my head up.

How do I deal with all this? I don't have a terrific answer to that. I work to retrain my brain through meditation, mental exercise techniques, consistent self-talk, and different holistic practices among other things on a daily basis to keep my sanity. It's hard work, and I certainly won't sugarcoat that for anyone.

Having said that, most of my decisions in life these days center around what will keep my chronic pain down. When I am anxious or depressed or get frustrated, the pain goes up. So, I do everything in my power to remain calm, rational, and be very selective on what I choose to let bother me. There's no magic pill for this, but motivation, hard work, and the conscious decision to live my life this way work for me. It started with small wins that added up over time to living a big life.

For example, I used to laugh at the absurdity of trying to navigate my wheelchair through a doorway that appeared to be designed for ninja squirrels. Dark humor for the win again. I did learn to drive my wheelchair eventually, and, with that success, I focused on that as a win.

If I falter for a moment, then I'm done for. As long as two of my pains are slightly in the background with respect to the noise level, I'm able to function. If all four pains are screaming at me at the same time, then I have to get to my bed, close the curtains, and reduce all light and noise to rebalance my nervous system. I suppose it's akin to working through a migraine. I don't sleep very well, but when I get a rare great night's sleep, my body kind of resets my pain batteries, if that makes sense.

As I read this chapter about my pain types out loud, my pain levels increased about 20 percent just thinking about them. Through the use of my self-hypnosis guided meditations, I've learned to detach my body from my pain. It almost feels like there are two of me—my pain me and the rest of me. I haven't named my pain per se, but she (yes, she's a female) normally gives me about 80 to 85 percent of what I need in a day, but when she starts screaming like a colicky infant, I stop everything to give her the day. It's a fair compromise, and one I humbly accept.

CHAPTER 21

All Things Must Come to an End

As we approached nearly three years of living in Kunming, I had a decision to make. My parents were now nearing their seventies. I had somehow thought we were going to live here for the rest of our lives. I hoped anyway, because life was pretty simple, and that's what I wanted. I had dozens of conversations with my sister and brothers to figure out the next steps in life as my parents were aging. If something went wrong, my siblings could not immediately come help. They were on the other side of the world.

I had no idea what the next chapter of my life would entail or what it would look like. My sister and I decided that I would move to Raleigh, North Carolina, to live near her, so we could be each other's support system.

My sister was also about to get married. I have always been the planner of the two of us. I agreed to plan her entire wedding, another reason to move back to Raleigh. This needed to happen in a hurry, because I had exactly three months to plan her wedding. It was a huge effort to once again pack up an entire life and move across the ocean.

I wasn't scared or stressed out. I was focused. I had endured so much. How much worse could it get? That's really a terrible question to put out in the universe. I could not have predicted the road ahead of me over the next year.

And, just like that, I was on the move once again.

CHAPTER 22

Prepared for a Life of Normalcy

I WAS EXCITED FOR the possibility of a new life. I had spent the past five and a half years going through hell. I was filled with the exciting prospects of building a new life, planning my sister's wedding, and finally getting "out there" for dating since my body shed the weight I had gained. I thought I looked pretty good all things considered with a quad body. I was definitely in good spirits.

When I arrived in Raleigh, my sister had hired several new caregivers for me. They were a disaster. In full disclosure, we had had countless traumatic experiences with caregivers, so I'm pretty sure I was also suffering from delayed PTSD around all this change.

I had become accustomed to my beautiful Chinese caregivers. Now I had to start over again with new caregivers. Many of the caregivers in my life were simply in and out and just collected their paycheck. They didn't seem to give a shit. It took me years to find good caregivers who are also good people. It didn't matter though, I was still in good spirits, bouncy, bubbly, and ready to take on the world.

I planned an epic bash for my sister's wedding with surprises and gummy bear dances where I had the men in my family dress up in these ridiculous costumes to sing and dance. I got brave and created an online dating profile. Just like that, I was ready to pick up where I had left off prior to my accident, psychologically speaking.

I talked to a few gentlemen and met a really nice guy through a mutual friend at a bar one night. I had not taken a sip of alcohol in nearly five years because of all my medical challenges, so I was ready to get tipsy. On one such occasion later, I may or may not have proverbially tipped over the line from tipsy to drunk. I can't really tell you what happened, but I do know I was over my brother-in-law's shoulder while my sister drove my wheelchair upstairs. To this day, my mother still reminds me to drink responsibly. Mom, it was that one time (says every kid)!

I was back, baby! I felt confident, sexy, I was out of adult underwear and went lingerie shopping with my mother, and most of all, I was thinking about plans for the future.

Losing My SCI Virginity

THE FIRST GUY I dated, let's call him Dave, was kind, loved to go out, fell in love with me in two weeks (that should have been a sign to run the other way my therapist now tells me), and we were so into each other. Looking back now, I think I just felt grateful that any man would find my quad body sexy. It took me a few years of therapy and a failed marriage to learn how to be truly confident in my own skin.

After Dave and I had been dating about two weeks,

I told him I had not had sex in five years, and I wanted to lose my paralysis virginity with him. You know that expression "curiosity killed the cat?" The same concept applies here: curiosity killed my virginity. This was true when I was a teen, and it was true when I was thirty-three. I admit that I'm devious and that I love to have casual sex. It was even more exciting because I had no idea how my body would react.

I made arrangements for Dave to come see me one afternoon. I had my mother dress me up in sexy lingerie, sprawl my body in a beautiful position on the bed, and I dehydrated myself all day, so I wouldn't have to pee into my catheter bag. I would say this was not a particularly intelligent idea, but I wanted to feel sexy.

And I did! I think I rocked paralyzed sex like 1999. I had my legs in the air, I had him flip me around in the bed, and you get the idea for the rest. *My God*, I thought, *I'm a bendable Gumbyesque goddess.* You can just throw me around and put me in any position you want. I was a paralyzed, bendable sex goddess—so I believed on that day.

How did it feel? Oh, it felt terrible. The moment he put himself inside of me, my blood pressure zoomed up. Dysreflexia again. Dammit. Not during sex, really? Could the universe not cut me a little bit of a break? I started sweating and the nerve pain started increasing. I couldn't feel sex through skin-to-skin contact anymore, but it did create internal sensations. It was horrible. I didn't care. I was having sex. A man desired me. I would just get over the rest. I told him it felt great. He didn't generally seem to care one way or the other.

Afterwards, I got dressed and met him at a bar for

drinks. I held my head a little higher, feeling like I just popped my cherry for the first time. Then I started to get dysreflexic again. I asked him to take me home immediately. I started to panic. The trauma from my China experience was on my mind. When I was laid down, I instantly felt fine. When I sat up, symptoms would immediately reengage.

As luck would have it, my mother had left for Germany the day after my date, so I called my sister. When pressure was put on my lower right abdomen, the dysreflexia would get significantly worse. We both came to the conclusion my appendix had burst. Please don't play Dr. Google, people! My sister rushed me to the emergency room where they did a battery of tests, told me nothing was wrong, chalked it up to a urinary tract infection, and sent me home.

Emergency rooms are really dangerous for people with paralysis because most of the doctors and nurses have minimal knowledge at best about spinal cord injury or associated secondary complications. Many quadriplegics have permanent indwelling catheters. When you have a permanent catheter inserted in your body, your body believes it's a foreign invader and is constantly trying to push it out, resulting in urine tests coming up positive for urinary tract infections. The long and short of it is that they were lazy, did not know how to deal with me, and sent me home with some antibiotics.

The next day things got even worse. We went back to the ER. Everyone was confused as to why I was returning. After much back and forth, the resident on call asked me if I had done anything different over the last several days. I don't know why I didn't think to mention sex right away, but I didn't. I did eventually bring it up. At first, he didn't think sex could cause this kind of reaction when I was sitting vertical in my wheelchair. He asked how I physically had sex. Oh, I was very excited to share this information with anyone who would listen. I explained to him and the nurses that I am flexible and bendable, and I had my leg literally behind my ears sort of like a pretzel. I'm sure I had a proud expression on my face in the telling, but there was a growing look of horror on their faces.

Then one of the nurses started laughing. I laughed with her. The resident? He was clearly not amused by either of us. Multiple trips to the ER could have been avoided had the resident asked the right question and taken the right imaging. If you ask the wrong question, you're not going to get the right answer. My dad taught me this actually. You have to be your own investigative reporter in your life so you can advocate for yourself. If you don't ask the right questions, you're certainly not going to get the right answers. Evidently, I did not ask the right questions.

It turned out I cracked my sacrum (it's the bone right above the tailbone). It was just a hairline fracture. What created the pain was my physical weight on the cracked bone when I would sit in my chair. I asked the resident what we could do about it, and he told me that I would need to be in bed for about eight weeks.

Oh hell no! Seriously? Not again. I managed to break myself through sex because I was eager, impatient, and just wanted to do it. Dammit. I had no one to blame but myself. However, if I was going to break another bone, at least I had a great story behind it this time.

I spent the next eight weeks in bed. My new boyfriend visited me regularly. I could not understand why he wanted to stay with me, but it was sweet. I was proud to finally have an injury from something moderately amusing, to me anyway. I accepted the consequences of my actions. We still found other ways to be naughty if you catch my drift, but I was prepared to do the time for my crime.

Ode to My Ass

PLANNING MY SISTER'S WEDDING, breaking my body from sex, going through new caregivers at a rate that would make your head spin, and building up a new social life all happened within a few months of moving back to the United States. I was really starting to get a handle on this new life, until . . .

I woke up one morning with my caregiver asking me "what is that on your butt?" My heart sank. Oh my God. I didn't even have to look. She took a photo. Stage I pressure sore. Giant red circle about eight inches above the rectum right over the small of my back. I knew what to do though. It was just a red mark, no problem. I was going to spend a few days in bed, put the right cream on it, roll back and forth on my mattress for weight shifting purposes, and be up and resuming normal life activities within a week.

Unfortunately, days turned into weeks and the Stage I pressure sore turned into a Stage II. I saw multiple wound doctors, because I like to have multiple opinions since medical teams have a habit of killing me. Multiple trips to the wound doctors, days in bed, ointments, and cleaning regimens for the sore were to no avail. This went on for a few months. I was taking diligent care of my wound, but I was also interested in living my life, dammit.

I would spend the daytime hours in bed and then I would get up, cover the wound, and go out. I frolicked around town with Dave, meeting so many wonderful characters. I wouldn't say this was a particularly brilliant idea, but I wanted to be able to do it all. Then came the day that one of my wound doctors told me he did not think he was going to be able to heal this wound, and I would likely need surgery. Unfortunately, insurance probably would not approve the surgery unless I tried multiple lesser invasive modalities first. That would take about a year of my time.

Nope. No thank you. Wrong answer. Try again. I fired all my wound doctors on the spot. My wound was getting bigger though I was doing everything I could to prevent that. I read countless clinical journals on the best way to heal different pressure sores, and I tried alternative therapies such as blue laser light therapy, massage, acupuncture, micronutrients, high protein intake, and the list goes on.

I went on a mission to find the best plastic surgeon in the state because what is a pressure sore after all? Yes, it can be an issue with pressure, but it is all about your skin. I rolled into the surgeon's office, flipped on my belly (well, inelegantly transferred onto the table and clumsily rolled onto my belly with my caregiver's help), pulled my pants down, and he pushed on the wound. I felt the pain through increased nerve pain. He immediately exclaimed, "Ah, yes, I see what's going on." I waited with trepid anticipation as he followed up by saying, "You have an extra vertebra in your tailbone."

It's not that uncommon. My mother has the same issue because when she sits for long periods of time, her tailbone hurts. He told me that because I lost muscle mass due to my paralysis, lost a lot of weight, and spent so much time sitting in my chair that this pressure sore was never going to heal on its own. The bone was literally going to make its way through the skin. This was not a diagnosis I wanted, but at least the problem was identified.

I asked him what the next course of action might be. He said he would first perform a very straightforward procedure called a coccygectomy. Basically, he would start with a straight-line incision to get access to my tailbone, saw off the bottom of the tailbone while not affecting the nerve bundles it wrapped around, and stitch me back up. He anticipated I would be back up and running (so to speak) in about six weeks.

Fantastic. Six weeks? Child's play. Let's do it. One challenge I didn't see coming was with my insurance. My surgery was scheduled the day after New Year's Day, and my insurance provider had switched with the new year. This resulted in my first fight with health insurance. I won, but this really started to rev me up on the injustices in our healthcare system related to health equity.

It was now January 2016. My relationship with Dave was hanging on by a thread. I didn't realize he had been diagnosed with bipolar disorder. He was treating himself with alcohol and marijuana. It was not a brilliant combination, and I was, once again, about to fight for my life.

I rolled into surgery with high hopes that it would be a success. Dave stayed with me during this surgery, but it was the beginning of the end of our relationship. I was going to be fully in bed once again.

Upon waking from my dreamless state of anesthesia, high as a kite, and just loving that feeling of not knowing my left from my right, the surgeon walked in. He said the surgery went as well as they expected. He said I should recover after about six weeks in bed on a special pressure relieving mattress and that I should come see him in a few weeks.

I did, in fact, own a special pressure relieving mattress, but not the right kind I later learned. Six weeks came and went quickly. The surgery, ironically, didn't increase my chronic nerve pain, so I was looking forward to getting back into the swing of things.

About three weeks into my recovery, I noticed something really odd as I was taking pictures of the wound each day to track its progress. The stitches were opening up, and it was really gnarly. I knew this was not normal, so I hired an ambulance company to transport me to the surgeon's office since I couldn't physically sit up. And no, insurance wouldn't pay for it—go figure.

At the surgeon's office, I was placed on an examination table. My heart was racing as I didn't know what he was going to do or say. Did I do something wrong? Did he do something wrong? Oh dear God. Dread. That is the only emotion I remember feeling in the moment.

He took a pair of scissors and cut open the stitches. He then proceeded to put his finger inside the incision site and said, "Hmm, yes, I see now." Dammit, what did he see? *Stop being so cryptic,* I thought, *just tell me, is my life over? Am I going to have to live forever in bed?*

He was quite a masterful bullshit artist trying to save his ass with respect to what had gone wrong. It turned out I was on the wrong type of mattress. I needed to turn more. He had not put a drainage tube in during the surgery, so the blood was pooling back into my body, eroding the tissue around it and causing the stitches to open up. The wound was 4 cm deep and down to my tailbone, which was completely exposed in the incision. Holy shit. I had to process this information in microseconds.

I had become pretty adept at analyzing situations very quickly, so I asked him why this happened. His response was quite pitiful. He said that he could have put in a drainage tube, but he didn't see the need at the time. I was essentially bleeding back into my body when I was supposed to be healing. Medical translation: He messed up just as they had done in Miami back in 2012 when I was bleeding back in my body from the cervical cancer. He, of course, did not admit his error.

I don't have time to cast blame. I just want to live my life. I wanted to fix the problem, and I wanted to move on. With my face down in the pillow and tears streaming, I asked him what the next step would be.

Just as the wound surgeons had suggested months earlier, I needed to undergo a procedure called flap surgery. However, insurance would not approve this surgery until I tried something called a wound vacuum[vi] first. In other words, I would have to be hooked up to a wound vacuum for three or four months, following their standard of care, before insurance would consider approving flap surgery. This almost killed me.

Wound Vacuum

I NOW HAD A quarter-sized hole 4 cm deep, down to bone itself, over my tailbone and then the hole sprawled out left and right (called tunneling) about 3 cm in each direction, and insurance was telling me I was required to try healing it with a wound vacuum.

This meant a wound nurse would come to the house and take these giant pieces of foam, cut them in the right shapes, and stuff them inside my wound. It was a good thing I could not feel my butt. I don't think this would feel very pleasant. Then the wound was covered with an airtight seal with a tube that ran to a rectangular battery box. There's science, negative pressure, and blood draining involved with all this that is meant to promote healing. What it meant to me was I basically had a tail. When I sat up in my chair, I would have a tube coming out the backside of my pants leading to the battery box on the back of my wheelchair. It looked freaking ridiculous!

CHAPTER 23

Bedrest Life

DÉJÀ VU ANYONE? BACK in bed again, no future in sight, chained up the machines once more, and not much of a community network established yet in my North Carolina life.

I couldn't believe it. I thought after five years that my life had found some normalcy. Let the medical hunger games begin again. In my spinal cord injury career, because it certainly was a career at this point, I had already suffered pulmonary embolisms, been diagnosed with hypothyroidism, developed cervical cancer, experienced a life-threatening spinal cyst, lived with chronic pain burning me alive daily, and battled multiple pressure sores. Surely this had to be a cruel cosmic joke. If there is a higher being—I'm still on a spiritual journey by the way—this latest occurrence sure was not doing me any favors. Had I pissed off fate in a karmic way? There are days I still debate this.

You may be thinking, here we go again, yet another life-and-death situation. Well, yes and absolutely no.

Something had profoundly shifted in my mental state this time around. I still can't tell you if it was because of my practically suicidal experience in China or everything I had been through, but truly, I was not devastated.

I was prepared to spend the next year of my life in bed, and I was prepared to do it with a different mental outlook. I don't know precisely why, but I didn't suffer from as intense chronic pain with this pressure sore as I did with a broken leg. I'm counting this as a win, and nobody can take that away from me.

So, I commenced using my wound vacuum. I called her my twirling twisted tail. My relationship with new boyfriend Dave went south, and I was sad for, I don't know, maybe a week? I was preparing for another medical battle. I didn't have the emotional ability to consider the feelings of a man who treated his bipolar disorder with drugs and alcohol.

I knew I had to create a strategic plan of action for the next year of my life. I really didn't know if I would survive the surgery, but survival was not my biggest concern. I was more interested in making whatever my time was quality time, living as fully as I could in the moment. I might have to be in bed full time, but I was determined I would make the most of it. How? Well, I didn't see this one coming. I don't see most things coming in my life quite honestly, and that's kind of what I find charming about life in general.

Connection

I HAD BEEN PRETTY lonely for quite some time in Raleigh. I had not fully established a group of local friends yet, and

I was pretty much just tagging along with my sister's yoga friends. They were delightful, but they weren't wacky like me. One night I was lying in bed, checking my Facebook account. I had not really used Facebook much over the past decade, but I decided to join some spinal cord injury and other disability groups. A few hours later I realized I was not alone. Oh my God, others were experiencing the same feelings and medical nightmares that I was. I felt sad for them, of course, but I felt connected to them too. Most of us tend to gravitate to those we feel authentic kinship with. It's kind of a natural attraction. I'm just very cautious not to dive into a "misery loves company" frame of mind.

Over the next few months, I eagerly picked up my phone, excited to hear from other folks who understood what I was going through just as I understood what they were going through. I don't know why I had not already built strong connections with the wheelchair community, but sometimes I've been known to be late to the party.

Structure

To PREVENT MYSELF FROM falling into a depression during this waiting year, I turned once again to productivity. I was going to be the most productive bed-ridden human you ever saw. I woke up each morning, worked with my caregivers, exercised with stretchy bands tied to my hospital bed, read at least fifty pages in something that interested me, day traded, and utilized micronutrients to help me heal faster with the wound vacuum. I also meditated daily. An amazing therapist came to my room to help me prepare for the upcoming flap procedure when the wound vacuum predictably would fail and insurance would approve my surgery. I researched health insurance plans. I researched corporate policy, read peer-reviewed journal articles, and started learning to fight small battles for products or services I was denied.

Okay, the community aspect of my life—check. Intellectual aspect of my life—check.

Bendable Goddess—2.0 Experiment

So, IN THE STATE that I was in, what did I do? I jumped right back into online dating. It was absurd in a way because I would only be able to jailbreak from my bed for a few hours at a time to go on a date. Technically, I was not allowed to move from my bed. I didn't care.

I wrote multiple iterations of different online dating profiles, giving me incredible enjoyment. On each one of these profiles, I put my paralysis and wheelchair life on the table, but I didn't say that presently I had a giant hole in my backside or that I would be off the dating market for quite a while when this mega surgery was approved. I didn't think they needed to know that.

Oh, and did it work. Holy cow. I received more attention than I had bargained for. As I have said several times now, I was certainly not going to let my disability insecurities hold me back. After all, I was not looking for a long-term partner.

I would go out for drinks and dinner with these gentleman callers, but I had rules. I would only go on three dates, and then I would move on to the next. I didn't know how long I had until the surgery was approved, but likely four or five months. I didn't know if I would survive, so I had no time to waste.

The first date would involve drinks to see if there was chemistry. The second date was dinner and a high school make-out session to see if they were a fantastic kisser. I had dozens of those dates. If one of my male suitors was lucky enough to get a third date with me, this is where things would get naughty and saucy. I called these "Underwear Dates." I would tell my date to meet me in my bedroom after work. I had Mom dress me up in sexy red silk lingerie. My caregiver would escort my date into the apartment and direct him to my room. Jaws always dropped. The look on my date's face when he entered my room was gratifying. None of these dates had any idea what was in store. They were probably wondering how they were going to have sex with a person with paralysis if I'm being honest.

Fun, sweaty moments ensued, then they had to leave. I had a strict policy of no more than three hours for an Underwear Date as I had to make quick work of putting my wound vacuum tail back on before going to bed.

My sexcapade experiments launched my blog, the Quirky Quad Diaries. The original tagline started out as a blog on "Sex, Sass, and Spinal Cord Injury Adventures." I designed (and printed) business cards with two ladybugs having sex when I was tipsy and added a whimsical line: Professional Quadriplegic and Dark Humor Enthusiast. Many years later I rebranded the Quirky Quad slightly, but I did keep the last part on my cards. The prompt in rebranding arose after handing my card with two ladybugs having sex to a judge. She laughed, I cried a little inside, and then I reimagined a new direction.

I wrote about my dating experiences without using names on the Quirky Quad by comparing the dates to fine wines and charcuterie platters. I had one guy who was twenty-six I think. He came into my room, engaged in a passionate make out session with me, and then just up and left. Not great for the ego. He called me and asked if he could come back about thirty minutes later. He brought his art supplies. He was an aspiring artist. He drew me with black charcoal. He then left again and ghosted me. I saw him many years later when I had hired a caregiver who was talking about her ex. We ran into him and, well, let's just say the caregiver did not choose to continue to work with me because he wanted to take me out on another date. Yes, it was very awkward.

One fellow did a strip tease for me down to a bright purple speedo. I tried not to laugh when he was on top of me, but I just couldn't help myself.

I then liaised with one gentleman caller who decided to tell me that he was married as we were having some private time in my bedroom. Classy, right? I mean I couldn't make this stuff up if I tried. He was literally and figuratively in and out in nothing flat.

I was back to my naughty Ali self and loving every minute of it. The days and weeks rolled by, and I was hanging out with four men at the same time (not at once!), and cycling them in and out. I became robotic with taking care of my pressure sore, my body, and simultaneously biding my time dating until I was approved for the surgery. I can't say many of my friends or family approved of my actions, but it wasn't their life on the line. It was mine. Truthfully, most of them don't approve that I put most of my life on the internet, but if it helps one person move forward, well, then it's worth all of the intimate details.

I still giggle how I was having the time of my life and was also a prisoner in my bed. The significant thing was that I was not a prisoner in my mind. This was the critical distinction to make in how I survived a year in bed.

Then along came my husband-to-be. I'll call him Derek. He was one of my gentlemen callers, and we didn't even hit it off that well in the beginning. He was really awful with communication. He eventually made the cut and came up for an Underwear Date. He was fantastic in bed. We engaged in scintillating conversations and spiced up our bedroom life in creative ways. I liked him, but I think he may have liked me more in the beginning. I was distracted with everything going on in my life at the time.

In order to engage in these Underwear Dates, my mother came to the rescue again. Before the date, she stuffed my wound with gauze wet with saline and bandaged it tightly. She was a great sport about this. I'm not sure she entirely approved of my lifestyle, but she supported me nonetheless. Some of my caregivers at the time did not approve of my lifestyle. That was their prerogative, but they were not in my life much longer.

After my Underwear Date left, my wound vacuum tail got put back on, and I defaulted back to my alter ego quiet life. That's how I did it. I was living two lives once again. I attribute my psychological survival through this period to my lifestyle choice.

CHAPTER 24

Surgery Is a Go!

THE TIME HAD FINALLY arrived. Just as girls have parties to become women for their Sweet Sixteen, or Quinceañera in the Spanish culture, I knew this was it. I had this gut feeling that this surgery, albeit long, tedious, and not without its challenges, would somehow change my life. Once again, I had hope. I felt like it would be my coming-out party, if I could endure the hardships ahead.

It had already been about eight months since the pressure sore first appeared, and the flap surgery ahead would leave me in bed for another six months. During this time I truly would not be able to get up for even a moment. I would not be allowed to move an inch on the specialized mattress I was going to have to sleep on.

Things were a little bit complicated because the specialized mattress I needed was called a Clinitron Air Fluidized Bed. It creates the same arterial pressure on your skin as the air does. Basically, it feels like you are floating on air. Your body doesn't have any pressure touching anything. It accomplishes this through thousands of small silicone beads and a power source that plugs into a wall outlet to constantly have these beads in motion. It's loud and sounds and feels like the ocean battering a wall in a hurricane, but I found it very comfortable. The challenge with these beds is that they were not approved for in-home use anymore. It's complicated, it's an inequity in the health insurance system, and I'll leave it at that for now.

So, I was going to have to choose a nursing home. Yes, a nursing home to get approval for this bed. I frantically drove around town looking at nursing homes with one smelling like death more than the other one, nurses and their aides not seeming to care, elderly people unattended, people with disabilities ignored, and basically a place where you go to die slowly (at least psychologically). I was terrified, but I had no choice because these mattresses cost around fifty thousand dollars.

In general, a patient is allowed to stay in the hospital for only so long before being sent to one of these homes. We are simply too expensive to care for in the hospital. In a stunning turn of events, my brother found one of these mattresses for a few thousand dollars, and I became the luckiest girl in the world because I was going to be able to recover at home. I couldn't believe it. If you would have met me back then you might have thought I had suffered some kind of psychological break because I was just full of beans, excited to have surgery, and ready to fight once again.

Right, so, what about the men? Well, as I was preparing all my bags for the hospital and planning the next several months of my life, I started systematically breaking up with all of the guys. I didn't make any connections,

I didn't promise anything, and when they asked what I was doing, I simply said I was leaving town. Well, I was, as I was going across town to a hospital for an unspecified period of time.

Not Derek though. He kept pushing me and pushing me. I finally fessed up to the entire story, and he called me back several hours later asking me if I would be his girlfriend. I hung up the phone. It was a reflex reaction. I don't know why I did that. I panicked. Why would this guy I had known for a few weeks willingly date a quadriplegic who would be laid up in bed for the next several months? I couldn't think of a reason. I decided what the hell . . . and called him back and said yes. I mean what was the worst that could happen? I certainly had bigger fish to fry with trying to stay alive.

Flap Surgery

HAVING NOW EXHAUSTED ALL options with different pressure sore modalities or therapies, the last option was the flap surgery. This surgery is no joke, will likely take up a minimum of six months of your life, and maybe as long as several years, lying flat in bed. It really affects a person's quality of life. However, it can be lifesaving.

During a flap surgery, typically the surgeons perform a procedure that essentially uses a cautery knife to cut out the dead tissue portion of the pressure sore. This will leave a significant hole in your body whether this is on your heel or your bum or thigh. The problem is the skin can't be stretched to close the hole, so they need to cut skin from another area, pull it over the hole in your body and stitch you up. There are other strategies, but this is the most simplified one. The beautiful thing about the glutes is that you have two arterial veins with really great blood supply on each side of your buttocks. This really does promote healing at a rapid rate.

The Day of Flap Surgery

I ROLLED INTO THE hospital at five a.m. sharp with a giant smile on my face. I met with a woman from the finance department so she could explain the costs I would have to cover for my surgery after insurance paid what it would pay. I was well-versed in reading corporate policy and health insurance plans by now, so I was aware of the several thousand dollars I was going to have to outlay after surgery. She was a nice woman with kind eyes, but she slightly raised her eyebrow when I said, "Oh yes, I know exactly how much I will have to pay the hospital to stay alive." I thought it was funny. I'm not sure she found it amusing.

My caregiver undressed me and positioned me on the gurney in my hospital gown. I put in my Bluetooth. I pressed play to listen to a specialized pre-surgery meditation I had found with one of my therapists. I closed my eyes, took deep breaths in and out, and envisioned a smooth recovery.

When I opened my eyes, my mom had her phone out and took a photo of me as I raised my arms in the air with a gleeful expression of "I'm going to kick ass in surgery." Still, I had written individual notes to my family members as I had done in China, just in case surgery went sideways. I still had things I wanted to do, but if things didn't go my way, I would be happy with what I had accomplished in my life.

I did not take this surgery lightly. Most people expect to wake up from their surgery. I do not. I know each time I go under anesthesia, let alone the surgery, there is a chance I may not wake up.

I had lovely scrub nurses and joked around with them as I love to build a great rapport with those who are going to be slicing into my body. We had a giggle as I was counting down 10, 9, 8 . . . I only remember getting to eight.

I woke up on the medical surgery floor and immediately thought, *Okay cool, I made it. Excellent.* Medical professionals were in and out of my room and my family was next to my side. The surgeon told me the surgery went as planned, but I was in for a long road because I had 400 stitches with about 200 staples on my behind. The plan was to keep me in the hospital for about a week until the staples came out. After that I could head back home to my specialized Clinitron bed for recovery.

A few days later Derek came to visit for the first time at the hospital. My dad and brother had a very puzzled look because they didn't know this gentleman who was walking into my room with flowers and a blue plush teddy bear. I told them he was my boyfriend. I wish I had a picture of the expressions on their faces. Priceless. My mom giggled.

Science has proven time and time again that happier people heal faster. I was going to do everything in my power to heal as quickly as I could from the surgery, so I was going to be happy. I had stuff to do!

About five days into my hospital stay after the staples

on my backside were taken out, my body went into dysre-flexia shock. I did try to tell my medical professionals about autonomic dysreflexia, but they dismissed me. They frantically tried to get my blood pressure under control, which they did, but then administered too much nitro-glycerin and my blood pressure tanked. I coded out. I was resuscitated. I tried to tell them! This must've scared them because I was immediately moved to the ICU.

I ended up spending about six weeks in the ICU. It was quite painful with constantly being revived and then passing out again, dealing with blood pressure issues, and with so many tubes in and out of my body. The more often I was revived, the bouncier I became. This is when I officially proclaimed myself the "Energizer Bunny on Wheels 2.0."

After coding on one particular night, I vividly remember telling my mom the next day that I needed her to help me create a moment of joy. In true Ali fashion as my family would say, with tubes sticking out of my body, I asked my mom to please lay one of my many little beach wraps around my naked body with tubes coming out of me. I wanted her to make me look as sexy as possible. I wanted to do a sexy ICU photoshoot for the story, the memory, and to lift my spirits.

My lovely and agile German mother climbed on a hospital stool like a monkey, shooting me from every angle. The nurses were giggling, I was laughing, and then the doctor walked in the room.

He asked to examine me. He was an endocrinol-ogist checking on my hypothyroidism (resulting from an autoimmune disease I have called Hashimoto's), and

I asked him to please wait a few moments until I finished my photoshoot. He did not look amused. He waited with a look of impatience on his face. When he started to examine me, I asked him before he proceeded to please find out if he was in my network. I was speaking about my health insurance in-network providers, which is what my health insurance company will cover as opposed to being charged full price for an out-of-network doctor. He did not know. I really didn't expect him to know, but fool me a dozen times, and I'm on to you.

This has happened to me so many times in my medical career. Doctors would come into the hospital just assuming a patient was in-network with their service. This is absolutely and categorically untrue. I don't blame the doctor, because he just wanted to treat me, but we, the patients, are left holding the financial bag if we do not ask these questions. Turns out he was not in my network, and I saved myself $453!

The lesson? My dad's "trust but verify" adage—politely, of course.

CHAPTER 25

Bed Life at Home

I WAS HAPPY TO return home to my re-designed bedroom with my specialized air-fluidized bed for another several months of full bed rest. I kept up the same routine as I had prior to the surgery with respect to connecting with the disability community, day trading, reading, studying, and with the added benefit of visits from Derek several times a week.

Recovery was tricky though. The incisions from my surgery made going to the bathroom really tricky. My mom was a ferocious lion and refused to let anyone do my bowel program except her to protect me against infections. You know what? Thank God. Again, my mother saved my life for yet another challenging chapter coming up in my life.

Truthfully, the next six months were quite boring. My specialized bed provided an unexpected blessing. My nerve pain was not screaming at me all the time. I was healing faster than they had anticipated because of the amazing self-care nutrition I rigorously followed. And I was in a real relationship.

After a few months, I was allowed to sit up for five

minutes, then work up to ten minutes, then fifteen minutes a day. I passed out more times than I can count because when you have been lying flat for months on end and you sit up, your blood leaves your head and that causes you to pass out. We eventually figured it out, and I was finally up and about in my wheelchair on a regular basis.

The end of 2016 was approaching, and by then I was pretty much vertical each day in my wheelchair, living my life, going out with Derek, making new friends, working, connecting with the disability community, and just going through the motions of a "normal" life as I knew it. This was the best normal I had experienced since 2010. As everything in my life started to settle, I found I wasn't quite sure what I wanted to do when I grew up.

I started to think a lot about this. I was no longer satisfied with just doing my trading work and talking to the disability community. After hearing so many stories from those in the disability community and the atrocities of a broken system pertaining to health insurance, a fire started brewing inside of me. I also recognized there were so many topics that most of us don't talk about because they are socially inappropriate or there is a social stigma surrounding them. My love to normalize really uncomfortable topics in life and in disability with dark humor, insights, and lessons was strengthened because there was, and is, a true need for these conversations.

The fire in my belly kept growing even though I still didn't know where it would lead me. I poked away day after day to learn more. I didn't have a plan. I started reading stories about health insurance fraud, collecting stories from personal friends, researching more on corporate medical policy, talking to folks all around the country who identify with a disability, and knew that I had to do something.

By the time the New Year rolled in for 2017, something amazing happened. For the first time in seven years, I was not in near constant fight or flight mode for survival. I had time for myself and found that I was ready for and needed a larger meaning in my life. A purpose if you will. Surviving was no longer enough. I decided to give my pain a purpose.

I didn't fully understand the concept of purpose per se yet, but I knew something was about to change. It took a few years to get there, but I was on the path and running on high octane, working toward something greater than myself.

PART 3

CHAPTER 26

The Start of a New Life

I SPENT THE FIRST few months of 2017 creating a new website for the Quirky Quad, building partnerships with advocates and communities around the country, speaking free of charge on health equity issues, writing for magazines around the country, day trading, and going out and having a fun time with Derek.

My writing was about sex, bowel and bladder issues, Ableism, other uncomfortable topics surrounding social stigmas in the disability community, and daily life as a quadriplegic and what that entailed. The collection of hundreds of my articles can be found at ***www.QuirkyQuad.com***. I had an earlier blog called The China Quad Diaries, about my life and adventures in China. Those articles were written with my dad's help. If you recall, he was once in the publishing industry. He refused to let me put an article online without proofreading it first. One day I wrote an article and there were just two little red marks. I felt like I had arrived. I have now reached the point of progress over perfection. I simply want to get my words out in the universe.

Blossoming Personal Life

SEVERAL MONTHS AFTER I healed from the surgery, Derek told me he loved me. Looking back, I remember saying to him a few weeks later that I was in love with him too. However, there was a pit in my stomach. I didn't know why. I didn't figure it out until years later with much therapy. It didn't matter at the moment. I was happy, we were traveling alone, we met amazing friends downtown, we went dancing, we dressed up in banana costumes for beer crawls, and attended Halloween parties.

On one such Halloween I had my dear hairdresser friend dye my hair pink. I put on the most fabulous makeup and put together a fun Barbie costume. I even had a sash made with "Paralyzed Barbie" printed on it. The printer called me to ask if I was serious about having that imprinted across this sash. I was serious. I thought it was hilarious and the best use of dark humor. I entered a Halloween costume competition and was beat out by a gay man dressed as Maleficent from the Sleeping Beauty adaptation. He did have a slightly better costume. I ended up giving them a ride on my wheelchair as I gracefully accepted defeat.

Paralyzed Mermaid Back in Action

I HAD REALIZED MY dream of getting back in the water once I moved back to the US. My time to enjoy this was short-lived with the onset of the pressure sore ordeal. However, once I was healed from the flap surgery, I was determined to get back in the water. Did I remember how to swim? Was I still a mermaid? Could I swim independently without my swim instructor and not drown?

The problem in North Carolina is you can only swim for about three months when the pools are open. I purchased new bathing suits and devised a plan with my sister on how to be piggybacked into a pool because there was no pool lift at my apartment complex at that time.

The moment my sister let me go in the water with my mother pacing nervously back and forth on the pool deck, waiting to see if I could still float, there it was. Instantaneous muscle memory for the win! I didn't forget a thing. I could roll over for safety, swim my adapted style freestyle and upright backstroke with ease. I wriggled around in the water. It was extraordinarily challenging for my sister to get me out of the water. I wanted to stay in. And just like that, the paralyzed mermaid was back in action. My YouTube channel has a well-done professional video of how I swim.

One of the challenges with spinal cord injury is the issue of thermal regulation. When you injure your autonomic nervous system, you do not have the ability to control your temperature. I'm always freezing. I sleep with heating pads on my chest and head, and my body thinks it's fifty degrees outside when it's really seventy. This can be challenging when you're swimming because you lose your heat in the water. I can only swim when it is over 80 degrees and sunny with minimal cloud coverage. One adaptation I added to my life with swimming is a floaty toy. Oh, a glorious floaty toy to use after I complete my sixty minutes of laps. I just bake in the sun. I probably should've worn more sunscreen throughout my life. I ended up getting skin cancer years later. I didn't care at that point.

My nerve pain still keeps me awake most nights. I can't even take a nap, because the moment I close my eyes, the burning pins and needles start screaming at me. It's a different story in the water. I can feel my nerve pain when I am basking like a walrus in my floaty toy, but it melts away with the external sensation of physically being free from the wheelchair and gravity and feeling the heat of the sun.

Pool time during summer weekends is my sacred time. I invite anyone to come join me, but there's absolutely no talking to me when it is my naptime. Seriously. I'll hurt you or roll you over. This is a religious-like ceremonial activity for me, and I will not let anyone take that away from me. You could say this is my ultimate form of self-care in the summer, and I treasure it because so often my time is spent working or traveling these days. Over the years, I've even given up social time because I just love the quiet, exercise, and lifestyle of pool life. Of course, it's not the same as growing up in The Bahamas, but I adjusted my expectations early on.

When I moved into my condo in 2020, it took me nearly a year to convince the HOA to allow a pool lift and then another six months to raise the funds for it. I'm not really into material stuff except for my wheelchair, wheelchair cushion, my adapted accessible computer, specialized mattress, and pool lift. I'm possessive about those. I will give you the shirt off my back, but if you attempt to stir up trouble around any of these inanimate objects that improve my quality of life and independence, we'll have a problem.

Let the Travel Begin Again

I DID NOT TRAVEL without my caregivers until 2018. It took about a year of dating Derek until I felt comfortable enough to teach him how to take care of me. For me, this is a very personal and very intimate thing. Someone literally has to go into my bum with suppositories to help me poop, bathe me, transfer me into my chair, and help me with my hair. I was completely terrified the first time I was rolled over naked on my side, completely exposed with my "quad belly" out and Derek was there with the glove on his hand with my mother while he was learning my bowel program.

Ah, the quad belly. Paralysis below the chest means that you have no ability to move or flex muscles. You may be very healthy, have a slim physique, and exercise, but there's no escaping the quad belly. Oh, the dreaded quad belly. We're unable to suck in our tummy muscles, so we have a little pooch. Plain and simple. I don't like mine. I live with her. I would love to get rid of her, but she's part of me. I've never met one male or female quadriplegic who is a fan of their little belly or big belly, depending on their size. I've always been super self-conscious about mine. I still hold that self-consciousness today despite learning to accept my body for what it is and what it can (and can't) do now. Back then, though, having my man see what I considered a deformed body was new to me.

Okay, now back to the bowel program. I debated whether I should write about this, but it's a necessary part of my authentic lived experience every day. Each morning I have another human being help me go to the bathroom, change my catheter, and get me dressed among other things. Now, to have a man I had only been dating for about a year take this on? Oh my God, I was mortified but knew if I wanted to have independence in traveling with him, he was going to have to learn. He literally had to put gloves on and put a finger in my bum to help me poop with the assistance of the suppository. You can Google bowel program if you want to know all of the intimate details, but I think you get the idea.

Honestly, it was his idea. He told me, "It's just poop. We all do it. It's no big deal." I hesitantly agreed, but I did express my concern that he wouldn't find me a sexual being anymore if he was in the day-in and day-out of my caregiving. No, he did not take care of me full time. He was a backup in emergencies and only did full-time caregiving when we traveled together. There are two schools of thought in the disability community on their spouses or partners taking care of them, but I decided to give it a go.

I don't have much physical control with respect to taking care of myself, but when it comes to my body, it has to be my way or the highway. It took us quite a while, but Derek did learn what he needed to. I wouldn't say he was fantastic at it, but it was just amazing that he tried. We were able to go on many successful trips because he could take care of me.

Cruise Time

WE VISITED MIAMI EACH year to go back to see my friends, go boating, drinking, popping around to a few tiki bars, and enjoying each other's company. We would drive from North Carolina down to Miami. We attempted flying to Orlando once, but driving was better. My mom joined us in Miami, so she was always a backup just in case.

We were gearing up to take a cruise with Royal Caribbean to go to Belize, tropical Caribbean islands, and a few other stops on our own. I did all the research on accessibility. I'm an avid researcher on everything, and I was confident a cruise was the right move. I'd never been on a cruise before. I did not have any interest in being sardined into a vessel with thousands of other humans, however, cruise lines are well-known for their accessibility. I thought it would be a great starter trip.

We drove down to Tampa, Florida. The ship was huge, the room was beautiful, and we made haste to explore every nook and cranny of the ship. Truthfully, the cruise part was quite boring. I didn't care for the food, the fat bellyflop competitions in the pool, bingo, or any of the other activities. However, I planned a few offshore trips with a third-party company to dip my toe into the water with accessible adventures.

I discovered a lovely accessible travel company in Belize. They took us on a two-hour drive in this semi-accessible van to the Mayan temples as I held on for dear life. When I had visited the Mayan temples on the trip to Belize with my mom, dad, and sister, I climbed the highest temple and bounced around like a monkey.

I didn't know how I was going to feel this time. The temples were quite off-road, but I was pushed by our guide in my manual wheelchair, which I use for adventures that a power wheelchair would be unable to handle. Derek climbed to the top of the highest temple even though we were not supposed to climb on the ruins, but as devilish Ali, I told him to do it anyway. I should not have done that, but the look on his face was completely worth it though we were chased out by the park officials. It was just amazing to be on an adventure again. This was my first outdoor adventure since 2010 when I was in Maui, Hawaii, for the wedding of a close friend. I returned from that wedding exactly two weeks before I broke my neck. I probably would've climbed another waterfall or jumped off another rock into the ocean had I known what was to happen. C'est la vie!

After the temple adventure, I upped my game a bit to see if I would be able to snorkel. I was extremely confident with my swimming abilities, but when we arrived to what was described to us and labeled as "Accessible Snorkeling" on a nearby beach from the cruise ship port, I laughed out loud. There was sand on the beach, but there were rocks lining the entire shoreline. There was one dock that involved walking up a few steps and then walking down a handful of very slippery and wet steps. There was no functional beach wheelchair.

Derek was a great sport. We ended up spotting a few bucks to the guys working on the beach to help carry me for a good five minutes down the beach, up the stairs, and then down the stairs into the water. The down part was tricky. One of the guys slipped, Derek lost his grip, and I went flying headfirst into the water.

Thank goodness I can hold my breath for two minutes. The guide and Derek jumped in the water to help me. The current was quite strong. I was wearing my goggles and ended up holding onto a life preserver while the snorkel guide pulled the line. It was still magical though. I had seen hundreds of reefs in my life, but simply being able to wiggle around in the open ocean with my paralyzed body was amazing.

Sand. Now that's another story. I didn't like sand getting between my butt cheeks before my accident, but now it's medically dangerous because it can cause pressure sores. I describe my skin issues as my quadriplegic curse. You look at me and I develop a pressure sore. Truly, if you put a cell phone with a pop socket on my belly when I am naked, I will get that little circle ring on my belly within five minutes.

The day at the beach ended with Derek placing me on a lounge chair with multiple towels. We were served ceviche and pina coladas while we basked in the sun. There was a price to pay. A Stage I pressure sore when I returned back to our room. There must have been a slight wrinkle in the towel I was lying on. That slight wrinkle was my arch nemesis after only thirty minutes.

Even when I go to bed now, I have to ensure all of the sheets under my body are completely straight, no wrinkles. Everything must be flattened. This takes about twenty extra minutes every night. I'm not trying to sugarcoat that it's a pain in the butt, and I do wish I could just plop in bed as most of my other quadriplegic friends do, but nope. So, I adjust accordingly.

In all seriousness, I take excellent care of my skin, check it multiple times a day, and do not mess around with any red mark. No more pressure sores on my watch!

CHAPTER 27

Planting a New Seed

HEALTH INSURANCE MADE THE years 2018 and 2019 very interesting. I was denied a thirty thousand dollar electrical stimulation bicycle. Think of a bicycle where little sticky pads are placed on my legs and cables from the pads are connected to the bike. The cables send an electrical current called electrical stimulation through my legs to "bike" my legs. Electrical stimulation increases blood flow, reduces muscle spasticity, promotes healing, and (hurray!) reduces the recurrence of pressure sores, so important for many of us with paralysis. The primary reason I use electrical stimulation several times a week while biking is, you guessed it, to increase the blood flow in my legs and butt cheeks to reduce the incidence of pressure sores.

This bike is quite high-tech and not generally covered by insurance companies. I had a bike back in 2010 that my family purchased for me. Fortunately, it did not cost thirty thousand dollars back then. By 2018, the bike had broken, so I needed a new one. I had built a wonderful relationship with the manufacturer, so we decided to fight back when insurance denied me. More accurately, the company fought. I paid attention.

My health insurance provider stated electrical stimulation was experimental technology or something of that nature. If I had been denied a product, service, or drug under the provision of "not medically necessary," I could have appealed the decision. But when a denial is given because something is considered experimental or a luxury or convenience item, there aren't many avenues of recourse to appeal the decision. Basically, denial is the final decision by the insurance provider in such cases. Most people just give up at this point. We did not.

There are multiple approaches on how to go above your insurance company when they have denied something that you need. As a private insurance matter, we decided to file a case with the Department of Insurance in North Carolina. (Medicare issues in this regard go through the judicial system.) The Department of Insurance has the authority to overturn an insurance provider's decision. It's a long, tedious, and laborious process.

I worked hand-in-hand with a helpful representative of the medical equipment provider, who walked me through every step of the process. We sent more than a hundred pages of medical arguments and peer-reviewed journal articles to back up the argument for medical necessity of electrical stimulation for individuals with paralysis or mobility challenges. It took about sixteen months, but then I received a letter in the mail.

The Department of Insurance overturned my insurance provider's decision, meaning that my insurance provider was required to cover this product. It was a glorious day.

I was in shock. I couldn't believe a patient could advocate for themselves in the health insurance system this way. It is certainly not a cake walk, but it's possible if your life or the life of a loved one depends on it.

Even after winning, I didn't fully connect the dots that this experience would shape the next part of my life, but I was intrigued. I had learned a lot. For the moment, I was simply elated to receive my new bike. I put health insurance to the back of my mind, because I was preparing for bigger things in my life at that moment.

CHAPTER 28

Here Comes the Bride

DEREK AND I HAD been dating nearly three years and things were quite serious. The next logical step was marriage. Back then, I truly believed that was what I wanted. However, when I reflect back, I think I was probably following the social norm of what most people do after dating for a period of time. They get married.

Derek believed he had planned a grand surprise, but it was not rocket science to figure out what he was up to when he invited our parents to Carolina Beach when we were participating in an adaptive surf event.

Surfing

EACH YEAR DEREK AND I would head to Carolina Beach where this incredible organization called Ocean Cure with the national organization Life Rolls On provides opportunities for disabled folks to go surfing. It was a blast. I was picked up by strong men, placed on my belly on the surfboard, and then I rode the waves with someone steering the surfboard behind me. It was a summer ritual each year. I enjoyed it as an opportunity to connect with other members of my disability community and enjoy time in the water.

One year my surfboard actually flipped over. Everyone lost me, and I was rolling in circles under the wave breaks. I just held my breath and assumed I would be saved eventually. There was a look of horror on many faces when they finally grabbed me. I was laughing. They were not. With what I have been through, I dare you to try to find something that can really shock me anymore.

Proposal

THE TIME CAME AND Derek kneeled on one knee. I had this tiny feeling. I couldn't quite put into words what the feeling was, so I pushed it down. If I had been aware enough of the feeling and brave enough to claim it, perhaps we would have been saved from a long road ahead. In the moment, however, I was gleefully excited that I was going to get married. I couldn't fathom in my wildest dreams that I, a C6 quadriplegic, could be married.

The engagement was short, about eight months, I believe. Originally, we wanted to get married in a pool to have our first dance upright together with a serious barbecue to follow. This was immediately shot down by my dad who, in no uncertain terms, made quick work of telling me that the wedding is about family and the honeymoon is about the couple. I thought that was fair.

I planned my wedding myself with a little help from my mom. I couldn't find a wedding dress. I didn't really want to wear one because I am not a dress chick in a wheelchair. Before my accident? I lived in beach dresses. I don't think wearing a dress in a wheelchair is particularly flattering to me, and I wanted to look my best for my wedding.

My plan was to wear a white top with white pants. I found this incredible costume designer from the Carolina Ballet who heard my story. She designed a beautiful French lace and silk top for me. It was stunning. I wear it with jeans these days and think it looks terrific.

I recall my wedding with the fondest of memories because of my family. We had about fifty family friends fly in from all over the world. It was a reunion of reunions you could say. Even though the marriage didn't last, I only have amazing things to say about that day. I could tell my family couldn't believe I had come so far. I couldn't believe it myself.

My family made my wedding comical as I did for my sister's wedding. We played oldies music with '80s rock 'n' roll. There was drinking, dancing, and merriment all around. Derek and I had practiced our first dance to "I Got You, Babe," by Sonny and Cher in our apartment garage a week earlier.

I would've been happy just having a life partner, but marriage did seem important to Derek, and I wanted to make him happy. There were several mistakes made that day though. Derek was incredibly hung over from the night before and looked it as I rolled down the aisle with my dad. I was recovering from bronchitis. I couldn't taste alcohol, so I ended up getting drunk like you see in those really bad movies. We did not consummate the marriage on the wedding night. I'm not really a traditional girl, so those kinds of things don't faze me.

I wanted to go to Tuscany and then on to Switzerland for our honeymoon. I worked with an international travel company to plan the entire trip. It was going to be epic and expensive. When I told Derek about it, he seemed keener to go to the North Carolina mountains. Right, well, I certainly wasn't going to spend that amount of money on a trip with a partner who didn't seem that engaged with the plan, so we went to the mountains for our honeymoon.

Asheville, North Carolina, was beautiful. We stayed at a gorgeous five-star hotel. Derek carried me from luxurious hot tub to ornate pool in this underground spa. We had tours of different breweries, checked out cute little bookshops, enjoyed decadent food, and made the best of a beautiful honeymoon.

Sadly, things started to go sideways in our marriage after a while. It didn't happen immediately, but it did happen.

CHAPTER 29

A New Home, New Life?

IN JANUARY OF 2020, we had heard rumors of COVID-19, but we didn't really make much of it at the time. Coincidentally, that winter we learned that our apartment complex was going to triple their prices, so it was finally time in my late thirties to start looking for a condo to buy. Derek wanted to move to the country, but that's not very accessible for me, so he acquiesced to my request for city life. I purchased a beautiful condo in a lovely garden setting and went to work making it accessible.

Derek and I were having dinner one night in a restaurant around the corner and learned that we were in the restaurant with a gentleman who had just been exposed to COVID. The entire building was locked down, and, hours later, guys with hazmat suits poured in with their sterilization equipment. We had no idea what would follow just several weeks later.

We had a big decision to make in a short time. We decided to move to the condo before the adaptive construction was finished, since things were not looking good with the pandemic. We made it in the nick of time. I'm talking one week before lockdown. The construction crew worked around us, and it was a little bit of a camping lifestyle inside the condo, but we were safe.

Pandemic Life

OUR RELATIONSHIP AND WHAT was working and not working took a giant pause. I think we rediscovered some of our closeness during the lockdown, so I kept holding onto hope that something would change. Something that would save our marriage.

We were getting along, but then Derek lost his job, as did so many others during the pandemic. This was really hard for us. I believe he was going through depression. I tried to be there for him, but after a certain point, it became very challenging for me to continue to have empathy. I've always been able to pick myself back up, so I don't think I fully appreciated how best to help him. To be fair, he wasn't really expressing what he needed. So many areas of lost communication. I also think I babied him too much, but, again, I'm sure he has very different perceptions.

The Beginning of the End

MY ADVOCACY LIFE HAD been steadily building in many directions, and I was hooked. Before the lockdown, I was traveling, speaking, researching, and ferociously trying to find the next step in life. I had not combined my advocacy and professional life together yet, but I just kept getting out there any way I could.

Derek had passed up a few job opportunities away from home for me. I didn't ask him to, but he didn't believe in long distance relationships. That's fair. I felt different on the topic. I grew up with a dad who was away much of the time for work, so it seemed quite normal to me. Derek ended up landing a job that took him away for twelve hours at a time.

Sadly, we just stopped talking. I felt like I was growing as a person, and our journeys started to diverge. I don't know the exact moment I started to feel that, but it kept building, though I tried to ignore it. I have always had the ability to compartmentalize my thoughts and feelings for my psychological and physiological safety. I did that with my marriage. I started going to therapy on my own and realized I was more and more unhappy in our relationship. I was unhappy with myself too.

I think this is where I actually shut down in our marriage. I had been changing myself to try to mold into what he needed, which I later came to realize was a big mistake, because I wasn't being my authentic self. I started focusing on myself because something really unexpected happened in the summer of 2020.

Lockdown Life

IT WAS HEARTBREAKING TO watch the world suffer in such a drastic way. It seemed everything in the world was changing. For me, everything changed in a different way. The summer of 2020 and on into 2021 was a critical transformational period for me in the best possible way. The lockdown gave me time to think critically about my life and what I wanted to change. I solidified my purpose in life for the first time and made plans to achieve it. I focused on what was in my control to move forward.

I listened to and read online about the devastation and social isolation wreaking havoc for many people from crumbling relationships to creating anxiety, fear, and depression. I, on the other hand, had a different take on it as did many in the disability community, especially in the mobility impairment community. So many folks in the disability community don't have the right accessible transportation, caregiving, or funds to move from place to place. As a result, and by unfortunate default, many wheelchair users are stuck in their home more than they would care to be. Many of us live in social isolation in everyday life. So, for many of us with disabilities, social isolation is the norm.

My dad has often said that he likes a job that starts hard. He's not wrong. I can't recall one time in my life, not once, where I ever learned anything the easy way or something I really wanted just fell in my lap. People think my speaking and my writing just flow, but whatever I write takes five to seven rounds of editing, and it takes three times as long for the finished product to come out as I had envisioned. I learned in school to put the work in to get the result out. I began putting the same kind of effort in my work, independent of what was going on in my personal life at that time.

People think I live a very adventurous life. I do, but in very defined segments of time. Most of the time I'm just doing my thing and am fortunate enough to work from home where I am at my computer and three screens all day long. During the weekdays, I pretty much live in social isolation because I'm working so much. Whenever I post on social media, I receive many comments about how I am able to live my life and travel like I do.

There's a reason I can do these things. I work really hard and then I plan a trip for a week or two to go rock it out like 1999. I don't take one-day federal holidays, and I work on weekends half of the year. I've intentionally designed my life like this because I like to take longer periods of time to go somewhere really exotic. This takes money, time, and planning. There's always a compromise somewhere, and this is where I make mine.

CHAPTER 30

Change in Life Trajectory

THE DAY THE BIG white envelope arrived at my desk sent from my insurance company my heart sank. If you have applied to a university, you may know the type of envelope I am talking about. If you are accepted into a university, they generally send you a great big envelope package welcoming you to their university. If you receive a rejection, you are graced with a letter-sized envelope with one piece of paper. The opposite is true with health insurance in general.

When I opened the packet, I read through all the bullshit telling me I was important, I had appeal rights, yada yada yada. I understood the crux of the matter. I was rejected for a power seat elevator for a new power wheelchair I had submitted for prior-authorization.

When you are a full-time wheelchair user you are generally allowed one new wheelchair every five years. My year was 2020 and COVID was running rampant. I was devastated. Some of the corporate policy laws had changed. The power seat elevator for my wheelchair was now classified as "a convenience/luxury item," meaning I had no appeal rights.

A luxury item my ass! Power seat elevators have so many medical and quality-of-life benefits for full-time power wheelchair users. A seat elevator allows wheelchair users to raise their chair up for mattress level transfer to reduce the risk of fractures and falling out of the chair. Many of us need to raise our chair up to kitchen cabinets for food or to our sinks so we can brush our teeth. The benefits go on. The insurance company didn't see it that way as this add-on costs approximately five thousand dollars. I was enraged. I didn't know what to do at first. Then I remembered the fight for the medical bike.

I went on the laborious mission of writing my own letter of medical necessity and backing up my argument with peer-reviewed journal articles to prove my point. I made the argument that without a level transfer surface onto my bed I could fall out of my chair, break bones, and pressure sores would follow. I used peer-reviewed journal articles about the long-term costs of such injuries and the importance of avoidance of secondary complications associated medically with pressure sores to prove my case the power seat was not a "convenience/luxury" item. This was frankly not a very hard argument to make, but AI was not in full swing yet, so it was quite a manual process. I spent dozens of hours reading peer-reviewed journal articles, citing them, researching how to write these research-like papers. It didn't matter though. I was denied at every turn.

Then I went to the North Carolina Department of Insurance to file an external review to try and reverse the insurance company's decision, as I did with the medical bike.

Not a runner. Not a chance actually. I was informed that unless I was denied under "not medically necessary," I didn't have a legal pathway to try to appeal this decision. I was stuck. I had no more avenues to try my appeal.

Fighting insurance companies is really like an unpaid day job. When I am on hold for hours, I adopt an alter ego persona. I pretend I am a kung fu-fighting, master FBI hostage superhero negotiator dealing with the Mafia. When I am on hold with the insurance company listening to terrible "Jeopardy" music, I recite, "It's not personal, it's business."

This went on for about sixty days with nothing but denials. I became more and more angry, which resulted in me becoming more productive. The more something frustrates me, the harder I work to overcome it.

The Fight Begins

I WAS ON MY own with this one, but I thought this denial was unacceptable for the entire disability community or anyone with complex medical diagnoses for that matter. I read tirelessly, contacted everyone in my disability network, and continued to write articles, all to no avail. I was practicing the definition of insanity often attributed to Einstein—doing the same thing over and over again and expecting different results. I was getting nowhere fast.

A wacky idea came to me to grab some traction for my cause. It was time to take charge, whatever that meant! Imperfect action is better than perfect inaction. I went on a mission and contacted fifty-seven investigative news reporters around North Carolina to talk about the injustices in our healthcare system. I talked to anyone who would talk to me. I emailed them, left phone messages, and started stalking them. I didn't do this once or twice. I did this dozens of times. I was just very pleasant and smiley despite my anger.

This is where my unofficial middle name emerged: "pleasantly persistent." It basically means I am a stalker with a smile, and I will follow up with you until I hear back from you. I've since amended this slightly to "pleasantly persistent with purpose." I do think it's an important distinction to add the purpose because a purpose is not just about you individually. That's passion. Passion is very individualistic and purpose is when you start working toward fighting for a cause greater than yourself.

Exactly three investigative reporters reached out to me. They were from Spectrum News, ABC 11, and NBC 17. We made quick work of video interviews, and the investigative reporters started calling the insurance company on my behalf. I even had an article published in *The News & Observer*, our Raleigh daily newspaper.

I started posting about my media wins in North Carolina and around the country. Many organizations I was working with promoted this story nationally to illustrate some of the health equity injustices in our system. My story spread like wildfire.

I made dozens of trips to the insurance office, but no one would see me. I sat outside their office. I even wrote letters weekly to the then president of the North Carolina division. This did not yield fruitful results, which is exactly why I deployed a multi-pronged and multi-faceted strategy for engagement.

Shame on You

I CANNOT TELL YOU exactly what happened from the internal side of things (albeit I can guess), but within several weeks, I received a letter from my insurer stating that my power seat elevator had been approved as medically necessary. Maybe they were trying to reduce bad PR. Whatever it takes!

There was a huge "but" attached to the approval. They stated that the power seat elevator would be considered medically necessary for me and me alone. This approval could not be considered a precedent. They were basically telling me that no one else in the country could utilize my strategy to help the broader wheelchair population.

Oh hell no. No way. Not today. No thank you. It was not ethical, and it would have been a betrayal to my disability community to stop fighting. This was not just about me anymore but about the thousands of others who also needed a seat elevator. This blossomed into a mission that was bigger than myself.

The ITEM Coalition

How could I fight for others in this area? I was going to have to change legislation. I had heard whispers about a group called the ITEM Coalition (Independence Through Enhanced Medicare & Medicaid). It's a group of more than sixty doctors, lawyers, advocates, and clinicians who were coming together to prove the medical necessity of power seat elevators and standing wheelchairs. They were trying to have Medicare change legislation to assign power seat elevators with a different code so they would be re-classified as medically necessary. In general, once you have something approved within Medicare, private insurance companies follow suit and approve the same requested equipment or service. I didn't know much about this, so the approach hadn't occurred to me.

I eventually connected with the ITEM Coalition and was invited to be their primary disability advocate for power seat elevators in their fight with Medicare. I accepted and the hard work commenced. Truthfully, the clinicians did all the hard work because they're the ones who prepared a report that was two hundred fifty pages long for Medicare. We had weekly calls for years, I attended congressional briefings and other advocacy events in DC on behalf of all power wheelchair users requiring power seat elevators, and we launched an awareness campaign. I made beautiful friends, built incredible partnerships, and this launched many other health equity initiatives I work on today.

I am incredibly proud to share the recognition with dozens and dozens of individuals who worked tirelessly on this mission for years. In June of 2023, Medicare officially changed their policy and re-classified power seat elevators as medically necessary for those who need them. It was a landmark legislation change for us in the disability community. There's so much more work to do, but this was a triumphant win because it had been about sixteen years since Medicare re-classified a different component of power seat elevator function as medically necessary.

Now, tens of thousands of power wheelchair users have access to a vital product to enhance their well-being and quality of life. This is the true meaning of the power of the network in my opinion. My professional health equity life exploded. I was now day trading while also working in the health equity space. My world was still quite separated from a professional and advocacy perspective.

Because I Am Cheeky

I DIDN'T WANT TO stop at a power seat elevator. I decided to systematically test my theory of appealing different pieces of equipment I needed not only to survive in my life but to thrive, knowing others in my community would have the same or similar challenges. I went on my own personal mission for a specialized hospital bed frame, shower chair, specific drugs, and other smaller pieces of equipment to improve the quality of life. I was denied at every turn under "not medically necessary."

That was great! I knew what to do next and did it. It was an arduous process each time, but I couldn't believe it. I started winning everything. I shared my resources, information, strategies, and partnered with organizations around the country. At this point, I was doing everything pro bono and, as situations or needs arose, learning key lessons[vii] as I went along. I share some of those lessons in my "medical notes" at the back of this book.

The point in recounting this is that during the COVID times, my life was moving at warp speed in directions I had yet to clearly figure out. This would launch me into an entirely new life.

CHAPTER 31

Ms. Wheelchair America

NEWS OF MY ADVOCACY efforts traveled. I was asked to run for Ms. Wheelchair North Carolina 2022. These competitions are not beauty pageants but rather are advocacy pageants. To be eligible you have to either have an idea or have executed an idea that contributes to advocacy in some capacity.

I was crowned Ms. Wheelchair North Carolina 2022 and then was invited to the National Ms. Wheelchair America competition to be held about eight months later. The woman crowned as Ms. Wheelchair America would serve as titleholder for one year. It was quite grueling to prepare for this competition, which was held in Grand Rapids, Michigan. Most of the women found the speaking challenging, but my challenge was making this eighth grade science board poster showcasing the highlights of my advocacy work and facts about my state. I don't have functional fingers, so this was extraordinarily difficult. My sister-in-law came from Atlanta to help me create my poster.

I drove with two caregivers about seventeen hours to

get to Grand Rapids. The competition was strenuous. It was pretty much seven days of activities for about twelve hours a day. We were all in wheelchairs or had mobility impairments, so I'm still confused why they pushed it so hard with all our medical challenges.

What I will always take away from this competition is the women. The camaraderie. The relationships formed. I made some lasting friendships. We were all in this together. I enjoyed the competition section. We had multiple individual sessions with judges. Because I really knew my stuff, had been doing public speaking for a few years already, and absolutely love talking to people, I think I excelled in this area.

The crowning night came when five of us were asked to stay on stage as the finalists. Throughout the competition, we each had to prepare a two-minute platform speech and then had to answer several impromptu questions from the judges.

There were two of us left on stage, and we were both smiling. If I had "lost," it still would've been a win. I know that's cliche, but the competition really wasn't about "winning." Truthfully, being crowned title holder would require a lot of travel and appearances at many events. My plate was already full.

They called my name and I was crowned Ms. Wheelchair America 2023. The next year was filled with so much travel, building a new life, gaining new professional opportunities in very different directions, and connecting with organizations around the world.

I had never won anything in my life except the business plan competition when I was in college. Oh, and

I did successfully guess the right number of jellybeans in a jar once when I was in first grade. You could give me a thousand scratch offs, and I probably still wouldn't win. It was and still is a great honor to have had that experience as Ms. Wheelchair America 2023. In fact, this experience launched the next evolution in my journey. I was still reinventing myself every few years and was ready to embrace the change.

CHAPTER 32

Back Home to The Bahamas

I WAS APPROACHED ABOUT an interesting documentary film project by a dear friend who owned a film company and whose family owned a home near ours on Cat Island. She reached out to me about filming a documentary on my life. Initially, I was hesitant but decided if it would help others feel a little less alone or maybe a little bit braver in their lives, then maybe it could be worthwhile.

The key request I had was that the proposed film should be funny, quirky, and with actionable life lessons. If people watched a movie of my life, I wanted moments for dark humor laughter, reflecting the way I have lived and still live my life.

I've watched so many movies and documentaries about the disability community, and while many of them are powerful, they are also quite sad. I wanted people to walk away from my documentary laughing and hopefully with a change in perspective.

I also thought this might be a fun adventure, especially when they proposed that we start where it all began—on

Cat Island, my home. Frankly, I had two thoughts. Even if this documentary never got produced, I had the opportunity to go back home to The Bahamas for the first time in more than twelve years. And if it did get produced, then hopefully it might help others going through their tough times. Either way, I would have a blast doing it.

I gather some of the funding fell through, but for nearly a year of my life, we met at different locations around the country with the team. They filmed my life in North Carolina at different disability advocacy events and even accompanied me to Ms. Wheelchair America 2023 in Michigan, where my winning the title was just a bonus.

This project involved quite a logistical undertaking to figure out how to get a quadriplegic down to a marginally accessible out island in The Bahamas. This took months of meticulous planning on my end, purchasing specific items such as a beach wheelchair, a foldable power wheelchair, and the right emergency medical equipment in the event of a catastrophe. They wanted to film every moment of going down to the island. We rented a single engine Cessna caravan cargo plane in Fort Lauderdale for the mission.

The challenge was I had to leave my power chair in the United States because there's no way I was going to be able to drive this four hundred pound piece of equipment around the island, often in the sand. Not to mention, we had no way of getting it shipped down to The Bahamas in time, and it certainly wasn't going to fit on a cargo plane with a weight capacity limit.

To make matters more challenging, when I arrived in my power wheelchair on the tarmac in Fort Lauderdale, the entrance of the cargo plane was at least five feet above the ground. How was I going to get into the cargo plane?

That problem was solved by some strong men who lifted me up into the plane, but I didn't make it much farther than that. I was lying on the floor of the plane, rolling around while they figured out the body mechanics to get me up on the narrow airplane seat. Eventually, they got me onto the seat, but I was bobbing around like one of those bobble heads you sometimes see on a car dashboard, because I had to sit on this 3-inch thick cushion to avoid pressure sores.

They finally tied me down like I was tied in the Chinese ICU, but this time I was laughing the entire time. I kept envisioning how the next twelve days of my life would go if we were having this much trouble before we even left the United States.

As we were approaching the runway on Cat Island, I could see the entire island. I wasn't sure what emotions I would experience seeing this vista that had offered me so much joy for 27 years but also took away so much from me in just a moment.

For many years, I had been devastated that a place I love so much could also feel like my nemesis. The arrival was being filmed and the camera was on me to catch my reaction, but I was just . . . neutral. I wasn't sad, mad, or crying. I was in disbelief. I had not believed I would ever get to return.

When we touched down, there was a band waiting for me on the runway. When I had been rushed off to emergency surgery back in 2010, there were hundreds of folks surrounding me as I departed. Now there were folks surrounding me as I returned. It was bittersweet. I was home again.

As we arrived at our family compound on Cat Island, the bougainvillea, palm trees, and hibiscuses were gorgeous. I couldn't get back to my original room because there were too many little steps here and there, so I stayed in the main house with my mother. I was in my manual chair, which is quite challenging because I can't push myself. I was going to be dependent on someone else to push me around for the next twelve days. This part was incredibly trying. I couldn't just roll into a corner to have a moment alone.

I was accompanied by a documentary crew of four, my mother, my sister-in-law, my niece, and two caregivers as well as my now ex-husband. So many loving people were down there for me, but they sort of ruined it for me. Naturally, I'm so grateful for their constant willingness to help, but there were so many different personalities trapped on a tiny island that I never caught a private break. I had to hear complaints of each party member about another person.

Before I returned to the island, I asked that everyone please try to get along for the trip. I am the person who calms everyone else down and works to find a happy medium. I just needed twelve days of psychological peace, but I did not get it.

I don't cry very often, but I cried every morning when I woke up because someone was mad at somebody or frustrated about something someone did. My husband was not much help in that department either. I just wanted to roll my wheelchair to a quiet little tiki bar, but I could not get there by myself. My niece was delightful though.

She would take me in the water, and we would disappear for an hour or two. My dear friend who was running the production company was also very thoughtful and took me for private swims every few days. She had her waterproof camera, of course, to catch my reactions.

I so wish I could report that this was a magical experience for me and that I had some kind of psychological breakthrough of peace. Instead, my experience on the island could best be described as a Facebook relationship status option: "It's complicated."

The island itself was still pristine with pure white sand and crystal-clear water where you are able to see down a hundred feet. The problem was I couldn't access any of it. I traveled along a small pathway around the house, was carried down to the beach and into the water, and back again.

I wasn't able to go frolic by myself in the back creek area, kayak out to these little cays where we used to go snorkeling, take the boat out, or just have a simple walk by myself. I had no privacy, not for one moment.

I was really heartbroken. It's challenging to have privacy as a quadriplegic, but at least in my power chair I have the ability to roll around by myself. In a manual chair, I felt more paralyzed than I had ever felt before. To be fair, it wasn't all bad. We did have some wonderful in-between moments.

For instance, one day my niece took me out in the floating beach chair to have a little girl time together. We noticed the tide going out a little bit too late, and we were being pushed out to sea. She could no longer swim me back to shore, so she left to go get a kayak to tie to the floating beach wheelchair and paddle me back in. This failed too. We were floating out to sea and waving our hands frantically for help. Someone on the beach saw us and jumped in a little inflatable powerboat to come out and tow us back in.

The documentary crew had their film equipment zoomed in catching the action. It was a conga line of towing. There was the powerboat with a ski rope line to the kayak that had a tow line connected to my beach wheelchair. I was in the back in the chair and everyone else was on the boat watching me. I realized the powerboat was towing me in too quickly. The beach wheelchair started to tip left and then right, and then more forcefully left and then right. I could see where this was going! They couldn't hear me call out to them. I knew I was going to have to hold my breath once again as I had twelve years earlier.

3, 2, 1 . . . arms crossed over my chest, I took a deep breath, and the beach wheelchair started to flip over. There I went. Once again I was floating face down, holding my breath waiting to be saved. Another déjà vu. I was prepared this time, as I knew someone would come get me. My niece and husband jumped in the water to flip me over. I was laughing. I thought it so absurdly comical that I was in this situation once again in the place it all started.

My niece was laughing with me, but I don't think anyone else was amused. The problem was they couldn't pull me up on the small powerboat, so my niece wrapped her arms around me as we both held on to a metal rod on the beach wheelchair. So, there we were, being towed in, holding on for dear life.

The powerboat was speeding up too quickly, and we found ourselves being keelhauled. I mean literally keelhauled as pirates did in the old days. We were dragged under water, held our breath, then we popped our heads up for air, and down we went again. It felt like a James Bond movie in live action.

When we finally made it back to the beach about ten minutes later, the entire documentary crew and my family ran to us to assess the damage. I'm not sure if they thought I was injured or they just were terrified of the idea of me drowning again, but there was not a giggle in town. I'm not sure if they captured the audio on camera, but I know they captured the video.

This may be my twisted dark humor coming into play, but that is truly the fondest memory I have of being on the island for those twelve days. Comical disaster with a happy ending on a beach.

I did experience a powerful moment when the documentary crew took me in a van to the tiki bar where I broke my neck. It was in complete shambles. From what I have been told, no one ever went back to the tiki bar to hang out or party because they believed my bad luck was caused by some kind of black magic voodoo. No, I'm not kidding.

This once happy little tiki bar, where we pranced around twelve years ago, was no more, just like my functional body. There was a deck with a few poles and green ocean netting flowing in and out with the tide on the beach. That was all that was left of it. I know this is the moment I should've felt something profound, but I didn't. I wasn't feeling anything.

I think at that point I had done a pretty great job of learning to overcome all of my obstacles, but it was just surreal looking into the past at such close range. That's just it though. It was the past. That moment wasn't my future, but I appreciated the opportunity to have one last look. I asked my documentary friend to cut off a piece of the green ocean rope so I could take it back as a memory.

The twelve days came and went, and I'm grateful for the opportunity to have gone back one more time. I am not sure if I'll go back to Cat Island again. Not because of any emotional uneasiness I have, but it's just not very accessible. I'd rather save my money and go on accessible exotic tropical adventures whenever I have the time. The thing is, now I know. I know what it would be like to go back. I faced everything I think I was supposed to, and I have genuinely moved on.

I found this letter I wrote to Cat Island several years after my accident.

Dear Cat Island,

You were the love of my life and you shattered my heart. You brought me more joy and love than any romantic relationship in my life had brought me at that time. While the love for my family is the most important thing in my life, you were a close second.

You taught me how to swim, find peace, gave me adventure, helped raise me to be the woman I am today, made me tough, taught me adversity, and opened your arms to me when I needed you the most.

How could you let me go like that? A few seconds—that's all it took for you to turn your back on me and take it all away. What did I do wrong? I was yours and you were mine . . . that was the deal. We were supposed to have each other's back, but you abandoned me. I am still so angry with you, but dammit, I still love you no matter how long I've tried to forget you. We shared a love so intense throughout my life that I cannot let you go. I don't want to let you go, but I just don't know how we will find a way to live together once again.

Cat Island, I forgive you, but I can never forget what happened. How will you treat me if we get back together? Will you help me find peace again if I come back to you? You make me cry just thinking that I've been away from you for years.

I'm going to find my way back to you, somehow, and someday soon. I need you to know that I am still so sad and may be for the rest of my life, but I'm going to give you another chance.

Cat Island, I'm coming home one day soon.

When I read it now, I am proud of how far I have come. I will always love Cat Island with the beautiful memories it created to shape my childhood. I swiped this letter on my phone during one of my stints in the ICU.

I do reminisce about all the wonderful times I had on Cat Island, but I can't change the past. There are moments that I think about my beautifully capable body, but I would not be where I am today on a singular, purpose-driven mission to help others if my life had not changed. My accident, along with a million other events over the last decade and a half, shaped who I am today.

Still, if I had a fairy godmother, I would wish not to be paralyzed. Of course, we can't change the past, but if I lived in an alternative universe, I would choose my former life.

CHAPTER 33

A Brand-New Life

WHEN MY HUSBAND LOST his job during the COVID time, I remember my brother-in-law having a conversation with him about finding a career counselor. Sadly, he did not take him up on that suggestion in a meaningful way, but I did. My life was still segmented with my professional life in one direction and my advocacy life in another. Many people like to have separation of their work and personal lives, but I wanted to intertwine the two. I didn't have a clue where to begin.

I worked for months with this incredible career counselor who has a daughter who was injured in an accident and became a wheelchair user. We were kindred spirits. She made really interesting career suggestions that offered me ideas. We think with ideas and not information, after all. This is another key concept my dad instilled in me as a child.

I revamped my resume, created a website, and outlined a career business plan for myself. I embarked on a professional quest around the globe, Zooming with

CEOs, corporate leaders, consultants, advocates, and other folks in the business world who centered their work around inclusion. I did not have a specific focus on disability inclusion yet, but inclusion in general.

I read thousands of pages and studied reports. I took many color-coded notes, researched, internalized, and put this knowledge to use. In hindsight, I think I probably should have received a master's degree for all this work as I soaked up so much information.

This was happening after George Floyd when the whole Diversity, Equity, and Inclusion (DEI) movement really started to grow some professional legs. The challenge with the DEI movement is that I think what underpins the D and E is the I—inclusion. Taking that a step further, I believe belonging leads people to an increase in cognitive diversity (diversity of thought), which results in many organizations experiencing higher profits, better corporate culture, and happier, more loyal employees.

As I was building up a global network of allies, I was simultaneously applying to corporate day jobs in the DEI space. Rejection. Rejection. Rejection. After about the tenth rejection, I started to notice a pattern. Initially, I thought I was rejected because I didn't have the corporate experience—even though I thought I was highly qualified—or have a fancy postgraduate degree behind my name. This may have been the case, but the rejections came after I talked to HR departments about my accessibility needs.

Approximately one in four people (one billion people) globally identify as having a disability with about 80 percent of these disabilities not visible. This can include people who are neurodiverse, have chronic ailments, or mental health issues. I am one of the 20 percent who has a visible disability. I cannot hide mine. I have to disclose my disability because I have specific technological access needs and physical accessibility requirements. I was completely open with the HR teams, but they didn't know how to ask the right questions. I could tell they were plainly embarrassed when they stumbled over their words. They did not take the time to understand my needs. So, rejections. So many of them.

I was quite disheartened, but I bounced back quickly. I may be paralyzed now, but I was labeled the "Bounciest" in high school for a reason. It's really hard to keep up with me. "No" is usually a starting negotiation point for me, and I will just keep at it until I ask the right question and then find the right solution.

In an interesting turn of events, I started receiving phone calls as the months rolled on from businesses around the globe offering me consulting positions on inclusion initiatives. I became a disability strategy consultant.

Today I operate in a global community for a beautiful disability-inclusive research firm, work with Employee Resource Groups to consult them on different inclusion initiatives to move the dial forward within their organization, and with organizations on disability inclusive hiring practices. I also consult with multibillion-dollar health care organizations, trying to improve patient advocacy for their products and services.

I am with some of my clients regularly year-round while others are on a project basis. It's the nature of being a consultant. You are always hustling, but I do find if you have an excellent work product, great interpersonal skills, and work your butt off, life has a way of handing you really interesting opportunities.

It was during this time that I realized public speaking is one of my favorite things to do. I've never been shy, and I do love to talk, but I didn't realize for quite some time that it could become a professional business.

I was also partnering on incredible legislative initiatives for healthcare equity on Capitol Hill, working on reforming airline travel for wheelchair users, speaking around the country, joining nonprofit boards in my spare time, and mentoring young women in wheelchairs, which keeps me humble. I firmly believe in dedicating 20 percent of my work week pro bono for different advocacy initiatives. There is so much work to be done.

My professional life was soaring, but my personal life crumbled around me.

CHAPTER 34

Marriage Comes to an End

DEREK AND I HAD been on the fence for a while. I felt like we were strangers passing each other while trying to catch a connecting flight. We didn't really talk anymore. I convinced him to give marriage counseling a try, but we didn't do the homework together. Well, that's not entirely true. I did try, but he seemed uninterested. I can't speak as to what was going on in his mind. I think when a couple splits, unless it's something incredibly traumatic such as physical abuse or extreme mental trauma, it always takes two to tango. Always.

I knew in the summer of 2022 things were over. I think that's why I put so much stock, effort, and time into my other life and professional ambitions. I was tired in my personal life. I didn't want to fight anymore. I just became numb. I was almost living in a state of indifference again. I think this is the most dangerous state of mind. I had lived in this state of indifference for four years after my accident.

Our relationship ended in the winter of 2022. He moved out, we didn't talk much, we did not reconcile, and

I decided to file for divorce. I know I broke his heart, and he told me as much. I decided to take on the role of the bad guy. I think he needed to hate me or be sad or grieve in whatever way worked for him.

The divorce was a smooth process for me because we did not have children, nor did we share any assets together. Filing for divorce simply involved filling out a few papers, getting them notarized, and showing up for my day in court. He did not want to accompany me to the courthouse, not wholly surprising, really.

I think we spoke maybe two or three times over the course of that year. He was devastated and said some pretty awful things when he left, but I know he was just hurt. I don't think either of us intentionally set out to hurt the other, but we were both hurt, and we simply couldn't find our way back to each other. I guess you could say we had a COVID divorce, as did many others.

I do take responsibility for the ending of our marriage in that I probably should not have married him. I only discovered this through intensive therapy. I stayed in the relationship too long out of loyalty. He was there in the beginning during some of my most tumultuous medical challenges, didn't see my disability, and was totally devoted to me. One would think this would be enough to stay in a marriage, but, fundamentally, I don't think we had the same values or belief systems. We certainly did not have those longer-term conversations about what we wanted our life together to look like. Not a great recipe for a successful marriage.

With two parties involved, there are two points of view, two perspectives, and two interpretations of the same reality. I'm sure if you ask him why we divorced, I could garner a pretty accurate guess as to his thoughts, and I would understand his viewpoint. I'm not entirely sure he would see mine. At the time of this writing, I have heard he is engaged to be married. I wish him much happiness. I always have and always will wish him the best. He is fundamentally a great human being.

As for me? I don't know what the future holds with respect to life partners or marriage or anything else. Of course, I think many of us want to have the connection of a life partner, but that takes so many different shapes, depending on what we want in our lives. A life partner can be a best friend. I was seen to go against the grain of societal norms despite trying to fit in over the decades, but not anymore. I've read countless papers and books on women approaching their midlife. Many of us apparently throw the societal playbook out the door and focus on what we want, not what our community or country or society calls for. It's very liberating, slightly terrifying, but wonderfully authentic.

You know by now that I always try to find something funny or comically disturbing when things don't go my way. I suppose it helps me find meaning in the midst of a psychological hurricane, but the comical circus on the day of my divorce in the courthouse is worth noting.

My sister and a dear family friend accompanied me to the courthouse. I thought we were going to see a judge one-on-one. I had no idea how the divorce court worked, only what I'd seen on television. About thirty couples were packed into one courtroom. We all had our filed and stamped paperwork ready to hand to the clerk when it was our turn. Each had to explain to the judge why they wanted a divorce, swear that their separation date was accurate, and, bam, they were divorced.

About a third of the couples messed up the date they were separated. The one piece of advice I received from someone who had been through the divorce process was don't mess up this separation date. You have to be separated legally for at least one year in North Carolina before the state will grant your divorce.

One gentleman stood up and read this really heartfelt love letter to his soon-to-be ex-wife, begging for her to come home. She did not blink. She did not falter. She did not smile. She said no. I felt a little sorry for the gentleman, but at the same time I couldn't help but giggle inside because I was thinking *Dude, seriously? You're professing your love in a divorce court in the County Clerk's office? Maybe you should have tried this before you actually went to court.* The woman had such a stone-cold look she would have given Medusa a run for her money.

Then there was a tiny, fierce woman wearing a purple wig who did not want a divorce. Her husband, a big burly guy, wanted a divorce. The judge asked when the last time was they had marital relations, to which she replied, "Last week." The husband laughed and called her a series of names, looked at the judge and said, "No, sir. No. Not me. I was in jail last week."

Seriously, not making this stuff up. She then proceeded to tell the judge how they had sex, what sexual positions, and how nasty he had been in bed with her. The judge stopped them both in their tracks. He could spot a bullshitter a mile away, I'm sure. He did not grant the divorce and asked them both to leave. The moment they both left the courtroom, the judge asked a police officer who was present to please go break up the fight that was surely going to ensue. That judge was good. That's exactly what happened.

The judge put his face in his hands and started laughing. He apologized to the courtroom but told us that in his thirty years of being in divorce court he had never seen a display like that. So, apparently this was not commonplace, but of course I picked the day where the monkeys escaped from the zoo. Everyone laughed as they awaited their turn on the chopping block with the judge.

When this happened, I was still not divorced. I felt like I was in a comedy show. I was laughing, my sister was in disbelief, and our German friend could only make out half of what was being said in English. Finally, it was my turn. It took all of five minutes to grant my divorce. I answered all the questions appropriately, I didn't stutter, I was to the point, and just like that, seven years of my personal life ended with a simple stamp on a piece of paper.

I think I had already processed the end of the marriage a year or two earlier, as I didn't have much of a reaction the day of the divorce. I do have the most amazing therapist. She helped me during the most challenging times when I didn't think I would have the willpower to leave the marriage. But I did. I learned from it. I grew from it. I was ready to start a new chapter in my personal life. I just didn't know yet what that might look like.

Several months earlier I was at the Dueling Piano Bar in Raleigh while some women were having a divorce party. I thought this was delightful. I joined in their fun, telling them that I was just a few months away from my divorce.

My mother threw me a surprise divorce party with my local Raleigh friends. It was so twisted, and I loved it as it reminded me of our sexy ICU photoshoot years earlier. I wore a crown with a sash, got tipsy, recorded a dance party in my bathroom with some friends, and posted it on Instagram as a divorce party dance party. I have that little post for the memory bank for sure.

CHAPTER 35

Midlife Crisis

PEOPLE HANDLE DIVORCE IN so many ways. I didn't really think about it at the time, but I believe I was going through a midlife crisis. I was now forty years old, a quadriplegic, and divorced. This was not exactly in my life plan, and, to top it off, I am the only one in my family to be divorced. There are times in life I wish I did not always have to push the envelope. I didn't really feel like an awesome winner, but I had to keep moving forward.

Looking back now. I think I handled my midlife crisis pretty damn well. I decided to take an all-women's pilgrimage trip to Costa Rica for nearly a month, get a few tattoos I had planned for the last several years, and add a new career direction to my repertoire.

I spent months meticulously planning the perfect trip to Costa Rica with my mother, caregiver, sister-in-law, and two close friends. It was a big trip and an expensive one, but it was worth every penny. Let's call this adventure Costa Rica Accessible.

We hired an accessible van with a driver to drive

us around while we were there. It's worth mentioning that many roads in Costa Rica are not fully paved, have treacherous potholes, and get quite muddy when it rains.

The Costa Rican jungle roads are precisely what you see in the movies. There are no guard rails, which can be unnerving, as you can see hundreds of feet down off the side of a mountain while turning a dangerous curve. I had a blast bouncing around. I was a little surprised but very grateful that my body allowed me to have my butt kicked around as much as it did on this trip.

We went zip lining deep in the jungle, where I was carried up the mountain by lovely Costa Rican men and transferred to eleven different zip lines hundreds of feet above the ground.

I even rediscovered scuba diving. I didn't think I would ever get back to the water as an adaptive diver, but I saw an option for this adventure, and I signed up. We woke up at five a.m. to drive two hours to this very remote beach on Costa Rica's west coast where we were greeted by the dive crew. I was lifted into a recycled manual wheelchair and rolled down the beach to a twenty-foot inboard engine boat. I wasn't sure where they were proposing I sit, but they lifted me, chair and all, and put me right in the middle of the boat.

I had learned to scuba dive when I was twelve and loved it, but I had not dived in years. Now I was going to do it again. Thankfully, I had already discovered that when you find a handful of really strong men, most things are accessible.

When we arrived at this gorgeous little beach cove, they pretty much threw me overboard into the water. I was rolled left and right to fit me with my buoyancy compensator, and I was given a five-minute speech on what to do and not to do.

I don't think that would fly in the US, but I was comfortable even though it had been quite a long time since I had dived. I'm very calm in the water, and I was paralyzed, so all I had to do was sit there. It didn't seem like a hard thing to do.

That moment though, oh God, wow, rolling face first into the water and submerging. Breathing into the regulator felt like second nature and off we went. The scuba site itself was not particularly beautiful and there were few reefs. The divers kept insisting it was the most gorgeous place in all of Costa Rica. I decided to let them hold onto that belief. I had been scuba diving around the world in places like Sharm el-Sheikh in Egypt, the great barrier reef, all of the Caribbean, in The Bahamas, and some of the Pacific Islands. My adventures have their own tales with the mischief I aroused, the boys I flirted with, exotic customs I engaged in, and sharks I dived with.

One reason I found scuba diving an incredible adventure is because it represented, and still represents, a place of peace and quiet with no one talking to me. All I can hear is the sound of my breathing. It's magical. Our forty-five-minute dive went by way too quickly. I was hooked. I knew this would not be my last scuba adventure, and it has not been.

The trip itself was exactly what I needed. I cleared my head, devised a new path forward as I meditated, and developed the confidence to be comfortable alone. I realized I didn't need a man, even if I would like one. I would like a partner, but he would really have to be the right fit. For way too long I felt grateful a man would want to be with me, but that was no longer true. I hoped to find a lifelong partner. There have been men, but when that right one really does come along, I'll know it because we will have built up a beautiful trust, communication strategy, and we will never forget to talk. That is my hope anyway!

The reality? As long as I have a strong community around me with a sense of purpose, I feel like that may be enough. It's important to note that while I do feel my life is enriched with respect to what I've created, life is by no means easy on a daily basis. It never again will be. I believe living a meaningful or fulfilling life broadly requires another beautiful expression my dad raised me with: "constancy to purpose." It's about putting consistent effort forth each day, toward what really matters to you, whatever it may be.

I always wanted to be "normal" growing up, to fit in, but it took me decades to realize, and as my dad says, that I march to the beat of my own drum. This, sometimes, can lead to being lonely and not quite fitting in with others. I'm finally okay with not fitting in. It only took me about forty years to get to that place, but I am there.

My life experiences have shaped who I am, where I'm going, and who I want to continue to be. I have many different groups of friends, colleagues, and professionals. Each of them offers something very special to me. Today, I focus more on being grateful for what is in my control.

As for men? Well, I decided to jump back on a few horses as they say. I didn't know where it would lead. I wasn't looking for anything serious right away. I just wanted to test the waters of online dating as a forty-year-old divorced quadriplegic.

I should note that the end of my Costa Rica trip set up the next year for my personal life. My tour guide and I had a brief romantic dalliance, giving me the confidence to get back out there. It was a great start after my marriage ended. There's nothing like a whirlwind romance in a tropical location to reignite your confidence.

Back in the Dating Game Again

As I DO WITH everything in my life, I researched carefully what was happening in online dating. There are times I am grateful for my research skills and others I wish I would have just jumped in—feet first, of course!

I spent weeks reading reviews on various online dating sites like Match, eHarmony, Plenty of Fish, Zoosk, and a bunch more. I wanted a dating site this time for grown-up men who were financially stable, funny, potentially interested in something more, and didn't have a lot of baggage. I also wanted a site that made you pay for access. If a man feels that paying a few hundred dollars a year to find a meaningful partner is too expensive, no thank you, please move on. At my age, financial stability from both sides is really important.

I signed up on two to begin with because my little paws get tired with swiping on my phone. Zoosk would be my lighthearted dating app and Match would be my more serious one. I was essentially recreating my online dating experiments from seven years ago, and I had no idea if I would be up for the challenge.

I spent a fair amount of time writing a three-thousand-character profile about who I am, what I stand for, what I love to do, my life philosophies, and a few other tidbits.

I made the profile lighthearted and quirky, but meaningful at the same time. I had some really great photos to add, some sexy, some serious, and some adventure. To my surprise, my inbox was immediately flooded.

This is the online dating profile I created:

> I grew up internationally, traveling the world with the most incredible family. My mom is German and my dad is American. I have always been full of life, energetic, adventurous, lived in China, Europe, and grew up on an out island in The Bahamas. I have been fortunate to experience so much in life. I moved to Raleigh, North Carolina, from China years ago and have built up an incredible life here.

WHAT WOULD MY FRIENDS SAY?

> Without a doubt they would say I am quirky, silly, thought-provoking, kind, empathetic, live in dark humor, love to make people smile and laugh, am a serious and curious thinker, and someone who is always willing to give the shirt off her back if it helps another human being.
>
> I am really one of those people who always finds the bright side of things, even in the darkest of

circumstances. I get that we all go through our challenges in life, but I think it's what you make of it once you get through a challenging time that really defines you as a human being.

Life really is about people for me and the connections you make. All the adventures will follow afterward. When you really find a person who gets you, you may or may not have all shared interests, but you learn to compromise with one another and find things you both enjoy doing.

PROFESSIONALLY

I am a disability strategy consultant for corporations, global keynote speaker, health equity advocate, and technical analysis day trader. I simply love to help other humans in life and center my career around this.

WHAT DO I LOVE TO DO?

I love people. I work hard but love to go on adventures and travel and meet great people. I love to go out socially on the weekends, grab some drinks, go dancing, or snuggle up for a great movie night equally. I'm incredibly passionate about all kinds of accessible travel adventures such as surfing, swimming, wake boarding, scuba diving, ziplining, etc.

I love talking about pretty much everything on the planet. I'm insatiably curious. I may not share your personal views, but I will always listen, and I really pride myself on seeing different perspectives.

WHEELCHAIR STORY

Let's get all the elephants out in the room. :-) When I was 27 and living at my home in The Bahamas, I took a shallow water dive, breaking my neck, leaving me a C6 quadriplegic (basically paralyzed from the boobs down, paralyzed hands, but upper body mobility is great). I exercise all the time, eat healthy, and stay in great shape for being in wheelchair.

My personality has quite literally never changed, but I just have to live my life in an adapted way.

I joke that a lot of people have their disability on the inside, but I just happen to have mine on the outside.

Okay I'll get some big questions out of the way that I get all the time. Yes, I can have sex. Anything about my disability is completely an open topic, and I'm a very open book. I am so open that my whole life is probably online.

I will always give you an honest answer if you just ask. Don't be shy. I'm not!

YES PLEASE

- Eventually want to find my person. Nothing starts out serious and is always casual.

  That's called dating. Looking for the intention of long-term, let's just have some fun first to get to know each other.

- Intellectual, curious, really funny, open-minded, thought-provoking, silly, sensual, fantastic kisser.

NO THANKS

- Only looking for sex—been there done that too many times. I love sex like the next person but don't want everything to be centered around it. Intimacy is different.

- Not adventurous, not open to new ways of thinking, too serious all the time (life is way too short not to laugh every day)

- Does not have a strong command of the English language (don't start out by saying what's up, whazz up, hey — I'm probably not your girl).

- Being evasive. Just say what you're thinking.

I was like a kid in a candy store. I viewed online dating just as I do trading futures. It's a numbers game. If a hundred men reach out to me, I would look for a 30 percent return on my investment with respect to dates or something further. The other 70 percent, just the cost of doing business. I wouldn't get caught up on one guy and kept multiple gentleman callers flowing. I became adept at sexy texting, spent hours on the phone way too late at night, and really felt in my element. I thought it was fun. I didn't have any expectations.

There were of course the weird trolls who just wanted to have sex with me in my wheelchair or on my wheelchair. Clearly, they did not read my profile! After one conversation it became quite evident which guys approached me because of my pictures versus reading my entire profile.

Men were curious because they had never come across someone quite like me. I went on lots of dates ending with a goodnight kiss, but not as much attraction on my side. Kissing is terribly important to me. I don't have a lot of deal breakers, but being a bad kisser is definitely one of them. I also had and have a policy of not spending more than a few days on the phone without meeting in person. I didn't want to waste my time, because when I meet someone in person, physical attraction can change in an instant.

I had one gentleman caller who would come over on random nights of the week and stay for hours. Then I would kick him out. He didn't seem to have any problem with this. I think I might have been his dream girl because I wanted no commitment from him.

I had another older and very sexy gentleman who

would drive down from DC on the weekends to visit me. Aside from his age, he was a pretty great fit. He was cultured, traveled, well read, enjoyed talking about philosophy, and was a tiger in bed. He wanted me to make a commitment though. I wasn't quite ready for that, but I did enjoy his company.

There were a few highly comical moments, one being when he rubbed my body with coconut oil, not really thinking about the aftermath for cleaning up as a quadriplegic. My caregiver walked in and just looked at me in disbelief. I was in disbelief too. She said, "Ah, um, right. I'm not really sure where we should start." I didn't know either.

So, I sent DC coconut guy out to get sushi while my caregiver and I figured out how to get slippery coconut oil off me as I was sliding all over the bed. We had a great laugh. I will always be thankful for the memories, but I couldn't commit to someone who was more than twenty years older than I was.

To my surprise and enduring delight, a real gentleman entered my life and, as of now when I am writing this book, he is still with me. It's been over a year. I hope things will work out. You never know where life will take you, but, even as a forty-year-old single quadriplegic woman, I think I've still got it!

Dating is a mindset just as with anything else. I do choose not to put my hopes and dreams on another person because those are really my own responsibility. I am happy with where my life is right now. I am living more than I lived in the previous fifteen years. Recently, I was chatting with my niece, who is in her early twenties, and we were recounting very funny boy stories together. She said to me, "Auntie Ali, I want to be living like you when I'm in my forties." Talk about making my heart melt.

Now, I'm sure she was talking about my naughty activities, but still, I like to think it is my philosophy in life she wants to embrace. She's pretty much my mini me and living the life I lived decades ago. I told her she can copycat everything except breaking her neck. That will not fly in my book!

CHAPTER 36

Adding a Third Career

I HAD BEEN SPEAKING around the country since 2018 on a variety of topics including inclusion, belonging, health equity, how to overcome obstacles, and coping with uncertainty. But it wasn't until 2020 that I discovered speaking is my passion and fulfills an enduring purpose in my life of helping others on a much larger scale.

Frankly, I hadn't realized you could get paid to be a professional speaker. A few years ago, I began to be invited to speak at events where meeting planners inquired about my fees. A very rational inquiry, but not anything that had occurred to me before.

I spoke professionally for about eighteen months with paid engagements before I realized I did not have a business surrounding this. I almost headed to the corporate world for health insurance reasons but soon realized this would not make me happy. I don't think I particularly excel when I am trapped in a box with a lot of red tape.

So, I joined the National Speakers Association and my local chapter in North Carolina. I have attended their yearly conferences, local events, and made friends with speakers just starting out as well as well-established global veteran keynote speakers. Whenever I meet someone for the first time, I ask questions. I listen to their stories, and I always learn something new. This is one of my classic Ali characteristics. You might hear me say, "It's great to meet you. I don't have a purpose for this call other than getting to know you as a person. I love to meet people, so tell me about yourself."

I don't know why this works so well, but perhaps it's because when we get on a work call with people, we often immediately dive into our history of work, not our stories of life. This is what matters to me personally. As a result, I've gotten to know so many incredible people in my life and built lasting friendships. I always tell everyone my "Rolodex" of contacts is open to them. I am more than happy to make an introduction, but what they make of the next steps in a new potential relationship is up to them.

It soon became clear to me that if I wanted to add yet another career to my life and shift gears slightly, I was going to have to be pragmatic, systematic, and focused. I hired one of my mentors as a professional speaker coach, created a professionally designed website, paid exorbitant amounts of money for speaker demo reel videos, backend business processes, speaker packets, and more. Truthfully, I've been adopted by so many incredible mentors who've encouraged me to speak more often.

As with any entrepreneurial endeavor, professional speaking takes commitment, time, money, and direction. It's no different from a baker taking out a loan from a bank to open a brick-and-mortar store than it has been for me to take a loan to make this business thrive.

The ability to reinvent ourselves at any age, if we choose, always astonishes me. The trick is figuring out how to live and even thrive with uncertainty, and, for better or worse, I have plenty of experience with this! Sometimes I focus keynote speeches on this topic, whether that be reinvention in your personal life or professional life.

TEDx and Beyond

ONE DAY IN JANUARY 2024, a professional speaker mentor emailed me a TEDx application. The topic centered around "The Next Chapter in Life." He encouraged me to apply and, truthfully, I didn't think I had the proverbial snowball's chance in hell of being accepted. I believed I needed to be much farther along in life or in my professional speaking career. I was playing the classic game in my head just making up excuses and not taking action.

I later learned that some people spend thousands of dollars on TEDx coaches, apply to dozens of locations, and keep trying for years until they are accepted. I was fortunate. I applied just once, and I was accepted.

Just like that. And I already knew exactly what I wanted to say. My speaker coach helped me condense all I wanted to say into the allowed eighteen-minute TEDx speech format.

I shared my personal story and my principles on responsibility, success, and happiness. I really love the section on being "happy enough." Every time we search for happiness, it seems to make us more miserable. I have designed an entire philosophy on this that I incorporate in workshops. More on this in my next book with science to back it up.

The most difficult thing about preparing for TEDx was making sure I kept the message under the allowed 18 minutes without speaking a hundred miles a minute like a teenager. I practiced. A lot. My caregivers even joked with me that, if I happen to pass out on stage with low blood pressure, they knew my speech well enough that they could take over. I practiced 241 times out loud to myself. I practiced while taking a shower, exercising, in front of my desk, in my head, and even at my condo pool, where I pretended the trees were my audience.

I've always had to work hard for everything. When I arrived at the location hosting the TEDx event, there were many wonderful speakers there, but I was in game mode. I didn't have time to socialize. I had to focus on the task at hand. Many of the speakers have since become friends, but I definitely did not engage in the social dinners offered at the event. Also, it took me hours to get ready compared to my able-bodied counterparts, so I needed the extra time to myself.

I was scheduled as the first up speaker. As I was introduced, I rolled right onto that little red circle, which by the way is incredibly challenging to stay inside of when you're in a wheelchair. Game time!

I was delivering my speech flawlessly when I forgot where I was about seven minutes in. Suddenly, my train of thought had just vanished. Thankfully, I am quite quick on my proverbial feet, so I just kept talking. Within about thirty seconds I was back on track. When I reviewed the video after the event, I would say you would not have been able to tell what had happened unless you knew the speech.

The biggest challenge I had was dry mouth. The medication I take for my regular muscle spasms gives me terrible dry mouth. I researched feverishly to find mints that prevent dry mouth for an extended period of time. I used little throat lozenges that I found. In the TEDx video, you could definitely see that I was tossing this little mint back and forth in my mouth. After about fifteen minutes, I simply needed water. However, it doesn't look brilliant in the middle of your TEDx speech to stop for water. It's the scenario of "suck it up, buttercup" for 18 minutes (or less).

I think I hit a homerun, and I'm really proud of what I accomplished. We all need to stop and appreciate the small and big wins in life. I completed the entire speech without a sip of water. That was truly success in and of itself.

I was building a professional keynote speaking business from the ground up. I learned from many of my mentors that it's important to have a TEDx under your belt and to write a book. This unexpected TEDx opportunity opened up countless doors for me in the speaking world. I've heard friends who have also completed a TEDx event report that the experience went nowhere for them and others who said it launched their career into the stratosphere.

Truth be told, what really put fire under my paralyzed butt to write this book was completing this TEDx. For the really high-end speaking engagements, many meeting planners simply require a potential speaker to have a book. It's kind of like when you are in the corporate world and you need an MBA or twenty years of corporate experience.

I had believed I was years behind being able to make writing a book possible.

Inaction seems to breed inaction and that seldom, if ever, results in success. I had thought I wasted seven years of my life in hospitals, but now I can see that I was just gathering powerful stories along the way to share with the world later in life. It took me a while to realize this. I started writing this book, submitted it to a publisher, and my manuscript was accepted.

Meanwhile, I'm no stranger to rejection. I play a dangerous game with rejection. When I get "rejected" medically, it usually ends up with me coding or enjoying another long ICU holiday in the hospital. That's not going to happen if I crash with a book or a speech or other (reasonable) actions, and who knows, I might, just might, succeed! I believe I succeeded with my TEDx talk. We'll see how the book fares.

It should be clear by now that I love to learn and that I am committed to action. I embrace the concept that failure is simply a learning experience. Every time something does not go my way, my next action is to figure out how to move forward.

Winston Churchill once cracked that "Success is going from failure to failure without losing your enthusiasm."

I wake up each and every morning and recite this quote to myself. I double-dog dare you to name one person in life who has succeeded without a misstep or two, or even more. Leaving aside that there were many other parties involved for the invention of the light bulb, it's estimated it took more than a thousand tries for Thomas Edison to find a workable filament for this creation.

CHAPTER 37

Moments of Adventure

WHAT KEEPS ME GOING as I work long hours toward a mission is adding fun to my life. I have to say, if there is one thing I'm really good at, it's rocking out life like it's 1999. Seriously!

Whether I'm in the ICU engaging in a sexy photo shoot with my mother's help, swinging from the trees on a zipline in a rain forest, or visiting a Mayan temple, there is one thing for sure. I will be having a blast in the moment. That's just it. How can we make the best moments?

I returned to Costa Rica for a second year with family and friends. We went white water rafting, ziplining, and, equally as satisfying, meditated by a pool overlooking a volcano. I had never been white water rafting before and while the rapids were seasonally low, it was quite a logistical mission to try to wedge my paralyzed booty into a boat.

I had multiple men from the rafting company carry me down about five hundred feet to the boat where I was flopping all around while we tried to figure out how to tie me down safely. It took us about fifteen minutes, but I was as snug as a bug in a rug when we hit those rapids. I could tell everyone else was a little bit nervous as they had no idea what would happen if I tipped out of the boat. I didn't know either. I couldn't think of a contingency plan for that one. Thankfully these were only Class I and maybe baby Class II rapids, but be assured, I will be attempting a more rigorous class of rapids now that I understand how my body mechanics work in a rafting boat.

I mentioned I would go scuba diving again, and I did. I found the most incredible accessible dive company in the Fort Lauderdale area. They took me scuba diving, and then they agreed to try something they had never done before. They had never taken a C6 quadriplegic on a tiny Gilligan's Island boat into the deep blue sea to go on a shark feed dive.

They lifted me in a PVC chair into the boat and strapped my arms and legs down so I did not fly out of the boat. This was not an accessible boat. When we arrived at our destination, four strong men lifted me with a hoist into the water to put on my buoyancy compensator and scuba equipment. Then we descended into the deep blue ocean.

This time there were no reefs; it was just blue ocean left, right, and down about eighty feet. As we descended, I felt only peace and tranquility. One of the dive folks on the boat brought out a big square chum cage with dead fish to attract the sharks. People think I've lost my marbles when I tell them the story, but trust me when I tell you that it's much more dangerous to be in the ICU than scuba diving with sharks.

One after another, mostly lemon sharks plus a few

black tips, started piling around the food cage filled with dead fish. Before I knew it, we were surrounded by a dozen sharks, who were getting very friendly with all of us. I was head butted by a few, and the divers around me were trying to protect the quadriplegic. I was in heaven. I felt more at home in the water with sharks than I feel on land.

There was a delicate Mozart No. 5 violin concerto playing in my head. I could've died that day, truly, and felt proud of my accomplishments and happy with the non-medical adventures I've been lucky enough to experience.

CHAPTER 38

A Different Kind of Daily Adventure

Not all my adventures end with experiences most would consider enjoyable. Many of my adventures are medical in nature, and I would wager many of you will find what I'm about to write, well, different. To which I would reply: it's an authentic part of my daily life.

When I returned to the United States in 2016, I started a personal blog called the "Quirky Quad" to normalize highly uncomfortable topics in disability and society, sometimes using dark humor.

In this blog, I write on health insurance battles, dressing, caregiving, my sex life, chronic pain, adventures, the sky is the limit. There really is no topic off limits for me. I even started a YouTube channel with this name. For example, one video is about how to have sex safely if you are a wheelchair user. In the video, I'm dressed on the bed with multiple caregivers in attendance. I am being filmed while they are flipping me around in all kinds of positions to demonstrate what I am saying. There were lots of laughs, but it's a very practical video and a very real topic.

It's incredible to me that it's not PC to talk about bowel or bladder or sex or religion or politics in mainstream conversations. Want to talk about taboo topics? Then I'm your girl!

I've actually had thousands of people reach out to thank me for my authenticity when I was just trying to address things that I know others feel really uncomfortable with. You will find all kinds of outrageous, insightful, and hopefully funny articles on the Quirky Quad and my YouTube channel. This is not gratuitous fluff, it's the real stuff.

Bladder & Bowel—Oh My!

MANY PEOPLE HAVE A general idea that folks in wheelchairs do not have full control of their bowel or bladder. I'm not going to get into the science behind all of the reasons why this is, because you can Google that, but I will simply say I don't have control of how I go to the bathroom.

I have something called a suprapubic catheter, which is a small tube that goes into my bladder, then goes down my leg where it is connected to a leg bag, and voilà, I pee into this little bag. A caregiver then puts a little cup under this pulldown valve, and there you go. I love my catheter and have named him Petey. Actually, my sister named it. After my surgery, she told me it looks like a penis and I'm like a hermaphrodite. True story.

I designed my own custom system so that I can close off the catheter to allow my bladder to fill instead of continually draining. When I have to pee, I get these little goosebumps because my autonomic nervous system tells me something is wrong. My blood pressure rises, and I need to do something about it. It is then that the catheter gets opened. Okay, that covers Petey.

As for how I poop. Everyone has their own system, and no two wheelchair users' systems are exactly alike. We may have a similar routine, but we each have our own life hacks. I cannot feel when I have to poop and early on after my injury I was pooping all over myself. My body was still trying to adjust. It took a few years, but I successfully created my own "bowel program" where I trained my body to poop in the morning with liquid suppositories that are inserted into my butt. I wait about fifteen minutes, poop comes out, then caregivers go in with a glove to get out the rest. Medically, this is called digital stimulation. I have since named it "scooping" because I think it sounds more fun.

We have fun in my house with poop conversations. I mean if you can't laugh about it . . . .

Typically, things go pretty smoothly in my bowel program, but occasionally I have diarrhea or a stomach bug or whatever. Able-bodied people can run to the bathroom, I cannot. What does this mean? I poop on myself. Yes, like a baby. There are many dark humor similarities between quadriplegics and babies and elderly folks. In any event, it's usually when I'm in bed at night time. I do have these disposable under pads I sleep on to make sure I don't get any wrinkles on my butt because of my skin issues, but they also serve a secondary purpose in case I have any bowel issues. The pad can be changed and the sheet is fine. Bowel accidents just suck, but they happen. I can't be embarrassed about them anymore.

This chapter was inspired by something that happened recently. I had not had a bowel accident in months, and I was pretty pleased about that. I go through good phases and bad phases. My diet or drinking or different foods also affect this. This is why I eat extremely clean, like a peckish bird actually, and exercise a lot. Consistency is key as a quadriplegic to reduce bowel and bladder hell.

Well, I was starting to get a little bit cocky. Oh yes. Every time I think I have something figured out, BAM! Life has this really twisted way of humbling me. I had a bowel accident.

I called my caregiver, and we were joking around about poop while she was cleaning me up, and then she stuck her finger in my butt and had the funniest thing to say that made the two of us laugh out loud. She said, "You know, Ali, while my finger is in your butt, it's really warm. I had not thought about it before. It's quite pleasant." We laughed so hard we were crying. It was eleven p.m. and we were both tired, but we were making the best of a shitty situation—pun intended!

Once everything was cleaned up, the adventure didn't stop there. At nighttime I use a larger catheter bag so I don't have to wake up in the middle of the night to pee. That night something on the tube broke. When my caregiver rolled me over, my entire bed was covered in pee. I have to say I pee on more people than you could possibly imagine. When they empty the catheter bag on my leg, they sometimes forget to close the clip. That means pee will flow out. If I pee on you, then it likely means I'm quite comfortable with you. If you can take it with grace, then we're likely going to be friends for some time to come.

Well, we got that all cleaned up, changed the sheet, and it was now nearly midnight. We still had smiles on our face. Then my stoma (hole) for the catheter that is inserted into my bladder started to bleed. It's not as dangerous as it sounds. It happens because there are dozens of tiny blood vessels in your bladder that don't really like to have a catheter in there because it's a foreign object, so it is always trying to push the catheter out.

About an hour later, that was all taken care of because this particular caregiver is a rock star and superfast. We gave each other a hug and went to bed. My body was in screaming chronic pain, but I was disturbingly happy. I just have to consistently remind myself that my body (actually my mind) really does give me 85 percent of what I need on a daily basis, and I have to be humble to give her (my body) what she needs the rest of the time. She may need to go to the bathroom, she may need to lie down, she may need a timeout day.

The point is that it's all about how you look at a situation. It's about perspective. It's about thinking about those ten things that happen in a day and focusing on the eight good ones, not the two bad ones. This involves dozens of small mental exercises based on applied neuroscience to redirect, reimagine, and then reframe any situation in life. Even if I wanted to be cocky or have any ego, I'm sure my spinal cord injury would find a way to kick my butt even further down in my chair than I am now!

So, how one defines an adventure is entirely based on your perception of life. Even a lousy situation can be a humorous adventure if you choose to look at it that way. I'm not sure what else I could say on that particular topic!

CHAPTER 39

The Art of Being
Responsibly Irresponsible

I'VE OFTEN BEEN ASKED in my life why I engage in so many risky adventures like moving halfway across the world for exotic surgery.

It's a great question, and the answer encompasses my basic philosophy of doing things for the story that later grew into living my story. However, as with every story there are plot twists and turns and, for me, an important caveat.

I live my life by being responsibly irresponsible. I'm a big researcher for pretty much everything, but after I conclude my research, I try to just go with the flow. I research the consequences of my actions if I take on any semi-extreme activity, and I weigh the pros and cons of proceeding. If I'm not willing to take the risk, then the idea dies right there.

For example, I had the opportunity to go horseback riding in Costa Rica. When I studied the saddle, I realized it was for someone paralyzed from the waist down, not chest down. I looked at the terrain and the weather. I assessed that I would likely fall off the horse, resulting in many broken bones, and keeping in mind my sensitive skin, I decided not to go.

I did the same with white water rafting. I assessed the bounce of the boat, the cushion, how they could wedge me into the boat, and the fact that it was only Class I-II rapids. I accepted the risk and went white water rafting. I also researched the medical system in Costa Rica and figured if something did happen, they have a pretty good medical system down there.

All this to say, with every decision I make, first I assess risk. My father taught me this at a very young age. Every day I try to actively live my story to its fullest while also working to ensure I live to add more to it another day. This philosophy sounds quite simple, but it's much more nuanced than first meets the eye.

I live each day as if I will not have tomorrow, because there have been so many close calls for me. I have an ingrained adventurous spirit, but I do assess risk as critically as possible. If I choose to accept the consequences after my research concludes, then any harm that may come to me is my responsibility.

We are often so quick to judge other people because others do not necessarily make the choices we make. I find people project their own fears onto those who want to try something that may not necessarily be socially accepted. What a different world we might live in if we switched consciousnesses for a day or a week with a person in another walk of life. Talk about a lesson in world empathy!

In any event, this is how I live my life. Others may

find great joy in a cooking class or a walk in the park. I like extreme adventures that are semi-accessible when opportunities present themselves.

After living in the hospital for years on end, I have decided I will not do that again. I will take every opportunity to do something interesting to me when I find it. And I feel incredibly grateful there are people who will take on these adventures with me.

CHAPTER 40

An Active Legacy in the Making

WHEN I WAS YOUNGER, legacy was something old people talked about. I didn't think much about it. If I called you old back then, today I offer you a heartfelt apology.

Now, in what I like to call the spicy middle of life, the concept of legacy is no longer theoretical. It's real. It's immediate. It rides shotgun with me every day.

Maybe it's because I don't have children. That's a choice I made, and I have zero regrets. I live a rich, messy, beautiful life, full of purpose and with some very unconventional twists. But I do often wonder what I'll leave behind. What will stick? What will echo?

If I'm lucky, someone, somewhere, will remember something I said on a stage or that I wrote in a post or shared in this very book and pass it along, maybe in a conversation with a friend, maybe in a bedtime story to their kid, or maybe in how they choose to live differently.

Legacy used to sound to me like marble statues and fancy awards. Now, I think it's something much quieter and more beautiful. And being a quadriplegic? Well, it comes with a daily reminder that life is fragile. And that I'm still here. That I get to keep showing up. And that matters.

In my mind, a legacy is a laugh that lives on. A story that gets retold. A flashlight you leave behind for someone to pick up in the dark. It's the flavor you add to life's Big Pot of Soup. Yeah, let's talk soup for a second.

The soup metaphor is how I've come to understand legacy. We're all tossing in our own ingredients. Legacy is when you add flavor, your dash of smoked paprika, your whisper of cinnamon, your wildly unexpected splash of hot sauce—something that still shows up in taste memory long after you've stepped away from the stove. And yeah, sometimes you're the clump of undercooked quinoa. It happens. The point is, you fed the pot. You added something. You seasoned the world. That's legacy. And if yours is the unexpected swirl of smoked paprika or a surprise kick of cayenne? Even better.

We live these perfectly imperfect lives. We try things. We screw up. We love people. We hurt. We heal. We laugh inappropriately. We care more than we admit. And if we're paying attention, if we're curious, we learn as we go.

Curiosity has been my saving grace. It's the throughline of everything I've survived, everything I've taught, everything I've built. It's why I'm still here. I believe that we don't always need the answers, but we damn well need the questions. Openness. The willingness to lean in when life gets weird and ask, "Okay, what's here for me now?" Curiosity is the antidote to despair. It's the spark that keeps us moving forward. It turns pain into progress, fear into action, and confusion into connection.

And that brings me back to stories. Because ultimately, this book is a story. My story. And stories matter.

We've been telling stories for thousands of years, long before books, before podcasts, before TikToks and TED Talks. Stories are how we make sense of chaos. They connect us. They teach us. They remind us we're not alone in the chaos of being human.

So, if you've made it this far in my book, congratulations—and truly, thank you. Thank you for holding space for this wildly weird and true narrative of mine. If I made you laugh (or snort), if I nudged your thinking or raised your eyebrow, if I offered you comfort or even just entertained you at the end of a long day, then I'm delighted.

My life has never been what most people would call typical or perhaps even advisable. But it's been meaningful. It's been mine. And if there's a legacy in it, I hope it's this. Live fully. Stay curious. Be kind. Tell your stories. And don't forget to feed the soup.

This is my story. So far. And I'm not done yet!

ALI'S MEDICAL NOTES

Quick Spinal Cord Injury Lesson[i]—p122

HERE'S A CRASH COURSE in spinal cord anatomy served up with just enough simplicity that you won't need a med school degree to follow along. I didn't know any of this before I broke my neck, and, trust me, it would've been nice to have had a cheat sheet. So here's yours.

Your vertebrae begin at your brainstem and then work their way down to your tailbone. You have different sections of your vertebrae, such as the cervical (top), the thoracic, the lumbar, and, finally, sacral (bottom) section.

If you are paralyzed on any of the cervical vertebrae of which there are six (C1 to C6) then you are probably going to present as a quadriplegic. What actually makes you paralyzed is not breaking your vertebrae at all. You can break all of your vertebrae and walk away.

What causes paralysis is damage to the nerve bundles that make up the actual spinal cord inside the vertebrae. The vertebrae just protect the nerve bundles. I'm simplifying all of this, of course, but I want you to have a very broad idea since it's important for what happened in my life over the several months after my accident.

The nerve bundles in your spinal cord can suffer and die from local bruising that starves them of blood flow. Think of a bruise on your arm. When you first hit your arm, you may just see a red welt, but then over the next several days the bruise will spread out and turn green, then blue, then it will heal. The problem with a bruise around your spinal cord is that if the bruise ascends to your brainstem, it will kill you immediately, so your body has to protect itself some way to prevent that ascension.

The body's protection mechanism for the spinal cord is to stop that bruise in place. The result is life changing. Your body saves itself from loss of all critical functions causing death, but now you're stuck with this bruise held in place around your spine. This bruise blocks blood flow to sustain the nerves and interferes with the passage of nerve signals to and from your brain. This is what causes paralysis.

Let's just take this one step further. You may be looking at two individuals who break their neck at C6. One individual can move their toe or maybe stand up a little bit while simultaneously having paralyzed hands. This is called an incomplete injury. Another individual, like me, may have no sensation or movement below the level of injury. This is called a complete injury. A complete injury is when you bruise the spinal cord 360 degrees around and no nerve signals can pass through that bruise, up or down. This is the worst kind of injury. You simply will not know if you have a complete injury for months, even up to a year or more, after you have been injured, because your body is still trying to regenerate itself.

If, after one to two years, you do not regain any meaningful motor function recovery or sensory improvement during rehab, you are considered to have a complete spinal cord injury. This means you likely will be paralyzed the rest of your life unless there's some sort of miracle breakthrough in your body or in the treatment of spinal cord injuries.

If you have an incomplete injury and you start to regain some function like moving a toe after a C6 injury or having feeling in your leg or abdomen, this is great. This means the bruise in your spinal cord is actually filled with little holes. Think Swiss cheese. These holes are amazing because they allow signals to pass up and down from the brain to the rest of the body, which results in a higher chance of functional recovery over the years. This is the "good" kind of spinal cord injury, if there is such a thing.

The longer it takes for a person to get to surgery, the higher the chances of the injury being a complete one. Why? In a word, swelling. While the bruise will not ascend with the swelling, it does expand laterally, which can cause any "holes" passing signals through your spinal cord to basically close up.

You may have heard about football players who sustained a spinal cord injury but are walking a few months later. Well, they have had the best of the best initial treatment on the field, they get immediate steroids while they're on the field to reduce swelling and pain, get rushed to the hospital, and they are in surgery very quickly thereafter. There are also hypothermic treatments where body temperature can be lowered for days on end to reduce the swelling.

This only really works, though, if you make haste to get to the hospital. The twenty-two hours it took me to reach Miami allowed time for my bruising to swell.

Okay, with Google you can dive into researching spinal cord injury and all of the complications associated with it, but now at least you have a little more understanding of what happens when you "break your neck" (or back). It's for sure not something you want to do.

Pressure Sore Lesson 101[ii]—p130

THIS ISN'T A GLAMOROUS subject, but it's an important one. I had never even heard of a pressure sore before my injury, while today I could write a dissertation on them. Here's what every newly paralyzed person, caregiver, and, honestly, every human, because we all have skin, needs to understand before learning about pressure sores the hard way.

Skin is a fascinating organ. It's so elastic and durable, yet it can ruin your life. When able-bodied people sit down, they naturally move their butt for blood circulation without even thinking about it. This is not the case for a person with paralysis. In this case, if your skin is pressing on something for more than two hours, the skin cells start to die inside. You may see only a small, red mark on your body, but inside your body, that is, under your skin, the cells are dying. This happens when sustained external pressure on skin is greater than the internal blood pressure that feeds skin cells.

The external pressure might be creating a giant wound on the inside below the skin surface. There are four levels for the progression of pressure sores.

Stage I: This is when you develop a small red mark on your skin. When you push on this red mark and it doesn't turn white, it means there's no blood flow in that area. You need to immediately figure out where the pressure came from. You may need to stay in bed (if you're dealing with paralysis) or at least tilt back in your chair to distribute your weight every twenty minutes or so.

Stage II: The red mark becomes an opening in the skin. Even if you just scrape your skin a little bit, it needs to be treated like the worst kind of pressure sore. For people with paralysis, this can take anywhere from a few weeks to a month to heal, if you tend to it properly.

Stage III: The wound now is tunneling down into the subcutaneous fat level of your body. You're in serious trouble now. This can take anywhere from a few months up to six months to heal, if treated properly. With a Stage III pressure sore you absolutely have to stay prone in bed to prevent any pressure on that wound from sitting up in a wheelchair or a bed. You must turn every two hours or so to relieve pressure from one side of the body to the other.

Stage IV: This is where the wound has multiple centimeters of tunneling and often is down to the bone. This is the most serious stage. If the pressure sore is anywhere on your back, legs, heels, or bum, you will be required to live in bed. You will very likely require a complex surgery called a flap surgery, and you can pretty much bank on spending the next year at a minimum in bed even if everything goes as planned. If things do not go according to plan, that's another story. You can easily get a sepsis infection and die.

Welcome to the glamorous side of paralysis, where

a red spot can derail your life, and skin becomes your most high-maintenance organ. Trust me, you'll never look at sitting the same way again.

Autonomic Dysreflexia[iii]—p139

IF YOU'VE NEVER HEARD of autonomic dysreflexia, you're not alone. I hadn't either, until it became a life-or-death reality. It's one of the most dangerous medical conditions most people outside the spinal cord injury world have never heard of. So let's take a moment on this, because this one, too, really matters.

Did you know you have two nervous systems? You have your central nervous system (think brain and spine) and your autonomic nervous system. Think of this nervous system as controlling the automatic functions of your body.

Your autonomic nervous system controls your sweating, your blood pressure, your heart rate, and a few other bodily functions that are basically automatic. You don't think about them. You don't control these functions, as normally your body does this automatically.

When you sustain a spinal cord injury, you injure your autonomic nervous system. That means so many of us with cervical level injuries have no thermal regulation capabilities, sit with very low blood pressure, and only sweat above the level of injury.

When your body experiences any kind of pain with a cervical-level spinal cord injury, your body's autonomic nervous system goes into overdrive. It does this through changes in those body functions it controls. Ultimately, this results in a dangerous increase in blood pressure, then stroke, then death if you do not reach a hospital in time or figure out the source of the distress and alleviate it. This could be from a hot coffee spill on your leg, a urinary tract infection, any type of infection, an ingrown toenail, an overfilled bladder, or whatever.

It sounds dramatic, I know, and it can be, but this is real life with a spinal cord injury. When your body can't tell you what's wrong the usual way, your autonomic nervous system throws a full-on internal tantrum. Ignore it, and the consequences can be fatal.

Spinal Cord Arachnoid Cyst[iv]—p157

JUST WHEN I THOUGHT I had wrapped my head around spinal cord injuries, life decided to throw in a plot twist: a fluid-filled cyst growing *inside* my spinal cord. Dealing with this required a rare and risky surgery, a top-tier neuro-surgery team, and the kind of medical obstacle course that makes *Grey's Anatomy* look like amateur hour. Buckle up, as this one's not for the faint of heart.

I developed a fluid-filled (arachnoid) cyst growing on the anterior (front) side of my spinal cord. The thought was that the cyst, which ran from C-5 down to my C-7 vertebra and occupied more than 50 percent of my spinal cavity, was likely the major cause of my chronic pain. Furthermore, sequential MRIs revealed that the cyst was growing, and this may have accounted for the pain getting worse and lasting for more hours each day. Between December 5, 2012, and April 13, 2013, (about 18 weeks), this cyst grew from 2.7 cm to 3.6 cm, an increase of more than 30 percent.

Day and night this cyst pressed hard against my spinal cord, causing neuropathic pain, and there was MRI evidence that the incessant internal pressure was causing further degeneration of surviving tissue inside my spinal cord. The proposed surgery needed to remove this cyst would be extremely challenging, as the cyst was on the anterior (front) side of my spinal cord.

My 2010 spinal fusion had involved screwing a metal plate between the C-5 vertebra and C-7 vertebra, because my C-6 vertebra shattered in the diving accident. Therefore, access to the cyst was blocked on the front side of my spinal column due to the metal plate being in the way. Access to the cyst would have to come from the back side or "dorsal entry."

This meant that between the point of surgical entry and lancing this cyst there were not only three intact vertebrae that had to be cut away but also the actual spinal cord itself had to be worked around. Some obstacle course! The objective was to reach the fluid-filled cyst on the front side of my spinal cord in order to cut it open and drain the fluid, thereby decompressing my spinal cord.

We learned that few neurosurgeons anywhere in the world have experience with a procedure this complex (some would say daring) and even fewer would be willing to attempt it. Fortunately, members of my five-man team (actually one superwoman, Dr. Zhu Hui) were all Kunming PLA Hospital veterans who had already performed this kind of surgery hundreds of times and exuded confidence they would pull me through this just fine.

We also discussed participating in a vigorous rehabilitation program to start just fifteen days after surgery.

This rehab was anticipated to play a significant role in my recovery.

To gain access to my spinal cord, the surgeon needed to create as wide an opening as possible. This surgical procedure is referred to as a laminectomy because it involves removal of as much as possible of the lamina (bone) on both sides. However, because a major artery passes through the articular process on either side of the lamina, there's a limit to how far the surgeon can go. Executing a successful triple laminectomy was said to be the "easy part."

Next, the chief neurosurgeon, Dr. Liu Yansheng, would have to decide whether to approach the cyst by making his way to the left or right around my spinal cord. Once a path had been decided, he would cut open the dura mater, the tough external tissue that protects the spinal cord nerve bundle and then cut ligaments that held the spinal cord centered, pushing aside my spinal cord very, very gently as he went. Next was the super tricky bit, absolutely no room for error.

Once Dr. Liu worked his way round to the cyst, he could not simply remove it because of the risk of tearing the pia mater that enclosed what remained of my spinal cord. He would have to cut the cyst longitudinally, sort of like slitting a balloon, so it could never again hold fluid.

Along the way, Dr. Liu would scrape away and remove scar tissue from my original injury, thereby untethering my spinal cord and restoring CSF ("Cerebral Spinal Fluid") circulation.

The goal was to restore my spinal cord as close as possible to its original design and orientation within the spinal canal. That means my spinal cord would no longer be compressed by the large cyst nor would it be tethered by strands of scar tissue left behind from my original spinal fusion surgery. Instead, my spinal cord would be floating free again with full CSF circulation, free once again, as Dr. Zhu Hui expressed it, to "dance with the rhythms of my heartbeat and breathing."

Restoration of free CSF circulation, meaning no impeding scar tissue tethering and spinal cord decompression with the draining of the large cyst, was believed to be critical to achieving the optimal results from work I was expected to benefit from in the Kunming Walking Program. At this point, frankly, I would have simply been happy with cessation of the persistent, severe neuropathic pain that made it pretty much impossible for me to focus on anything else.

Now, of course, cutting away so much bone critically weakens the spine. In my case, the surgeon would have cut away altogether significant parts of the C-5 through C-7 vertebrae.

So, once this access "door" is cut open, there's an obvious need to build a frame around the opening to reinforce the spine. This requires the installation of two vertical titanium rods and one horizontal rod to provide lateral rigidity, all held in place by six screws after the cyst had been cut, tethering scar tissue removed, and the dura mater sutured back together. Then my neck muscles would be pulled back over the titanium framework, and finally they would suture my skin back in place.

All I wanted was relief from the pain. Instead, I got a crash course in spinal architecture, world-class neurosurgery, and the terrifying beauty of what it takes to give a spinal cord the chance to dance again.

Kunming Walking Program & Adaptive Behavior vs. Motor Function Recovery[v]—p174

First An Important Disclaimer: Let me start with a big, bold disclaimer. I'm not a doctor. What follows is not medical advice. Rather, it's simply my lived experience, filtered through years of sweat, stubbornness, and observation.

When I joined the Kunming Walking Program in China, I didn't know exactly what to expect. What I found was a world-class facility, a lot of sweat equity, and a deeper understanding of the difference between getting stronger and actually recovering function. Here's what I learned and what I think anyone considering this path should know.

Spinal cord injuries are vascular in nature, and therefore every injury is unique. This makes it especially challenging to generalize about what you might or might not gain from participating in any rehab program anywhere in the world.

When you break your back or, as in my case, neck, the damage to spinal cord neurons occurs from inflammation inside and around the spinal cord that kills off many neurons. This internal bruising chokes off nutrients to the spinal neurons, and, as a result, many neurons die.

But unlike with the Peripheral Nervous System, these Central Nervous System neurons cannot grow back. This means the signal transmission up and down the spinal cord is seriously disrupted and often irreversible.

You might want to think of spinal cord injury as leaving survivors with a permanent internal bruise (actually scar tissue) that can have occurred in as much as a 360 degree arc (all the way) around the cord and running higher or lower than the named broken vertebra.

The bottom line simply is that no two spinal cord injuries are alike, and therefore how many neurons and their associated axons survive the injury is unique to each individual. That's fundamentally what makes generalization about any physical therapy program or even subsequent spinal surgery so tricky to express in a helpful way.

Okay, so what was on offer in Kunming?

I have received many e-mails from SCI patients around the world, each asking pretty much the same question: "Are you or the other patients in Kunming gaining strength and improved function?"

This is a particularly tricky question to answer, but I am going to tackle it head-on, as I have developed clear views on the underlying issue here.

Adaptive Behavior vs. Motor Function Recovery

A SPINAL CORD INJURY survivor generally spends one to three months in the hospital and then at a local rehab center, using either a back brace or some form of a neck brace. As a result, during the first few months after an accident, many SCI patients are mostly bedbound.

Other than some light stretching, most SCI survivors do not initially engage in intensive rehabilitation to allow time for their spinal fusion surgery to heal.

According to an NIH paper published in January 2023 on the rate and assessment of muscle wasting during critical illness, when a body remains immobile, it loses approximately 5 percent of its muscle mass per week and up to 30 percent of muscle strength within just two weeks of immobilization. In more severe cases, such as critically ill patients, muscle mass loss can exceed 15 percent in a single week.

This means when the typical SCI patient begins intensive rehabilitation, he or she has already lost much of their muscle mass, even in the muscles that are not paralyzed. These atrophied muscles can be very deceiving, because they mask themselves as paralyzed after not having done any real work for so many months.

Therefore, when you start SCI rehabilitation, it can be very hard to determine whether a muscle is actually paralyzed. That is, whether there is loss of motor function or just muscle atrophy from lack of exercise, something that can be recovered with the right exercises.

Consequently, after intensive physical therapy begins and has progressed a few months, experienced clinicians and patients alike regularly confuse what is known as "adaptive behavior" with real motor function recovery.

And, indeed, it's often hard to tell what's going on, as the patient gets stronger and stronger and still-working muscles take on new assignments. An example of adaptive behavior is how today I can raise my arms over my head with no working triceps.

I am a so-called C6 (ASIA A Complete) quadriplegic. This means I am paralyzed from the chest down, my triceps are paralyzed, and my hands are paralyzed. I also have no feeling below the level of my chest. However, the muscles on the front of my arms including my shoulders, biceps, forearms and scapula muscles on my back are fully functioning.

I was laid up in the ICU in Miami for about four weeks before I was sent down to the rehabilitation center to start my rehab. When I first arrived in rehab, I could barely raise my arms, which I'm fully capable of doing today. I started slowly lifting weights and doing various training exercises, and, as the weeks went by, my arms started to get stronger above my level of injury.

Remember, everything below my level of injury (anything from my chest down, including triceps and hands) did not regain motor function because those muscles do not receive nerve impulses.

However, I was getting stronger and stronger and was able to shift my body on my own when I was on the mat, and I began to lift heavier and heavier weights as muscles that still worked adapted to new uses.

This is where it becomes very easy to confuse adaptive behavior with actual motor function recovery. As I was gaining strength in my muscles that were not paralyzed and building muscle tone, I was also learning to adapt these muscles for practical functions they'd never handled before, like picking up my phone by twisting my wrist or being able to lift my arms over my head.

To a casual onlooker, it appeared as though I was starting to recover hand function, but really I just learned how to manipulate the muscles that were not paralyzed to perform new and useful functions. After a year in Miami working out regularly four to six times a week for several hours a day, my muscles that were not paralyzed were again in tip-top shape.

Nonetheless, I did not actually regain any motor function below my level of injury. It just looked that way.

Essentially, no muscles started firing in my hands or my stomach or my legs. This is very typical of a so-called "complete" injury, and many people do not recover any motor function below the level of injury. If you are labeled "incomplete," and there are more surviving axon tracks in your spinal cord, then the likelihood of improving and reconnecting workable nerve-muscle relationships is greater.

The Complete v. Incomplete Game

A NOTE OF CAUTION with the terms "complete" and "incomplete."

Some doctors strike me as throwing around the term "complete" in an almost judgmental way and do their patients a consequent disservice. I want to make clear my view that the term "complete" does not mean what it seems to mean, as in, end-of-the-road.

Unless your spinal cord has been sliced right through like by a knife or gunshot wound (in which case you're not likely to have survived), there are surviving connections even to your lower most limbs. Just not enough to get local muscles to recruit and do useful work.

Surprised to learn this? Researcher Christa Moss, working in Dr. Hunter Peckham's lab in the Department of Biomedical Engineering at world-class Case Western Reserve University in Cleveland, Ohio, undertook a study in 2011 of 12 long-term "ASIA A Complete" quadriplegics. The results of that study suggest that voluntary activity is present and recordable in below lesion muscles even after a diagnosis of clinically complete SCI.

This discovery could impact the chronic SCI patient's potential for recovery. You can read this short article here: *http://www.ncbi.nlm.nih.gov/pubmed/21693772*.

So, coming back to adaptive behavior vs. motor function recovery and how this relates to Kunming. When we were researching the Kunming SCI Program back in 2012, the program's founder and leader, Dr. Zhu Hui, explained to us that compelling the body to support itself vertically, bearing 100 percent of body weight, induces the brain to force new neural connections as well as to wake up dormant connections to "speak" to the body's core and eventually also to the limbs.

While this theory is interesting and may have merit, I did not personally observe this to work out in practice, either for myself or for other patients I met over the year I was in the program.

Nonetheless, the Kunming Walking Program offers patients the opportunity to "walk" several hours a day at least five days a week, which can definitely improve adaptive behavior and even potentially improve their chances of motor function recovery from surviving axon tracks.

From my personal experience, and I want to be clear that I am not a doctor nor am I advocating for or offering specific medical advice, I believe adaptive behavior is still frequently confused with motor function recovery. Many of the patients who joined the Kunming program while I was there had been injured from several months to as long as several years prior and had never engaged in structured rehabilitation or even meaningful exercise of any kind.

So, new patients enrolled in the program in Kunming were deconditioned and very weak. However, after several weeks in the program, they experienced great improvement in their balance and ability to use their upper body.

I observed many SCI patients in Kunming closely over the course of that year I was there, and, since I speak Chinese, I even interviewed them.

I feel confident in reporting that the Kunming Program is inexpensive compared to many Western rehabilitation programs and that an SCI survivor can work out several hours a day to get strong again as well as to stay healthy and fit.

However, apparent improvements in motor function appeared to me to be, for the most part, attributable to adaptive behavior, especially for chronic SCI patients. Again, I speak as an observer, not as a clinician of any sort.

I worked out daily alongside dozens of the "complete" quadriplegic and paraplegic patients over my year in the active Kunming program. I did not observe improvement in motor function in chronic SCI patients. This is not to say that SCI motor function recovery is not possible but just that I did not observe this outcome.

Better Outcomes for Acute Patients

ON THE OTHER HAND, in Kunming I observed several "acute" SCI patients (that is, those with classified "incomplete" injuries from one month to one year old) gain meaningful motor function recovery. As I wrote earlier, every SCI patient is unique, and the outcome depends on a combination of how many axon tracks survived the injury and how hard the patient works at rehab.

Further, I noticed that the Kunming program seemed to benefit chronic paraplegic patients slightly more than quadriplegic patients. Paraplegics can hold themselves up on the Kunming walking frame and really work on improving their adaptive behavior and balance. It is a little more challenging for quadriplegics with no upper body strength, because we cannot hold ourselves up in the Kunming walker without substantial assistance.

Summing Up

BASED ON MY PERSONAL experience, the Kunming SCI Program is an option for a general all-around SCI rehab program, because it is really hard to find an affordable, dedicated SCI rehab program in North America or Europe in which one can work out vigorously in a dedicated facility multiple hours a day up to six days a week for months on end.

With respect to attending the Kunming program to regain motor function, from my observations, I cannot in good faith encourage high expectations for motor function recovery.

Perhaps some combination of an as-yet-unproven regenerative medicine therapy combined with rigorous Kunming-style rehabilitation may turn out to be the ideal combination for meaningful motor function improvement.

The Kunming program gave me physical strength, rehab structure, and community, and that combination is no small thing. But in a world full of miracle headlines and false hope, I feel a responsibility to tell it straight: recovery is never guaranteed, and there's no one-size-fits-all path. We each have to travel, however that looks for us, our own version of forward.

WOUND VACUUM[vi]—p205

ON PAPER, WOUND VACUUMS sound like miracle machines, and, to be fair, they kind of are in some ways. But like a lot of things in spinal cord injury recovery, their effectiveness depends on more than just the device itself. Here's what I learned the hard way.

A wound vacuum (Vacuum-Assisted Closure or VAC) is a medical device that helps heal difficult wounds more quickly by creating a controlled, low-pressure suction on the wound area. The wound VAC uses gentle suction to draw fluid and reduce swelling around the wound.

If you have a wound that is open and cannot be closed by sutures, then this device promotes faster healing, reduces infection risk, minimizes tissue damage, and helps improve mobility.

This is all true, but the success of these devices varies greatly and depends on a multitude of factors.

SCI patients with very limited mobility and poor blood flow to the wound do not experience a high success rate in healing pressure sores from their level of paralysis on down.

For some, a wound VAC can be a game-changer. For others, especially those of us with limited mobility, it's just one more thing that might help, if the stars align and your skin decides to cooperate.

KEY LESSONS DEALING WITH
INSURANCE PROVIDERS[vii]—p256

AH, MEDICAL INSURANCE, THE invisible hand that somehow manages to hold everything up. If you've ever tried to get coverage for anything beyond the basics, you probably already know how maddening it can be. But when you're living with a spinal cord injury, "maddening" becomes "potentially dangerous." Here's a glimpse of what that looks like from the inside.

The problem is there are defined, coded protocols involved, whether it be for a drug or service or surgery, with respect to what insurance will or won't approve at a given moment. Essentially, medical insurance companies, which vary in their protocols, usually want you to try the path of least resistance and the least expensive option first before moving on to something more major.

The challenge for someone with spinal cord injury is that these protocols don't take into consideration the added secondary complications we have, such as low blood circulation where paralysis occurs means that we don't heal as quickly, and standard modalities don't work for us as well as they do for able-bodied folks.

Dealing with insurance isn't just paperwork. Rather, it's a full-time job with its own language, secret handshakes, and maddening loops. After years of navigating this system while living with a spinal cord injury, I've picked up a few key strategies that have saved me time, sanity, and occasionally, my actual health.

Here's what I've learned and what I wish someone had taught me sooner. These are very specific strategies on how to increase your chances of success in the prior-authorization process.

- You are legally allowed to have an internal representative from your health insurance provider guide you through the entire prior-authorization process. This is critically important because otherwise you would be dealing with a different person each time, which complicates and confuses the situation, generally providing a less than desirable outcome.

- If your provider is out-of-network, and you do not have a reasonable alternative-in-network within 50 miles, you can make a very strong case to have a product, service, or drug authorized for your network.

- It's very important to understand stakeholder engagement. Who has control of the necessary information that needs to be sent to your health insurance provider so a decision can be made? Is it your doctor? Is it your physical therapist? Is it a specialty doctor? Is it a durable medical device provider? The reason this is important is because so much paperwork gets lost throughout the faxing or emailing process. Often times the wrong code is entered on paperwork, or there's a missing signature, or other seemingly small details are awry. Missing such details will automatically result in a denial, and then you have to start the oh-so-fun appeals process!

The system doesn't always seem fair, and it's definitely not easy to navigate, but understanding how the system works gives you a fighting chance. And, in the world of insurance, sometimes a well-placed code is more powerful than a well-written appeal.

AUTHOR'S NOTE

AT THE HEART OF my work is a core belief: Reinvention isn't just for crisis. Rather, it's for anyone, at any time, who's ready or forced to shift how they think, lead, or live.

Whether you're navigating burnout, caregiving for a parent, recovering from loss, climbing the next mountain in your career, or just waking up and thinking, "I didn't sign up for this version of adulthood," the truth is, life keeps on "life-ing." And change will find you, whether you're ready or not.

For years, I applied tools I couldn't yet name—strategies I had created to survive and then later to thrive. I wasn't trying to build a framework or brand or write a book. I was just trying to make it through. But over time, I started to see the patterns. I began naming the things that worked. I studied them. I tested them. I taught them. And I watched them help others move forward too.

So now, with a whole lot of real-world experience, a heaping dose of dark humor, and a deep belief in the power of human resilience, I'm excited to keep sharing what I've learned—in a more bite-sized, practical way.

My upcoming (shorter!) books will explore ways to keep moving forward in your life. Each of the three books in the **Keep Moving Forward Series** is rooted in lived experience, backed by research, and designed to meet you exactly where you are.

These books aren't about fixing yourself. They're about understanding how you think, how momentum actually works, and how to move forward—especially when things feel messy, uncertain, or stuck.

The Art of Being Pleasantly Persistent: Getting to "Yes"— available in March 2026

- Great leaders don't get more yeses because they push harder. They get more yeses because they understand people, timing, and what the brain does when it encounters friction.

- This book blends business strategy, real-world storytelling, and applied neuroscience to redefine what effective persistence looks like—in leadership, influence, and everyday life.

The Activation Method

- A simple, brain-based way to move forward when it matters most. This isn't about inspiration or motivation. It's about activation—because inspiration fades, motivation fluctuates, but activation is what happens when you understand what your brain is doing in real time and know how to work with it instead of against it.

- You'll learn how to:
  - See differently when chaos hits
  - Think differently by rewriting the story running in your head
  - Act differently by choosing your next move and taking ownership of it

Being the Scientist in Your Own Life

- A practical guide to examining your beliefs, questioning inherited stories, and running small, meaningful experiments in how you think, decide, and show up.

- This book is about curiosity over certainty—and learning how to test what actually works for you, rather than defaulting to patterns you never consciously chose.

These books won't be sugar-coated. You'll find honest reflection, transparent thought, practical applications, and yes, plenty of dark humor to help you laugh and learn simultaneously.

I've come to believe adversity is not the enemy, rather it's the training ground. Uncertainty can activate your superpower. And you don't need to wait for permission, a rock bottom, or a midlife crisis to decide to live differently. So, wherever you are in your own story, I hope this book sparked something for you—an idea, a perspective, or maybe a question you can't shake. I hope you carry that forward.

And when you're ready for what's next, I'll be right here, cheering you on and writing what I think can help. Let's keep this conversation going. Let's keep evolving. Let's stay curious, courageous, and wildly unbreakable(ish).

https://aliingersoll.com